vien Dotti *R*

Sigi Grabner
N

Anders Löun
CE

S
PAOLO BERTANI

GG
ami HYRY

Stuart Brass
S

SANI ALIBABIC
GG

GG
I. FERNANDEZ

GG
Maureen ter Horst

Snowboards

Call for new '97 catalog of the *boards, boots, bindings, and clothing* that we ride. / **European Rider Hotline +43 512 22 82 0 82** / www.burton.com

0512 2282082   *I* 0464 519597   *B* 050 622794   *NL* 071 4076010   *DK* 45 824513   *N* 73 893040   *SF* 90 650 530

S 0565 10100   *F* 50 273838   *CH* 081 322 88 33   *D* 07432 9560   *GB* 01784 423693   *E* 93 263 3853

INGEMAR

ATLANTIS SNOWBOARDS INC.

449 SANTA FE DR. #215 ENCINITAS CALIFORNIA 92024

First published 1996 by
Low Pressure Publishing Ltd ©
Unit 33, Pall Mall Deposit
124-128 Barlby Rd
London W10 6BL
Tel/Fax +44 (0) 181 960 1916

Low Pressure Europe +(33) 558 77 76 85
Creation of all maps, graphic arrangements
and devices, pictograms, text and index,
© copyright Low Pressure publishing (1991) Ltd
Relief maps copyright Mt High Maps.

A catalogue record of this book can be obtained from the British Library.

ISBN no : 0 9519275 1 5

Front cover pic: Jeff Webb - Saas Fee

This page pic: T. Rainger

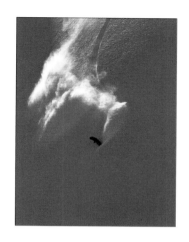

the snowboard GUIDE
europe

LOW PRESSURE publishing©

snowboard
europe

Commissioning Editors
Tim Rainger and Ollie Fitzjones

Publishing and Photo Editor
Tim Rainger

Editor and Co-Ordinator
Ali Hanan

Information Designer
Dan Haylock

Designer
Jamie Asher

Design Assistants
Gareth Parkinson

Advertising, Marketing and P.R.
Suzanne Alleyne

Copy-Editor + English Proof Reader
Sue Heady

German Translator
Angelica

German Language Style and Editor
Christian Shartner

Key Researchers
Drew Stevenson/Austria
Antony Colas/ France
Marc Hare/ France
Tim Rainger/Switzerland
Deidre Gaspari/Italy
Christoph Sumo/Germany
Peter Grant/ Scandinavia
Martijn Drenth/The Lowlands
Steve Davis and The B.S.A./England
Jose Lekenda - Tres 60/Spain

Contributing Journalists
Danni Kiwi Meier, Martin Willners, Reto Lamm, GoGo, Tim King, Johnny Barr,
Sara Bovo, Scharti, Ollie Fitzjones, Lloyd Rogers, Danni Burrows, Ian Trotter,
Ross Woodhall, Adam Barnes, John Bush, Gina Dempster, Bruce Sutherland

Photographers
Richard Walch, Jeff Webb, Tim Rainger, Helmut Wahl, Søren Egeberg,
R. Reichenseld, F. Witmer, Katja Delago, Sang Tan, Nick Hamilton, J. M. Favre, Scalp, Nagel
photo, Danial Strasser, Mark Junak, Mark Frederick, Peter Mathis, Andy Jackson, Al Green,
Tim King, Robbi Trabbuci, Martin Willners, Peter Grant, Marc Hare, Jakue Andikoetxea, Claude
Etchelecou, G. Grübl, Reinke Weber,
Calle Eriksson, Face Shots, Stig.

Special thanks to
Bruce Sutherland, Stephen Jenkins, Kore Antonsen, Urs Eberhard, Anna Watson, Danni Meier.

Thanks to
All our advertisers,
Air Engadina, Swiss National Tourist Office, Austrian National Tourist Office,
French Government Tourist Office, Andorran Tourist Authority, Camilla from
the Swedish Travel and Tourism Council, Norwegian Tourist Board and
Susie Golding from Rhone Alps.

To everyone else who helped in any way... you know who you are... thanks for everything
... we hope the work justifies your faith.

LOW PRESSURE publishing©

in association with

ONBOARD

Sprite®

"Great things happen when men and mountains meet. This is not done by jostling in the street" William Blake. 1757-1827.

This book is the first ever detailed guide to the snowboard resorts of Europe. Like *The Stormrider Guide*, it was written with assistance and input from a huge range of people in every country covered. Some made big contributions, others made smaller ones; all were of crucial importance.

We have tried to leave the various writing styles intact, so don't be alarmed at the mix. It's a lot like taking a trip through the old world... everyone seems to speak a different language or dialect; indeed it's one of the great things about riding in Europe. But while the huge variety of languages spoken across the continent indicate the wide cultural differences, we're concentrating on a sensation that is totally universal and something in which we all share - snowboarding.

It doesn't matter who - or what - you are, launching down a mountain covered in fresh snow is one of life's most intense and beautiful sensations!

By a process of information osmosis, we identified the 80 or so most popular snowboard resorts in Europe, and have covered them in great depth. To try to cover them all would have been sheer folly... Austria alone has nearly one thousand lift installations, while France has five hundred. At the end of the day, the vast majority of the snowboard community ride at the resorts reviewed within this guide, although some notable exceptions are missing for reasons too boring to detail. Suffice to say, the next edition will be expanded, and we will welcome feedback and constructive criticism on any relevant topics.

We hope this compilation of reports and hand-drawn maps will encourage riders of all nationalities to explore the vast, awe-inspiring mountains of western Europe. Likewise, the folk who inhabit them.

Thanks to the hundreds of amazing people who helped us during our travels and took us riding. They are all out there now, patiently waiting for good conditions. Take the time to listen to these people. It is their experience that makes this book valuable.

Use the knowledge wisely.
Love and respect the mountains.
Increase the peace.
Ride!

ph: Peter Mathis - St Anton

Contents

pic: Peter Mathis - Lech

Mountain Etiquette

The Ten Commandments

1. RESPECT FOR OTHERS
Slope-users must always behave in such a way that they do not endanger others, either through their actions or their equipment.

2. BE IN CONTROL
All slope users must adapt their speed and behaviour to their personal capabilities, as well as to the general conditions of the slope, weather, snow conditions and density of other slope-users at all times.

3. GIVE WAY
People ahead of you have the right of way - it's your responsibility to avoid them.

4. CHECK WHAT'S COMING
When joining a piste or setting off, always look uphill and give way to others already coming down.

5. BE WARY OF WHERE YOU STOP
Don't stop where you block a trail or are not visible from above. If you fall in an obstructive position, move out of the way quickly.

6. THE SIDE OF THE SLOPE IS SAFEST
Any slope users walking uphill or downhill must keep to the side of the slope, away from the line of other users.

7. RESPECT SIGNS ON THE MOUNTAIN
Whether concerning weather, slope or snow conditions, these signs are there for a reason. Keep out of closed areas.

8. ASSISTANCE
Any person who is a witness to, or instigator of, an accident must give assistance. Should the need arise, first raise the alarm and then, if asked by the mountain rescuers, help out.

9. IDENTIFICATION
Any person who is involved in, or a witness to, an accident must identify themselves to the Piste Patrol or emergency services, as well as to any others involved in the accident.

10. EQUIPMENT SAFETY
Lay your board on its bindings when on the snow and be aware of others while carrying your board, especially when in queues.

ZEN AND THE ART OF LIFT QUEUES
Quite frankly, the art of stress free lift queuing in Europe is one of the continent's least developed. Compared with the order which prevails at most American and Southern Hemisphere resorts, Europe's are a rugby scrum by comparison. It's not so hard to be relaxed in such situations, and not aggravate an already difficult situation. Just breath slowly and enjoy the view. Be cool in the lift queues. Be friendly, polite and generous. You'll make many friends this way.

THE ALTERNATIVE TO LIFT TICKETS
Swatch Access is a cool new watch that not only tells the time, but opens gates as well. This piece of high-tech wizardry, developed jointly with SkiData, comes with a micro-chip and a ring shaped sensor. The chip stores details of your pass, and the sensor opens the gate; all you have to do is point the Swatch Access towards the gate, and it's open sesame. Even if it's under your clothes. When your ticket expires, you get it reprogrammed at the cash desk. The resorts using this system that are covered in this book, are noted by the inclusion of the Swatch Access logo under lift information.

A RUBBISH RAVE

One of the big environmental problems affecting every resort is plain old rubbish. It's worth taking a couple of minutes to realise that rubbish doesn't disappear by magic. It all has to be taken off the mountain somehow, otherwise it will stay in the back-country, where it will fester and suppurate, spoiling the very environment we treasure so much.

Most things take longer to decompose than you think. That cigarette butt stubbed out and covered by snow isn't gone. It will stay on the mountain looking ugly for a few years. Or else wash down in spring thaws and choke some unsuspecting fish. Even human shit takes nine months to decompose.

For people walking in the mountains in the summer, rubbish is ugly, unsightly and ruins the concept of the wilderness. Who wants to be outdoors, appreciating the tranquillity and beauty, only to come face to face with a wadge of used toilet paper?

THE ETHICS OF TREE RIDING

The forests of Europe are having to cope with 'a serious drug problem' called acid rain. The Alps account for something like twenty five percent of Europe's tourism, which is great for the economy, but a problem for the woodlands because of the many resulting pollutants. Acid rain, far from being an enjoyable hallucinogenic substance, is death to trees.

The by-products of fossil fuels are the prime cause of acid rain, the effects of which are equivalent to genocide in wooded areas at elevations between 800m and 1000m. The rain, which hovers as mist, interferes with photosynthesis and thus starves the trees. Weakened by these effects, the trees are rendered defenceless against parasites and viruses.

As car exhaust fumes are in part responsible for the holocaust, think whether it's necessary to take your car with you when you head for the mountains, or whether you can team up with others, taking one car as opposed to two.

MAKE A DIFFERENCE

When you next go tree-riding, take care. Forests act as the planet's air filter, so give them a break, don't break them. The trees of Europe have enough to contend with, without you amputating their limbs or squashing their young.

Wooded areas are also home to wildlife and if people scream through the trees every day of the year, the local inhabitants' hunting habits, mating rituals and general habitat are disrupted. Think about it - it would probably be akin to having a boardercross through your living room!

So, if trees are roped off, it's generally because they need protecting or are regenerating. If there's a 'no entry' sign, don't go there!

Remember, go quietly and cautiously in forests.

pic. P. Bradley

"THE TIME HAS COME WHEN WORN-OUT, STRUNG-OUT CITY PEOPLE NEED TO ESCAPE INTO MOUNTAIN RESERVES; IT WILL DAWN ON THEM THAT THESE PLACES NOT ONLY HARBOUR PEACE AND TRANQUILLITY, BUT ARE THE FOUNTAINS OF LIFE. RESPECT THEM"

Yellowman, Yellowsnow site, The Internet.

Besides being unsightly, rubbish endangers the fragile ecosystems of the forests and mountain grasslands.

Many people take small, seal-top plastic bags up on the mountain, empty them appropriately and then recycle them - where possible - at the bottom of the mountain.The message is very simple; what you take in, take out!

Friends of the Earth point out that recycling benefits the environment in three main ways; by saving energy, avoiding pollution associated with waste disposal and slowing the consumption of the planet's raw materials. Recycling helps to save up to 22 percent of the energy necessary in the making of glass, 70 percent in that of paper and a huge 97 percent in that of aluminium. The side effects of too much energy production and consumption (such as global warming and acid rain) only increase problems of warmer winters, receding snowlines and skin cancers. All are major downers for mountain users!

pic: Martin Willners - Are, Sweden. rider: Daniel Engström

• **Ride in a group** - three is the minimum. If an accident occurs, one can stay with the buddy in bother and one can alert rescue services. The better riders should go first and last - to pick out a good line if first and to come to the rescue if something terrible should happen. The last person should always carry a shovel and probe.

• **Always descend one at a time** - waiting for the others in a safe spot. The later riders should always watch those who descend ahead of them, just in case someone gets avalanched and needs help.

• **Digging a snowpit** - will enable you to look at the composition of the snow pack. A cross-section will show you how many snowfalls there have been, the depth of each one and the type of snow involved - how hard it is and how well it has bonded to the previous snowfall. If you're digging a pit and looking at the cross-section, always look for the presence of loose, sugary snow. Known as depth hoar (or sugar snow), it gives rise to a dangerous, unstable snowpack.

• **Clothing and equipment** - don't be a fashion victim. Buy proper breathable, waterproof clothes and, if riding in isolated areas away from the ski area, take a bivouac, energy food, an emergency flare and a torch.

Freeriding is the ultimate for any self respecting snowboarder. It offers the snowboarder a sense of freedom and excitement not found within the limited bounds of a ski field. The mountain is a giant playground in which you are only limited by your own fear. But within the great expanses of untouched powder fields, comes a certain responsibility not only to protect yourself, but also your fellow mountain users.

When you go back-country, think ahead and plan. Prepare for all eventualities and take an Ortovox transceiver, a shovel, a probe and energy food with you - they could save your life. Push yourself to your limit, but not beyond your limit.

pic: Mark Frederick

WHAT ARE AVALANCHES?

There are two main types of avalanches.

• **Loose snow avalanches** start from a small point, fanning out as they travel downwards and gain momentum. They can be started by a falling rock, an explosion or - more commonly - a skier or boarder, and they can occur in both wet and dry snow conditions. Loose snow avalanches can be huge and are, therefore, extremely destructive. Even the air blast in front of one can reach speeds of 100mph.

• **Slab avalanches** occur when the snow pack is not robust enough to cope with the weight of additional snow building up on top of it. The weight of a snowboarder cutting across a slope of this nature can overload the snow pack, causing it to break away along a fracture line. These fracture lines can be hundreds of metres in length and several metres in width, and can bring down thousands of tons of snow. There are two main types of slab avalanches.

* Most **soft slab avalanches** are caused by the rapid loading of fresh snow on slopes with a gradient of between 25 and 45 degrees, and are therefore released during, or shortly after, snowfalls. They can be easily predicted, as they occur at the surface layer of snow and the attachment to the new snow to the base can be examined with the help of a probe. Wind during the snowfall will increase the risk of soft slab avalanches (see the following note on wind).

***Hard slab avalanches** occur from a well defined fracture line, which can be of any depth and may not necessarily be only the upper layers of snow. A prolonged period of very cold weather or any sort of heating beneath the snow pack (i.e. large rock bands warmed by the sun) can cause the crystals of snow to change drastically in shape, resulting in an unstable layer well below the surface. Hard slab avalanches are, therefore, very difficult to predict, because the top layer of snow can look and feel very safe. Only if a snow pit is dug, allowing examination of the various snow layers, will a weak layer be revealed.

WHAT TO LOOK FOR

• Gradient

In general, avalanche danger increases with the gradient of the slope, so the greatest possibility of an avalanche occurring is between 25 and 45 degrees. Of course, there are exceptions to every rule, but it is rarely that slopes above 60 degrees avalanche, because the sheer force of gravity prevents snow forming to dangerous levels.

• Convex slopes

The most dangerous! On a convex slope the weight of the snow is on the steeper side. Pulled by the force of gravity, tensions slowly build up along the upper reaches of the slope. All that is required to tip the fragile balance - and send the weight of snow crashing down towards the mountain floor - is the cut of a snowboard into the snow's surface.

• Concave slopes

These are considered the least dangerous for two reasons. First, it is much more daunting to ride onto a steeper slope where an avalanche run out zone and/or debris can be seen. Secondly, the volume of snow that could avalanche will be slightly less. For example, one metre of new snow will be one metre deep on level ground, but it is only half a metre deep on a 45 degree slope.

• Bowls

They look absolutely fantastic and inviting, but are a death trap if the conditions aren't perfect. Bowls tend to have well-rounded concave sides and a relatively flat bottom. If a boarder were to start an avalanche in any part of the bowl, the movement and the air blast might well bring all three sides of the bowl tumbling down. If this were to occur, the depth of snow at the bottom would be immense.

• Nature of the terrain

Certain ground surfaces are less likely to produce avalanches than others, but you have to be really familiar with the area to know what lies beneath the snow. For example, a smooth grassy slope will have a lot less cohesion than a rough bouldered slope. If the snow depth is not great, it may be possible to dig down and have a look or to see the undulations on the tops of boulders. With increasing snow depth, an exploratory dig becomes much more difficult.

• Geographical position

The composition of the snow is also affected by the sun. The sun changes the temperatures and the temperature changes the structure of the snow pack. South-facing slopes are generally safer in the middle of the winter, as due to the heat variations the snow settles down and the layers combine with each other. In the spring the heat causes massive instability and the slopes should not be boarded after the midday sun. But 80 percent of avalanches occur on north-facing slopes, as because these are in the shade, the layers do not adhere easily and are likely to slip.

• The Weather

There are two important factors to consider.

* **Temperature**: A long hot day may change the very structure of the snow crystals, with the result that some may bond better than others, forming a combination of weak and strong layers.

* **Wind** - affects the consistency of the snow pack structure, thus increasing the risk of avalanche. Strong winds can create an uneven riding surface and at the same time prevent the formation of a sound base. Strong winds also create cornices on the tops of ridges and bowls, which can easily break away under the weight of a single person. Whenever there are signs of wind during or after a snowfall, it pays to be extra vigilant.

One last thing to remember. It's no use just looking at the terrain on which you are about to ride. People have been killed because they did not look to see if there were any dangerous snow deposits above them. And never stand on a cornice or a suspect slope to view or test it, unless you are properly anchored.

This better have whetted your appetite - maybe you've realised what you should know. Go and learn more - do a course organised by a climbing association - it could save your life.

Most avalanche victims die within the first 20 minutes of being buried. The key to rescuing victims alive is to locate and evacuate the victim as fast as possible. The following tools may help.

• Avalanche Transceiver (Ortovox)

This is a small device carried by an individual, which constantly emits a series of high frequency beeps that are inaudible to the human ear. However, in the event of a wearer being buried, anyone else's transceiver can be switched from emit to receive, so that the buried individual's receiver signals can be detected and the victim located.

• Avalanche probe

This is important in pinpointing the exact position of the victim. Apart from searching for buried friends, probes can be used to check snow depths, look for crevasses etc.

• Collapsible shovel

As time is of the essence, searchers need all the help they can get. It is crucial, therefore, to carry a shovel to aid in the speedy recovery of the victim.

pic. T. Rainger

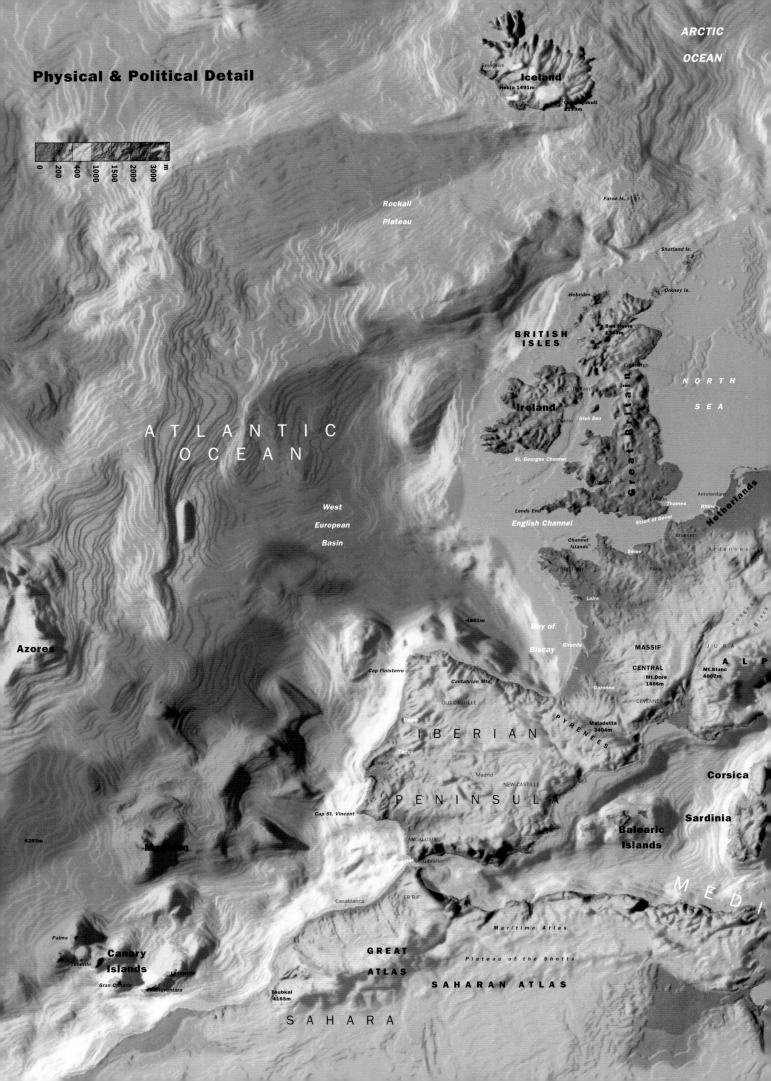

Physical & Political Detail

0 200 400 1000 1500 2000 3000 m

ARCTIC
OCEAN

Reykjavik
Iceland
Hekla 1491m
Öraefajökull
2199m

Faroe Is.

Rockall

Plateau

Shetland Is.

Hebrides
Orkney Is.

BRITISH
ISLES
Ben Nevis
1343m

Edinburgh

N O R T H

Belfast

S E A

Ireland
Dublin *Irish Sea*

Great Britain

A T L A N T I C
O C E A N

St. Georges Channel

Cardiff

London
Thames

Amsterdam

Rhine

Netherlands

West

European

Basin

Lands End
Channel
Islands

English Channel

Strait of Dover

Brussel

Ardennes

Seine

BRITTANY

Paris

Loire

Voges

Black

Bay of

-4861m

J U R A

Azores

Biscay

Gironde

MASSIF

A L P

Cap Finisterre

Cantabrian Mts.

CENTRAL
Mt.Dore
1886m

Mt.Blanc
4807m

Garonne

OLD CASTILE

CEVENNES

P Y R E N E E S

Maladetta
3404m

I B E R I A N

Douro

Tagus

Lisbon

Madrid

Corsica

NEW CASTILE

P E N I N S U L A

Sardinia

Balearic
Islands

Cap St. Vincent

6293m

M█████

ANDALUSIA

Str. of Gibralter Gibralter

M E D I

ER RIF

Casablanca

Palma

Maritime Atlas

Canary
Tenerife
Islands

GREAT

Plateau of the Shotts

Lanzarote

ATLAS

Gran Canaria
Fuerteventura

Toubkal
4165m

SAHARAN ATLAS

S A H A R A

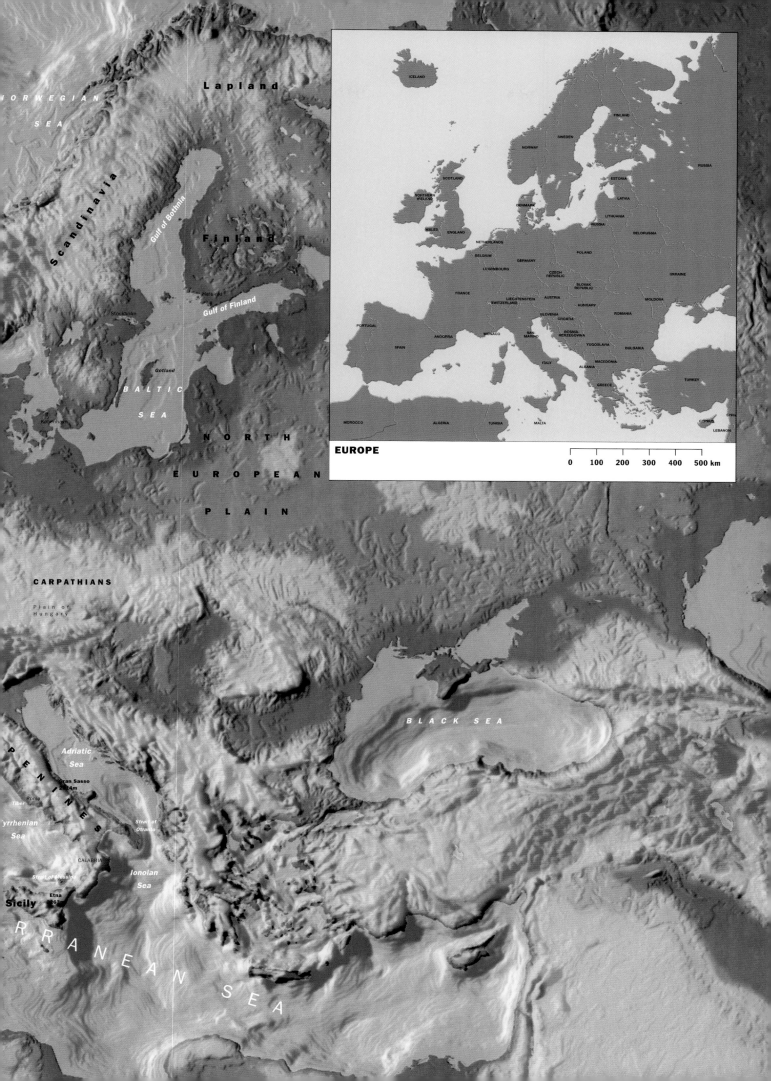

NORWEGIAN SEA

Lapland

Scandinavia

Finland

Gulf of Bothnia

Helsinki

Gulf of Finland

Stockholm

Gotland

BALTIC SEA

København

NORTH EUROPEAN PLAIN

CARPATHIANS

Plain of Hungary

BLACK SEA

PENINES

Adriatic Sea

Gran Sasso 2914m

Rome

Tiber

Tyrrhenian Sea

Strait of Otranto

CALABRIA

Ionian Sea

Strait of Messina

Sicily

Etna 3263m

MEDITERRANEAN SEA

EUROPE

ICELAND

FINLAND

SWEDEN

NORWAY

SCOTLAND

NORTHERN IRELAND

RUSSIA

ESTONIA

LATVIA

LITHUANIA

BELORUSSIA

WALES

ENGLAND

DENMARK

RUSSIA

NETHERLANDS

BELGIUM

GERMANY

POLAND

LUXEMBOURG

CZECH REPUBLIC

UKRAINE

FRANCE

LIECHTENSTEIN

SWITZERLAND

AUSTRIA

SLOVAK REPUBLIC

HUNGARY

MOLDOVA

SLOVENIA

CROATIA

ROMANIA

PORTUGAL

ANDORRA

MONACO

SAN-MARINO

BOSNIA-HERZEGOVINA

YUGOSLAVIA

BULGARIA

SPAIN

ITALY

MACEDONIA

ALBANIA

TURKEY

GREECE

CYPRUS

MOROCCO

ALGERIA

TUNISIA

MALTA

SYRIA

LEBANON

0   100   200   300   400   500 km

Jonas Roeser by Jimmy Clarke.

Danny Wheeler by Nick Hamilton.

Tor by Matt Woxland.

Kevin Young by Dano.

westbeach

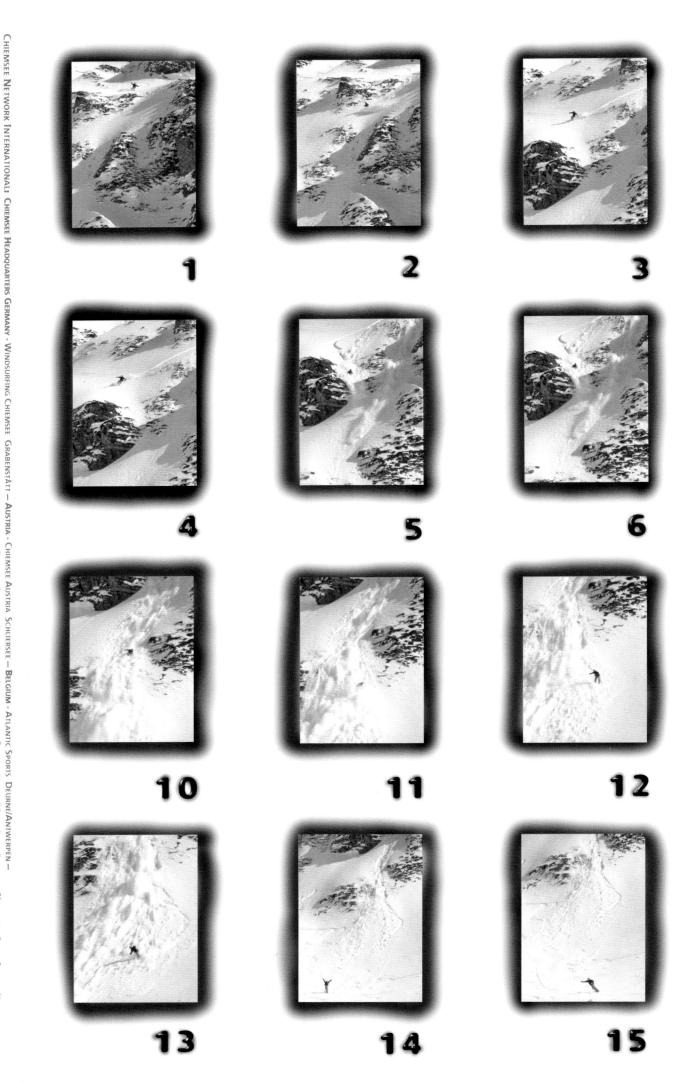

7 8 9

KEEP YOUR ASS DRY

The Chiemsee Defrost Collection 1996

Rider: Christian Ruggaber Photo: Thorsten Indra

Windsurfing Chiemsee — Chiemingerstrasse 19 — 83355 Grabenstätt — Telefon *49 · 8661 · 9888 · 0 — Fax +49 · 8661 · 9888 · 25 — Internet: http://www.chiemsee.com

Austria

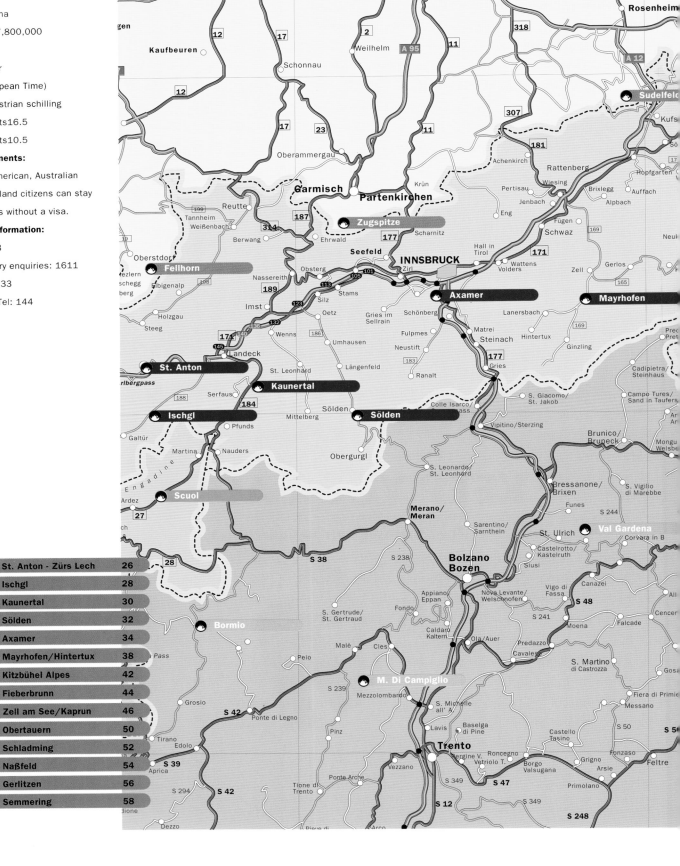

Further Inromation

Tourist board details

Austrian National Tourist Office

Margaretenstr 1

1040 Vienna

Tel: 01-587 2000

Fax: 01-588 6620

Youth organisation

Oesterreichischer

Jugendherbergsverband

Helferstorferstrasse 4 1010 Vienna

Tel: 01-533 3062

Fax: 01-533 3063

National airlines

Austrian Airlines - Tel: 0171-630 7300

Lauda Air - Tel: 0171-630 5924

Train travel information

Austrian Railways and timetable

information service - Tel: 0891-517 175

Bus travel information

Tel: 01-711 01   Fax: 0660 5188

Weather reports

All newspapers and after the

evening news.

Snowline telephone information

Vienna, Lower Austria, The Styria -

Tel: 1583

Salzburg, Upper Austria, Carinthia -

Tel: 1584

The Tyrol, Voralberg -

Tel: 1585

National snowboard magazine

Onboard

National snowboard association

Leopoldstrasse 4, Innsbruck 6020

Tel: 43 512 5656 75   Fax: 43 512

5656 76

Western Tirol

Arlberg - St Anton, Zürs, Lech
Ischgl
Kaunertal
Ötztal - Sölden
Axamer Lizum

Arlberg St Anton/Zürs/Lech

Mountain Information

Mountain chain:

Arlberg Region

Vertical metre range:

1,304m - 2,811m

Length of season:

end of December -

beginning of May

Number of lifts:

1 funicular railway,

9 cable cars,

36 chairlifts, 30 T-bars

Snow-making facilities:

Snow-making facilities cover

0.77km of piste when needed.

Safety:

There are avalanche indicator

boards at the bottom of all the

major lift stations.

Lift pass prices:

1 day: Ats430

6 days: Ats2,500

Season: Ats8,000*

(* Half the cost of the season pass

is redeemable if you work in St

Anton for 85 days in winter.)

Linked resorts

St Anton, St Christoph, Stuben,

Zürs, Lech and Zug are all included

in the Arlberg Pass.

Other:

The Arlberg region is the only area

in Austria where you can heliboard.

Book through Alpine Faszination,

the Arlberg Ski School or the

St. Anton Ski School. The price

for a group of four to make one

run is Ats5,600.

 ON THE MOUNTAIN

St Anton has a wide variety of terrain, but the mountain is renowned for its incredible, and intoxicating, extreme topography. Sit in the Ulmerhütte, look at the Valuga and Schindler peaks, and you'll feel the might and immensity of this huge powder playground. The terrain is endless and, long after the last snowfall, you'll still find fresh tracks. St Anton certainly won't disappoint.

 Snow conditions

When it snows, it dumps. Although most of St Anton is south-facing, due to its altitude the snow hangs around longer than most places.

Freeriders

The area available off one lift pass is huge. If you are an intermediate rider, Rendl, along with Gampen/Kapal and Galzig/Kandahar (on the adjacent side of the valley), are great mountains to sharpen your skills.

Stuben and Zürs offer powder hounds, cliff-

Rider Julian Ettel pic: Richard Walch

droppers and back-country boarders some of the most extreme terrain available worldwide. Experienced boarders should try the Rendl's 'Tunnel of Love' and 'Wannele' or go over to the Galzig side, high above the Ulmerhütte, and drop into one of the five Schindler chutes, which are located straight off the left side of the Schindlergratbahn and have 45 to 50 degree pitches. NB: the north face of Rendl and the Schöngraben Valley are both avalanche prone, and thus dangerous.

 Freestylers

On Rendl, there is a halfpipe, which is maintained regularly but is often not that good, located just above the restaurant. At Lech, there is a giant funpark with quarterpipes and a halfpipe, which are kept in good condition and are functional for most of the season.

 Carvers

St Anton's terrain is quite steep, so alpine boarders have little chance to experience the velvet finish of a high speed carve. The exception to the rule is the blue Osthang, which is located at Galzig. Lech, on the other hand, has autobahns of corduroy to carve - kilometres of fun.

Lifts to avoid

In Rendl, the Masslift and the Tuberlift are two seriously long, steep, groin-destroying T-bars, behind Galzig (Alremander) die Feldherrnhügel.

Mountain fare

The Rendl Beach (so-named because it's like a beach when the sun shines!) has great food and is the place to hang-out - hire lying stools and kick back for a sunny snooze. The Ulmerhütte is the place to soak up the view - one of the finest in the Alps.

pic: Peter Mathis

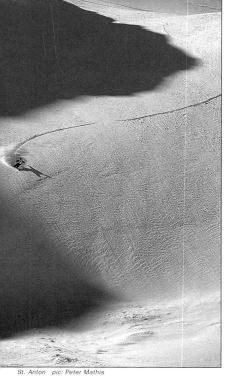

St. Anton   pic: Peter Mathis

Zürs/Lech   pic: Peter Mathis

FRESH TRACKS

 ABOUT TOWN

A small town lying at around 1,300m, St Anton is located just under the Arlberg Pass at St Christoph (1,800m). In winter, it swells to accommodate the masses that come to challenge the staggering amount of terrain. As it has everything, including lots of restaurants and nightclubs - you'll never know a dull moment!

 Getting there

By plane: The nearest international airports are Zürich (a 200km transfer) and Munich (a 250km transfer).

By train: The Arlberg Express travels directly from Zurich airport to the centre of St Anton - prices are from Ats350.

By car: There's an Ats150 toll on the Arlberg Tunnel, but take the Arlberg Pass if it's not snowing as it's free, it's only a ten minute longer drive and it's much more picturesque.

 Accommodation

Fax the tourist office in St Anton and ask them to send you the Hotel and Guest Guide, a list of all available accommodation, a map of the town showing the location of the hotel, plus details and prices of those listed. In the high season, expect to pay Ats250-300 per night. For a cheaper one or two weeks in St Anton, check with your travel agent for last minute specials.

 Food

St Anton caters for just about every culinary desire, from five star restaurants costing Ats1,000 per person to budget eat outs. In the latter category, try the Amalien Stuben in the centre of town or the Pizza Pomodori near the information centre.

For lunch, go to the Spar supermarket before midday and stock up on pre-made sandwiches for Ats12. In the evening, for a sit down meal with a glass of wine in a restaurant, expect to pay Ats200. On the mountain, the Rodelalm is one of the more traditional rustic restaurants and serves enormous portions of local fare, such as chunks of 'Schweinshax'n' - huge chunks of roasted pork.

 Nightlife

The nightlife is quite phenomenal, kicking off with après-ride drinking sessions, which can often be completely out of order by the time the sun sets. Your best bets are the Mooserwirt and Taps, where you're advised to sample the lethal local schnapps, the 'Obstler' and the 'apzfel'. Later, there is a healthy abundance of nightlife all within a 500m radius of the town centre. The Club Amadeus, which draws a mostly boarding crowd, offers a range of games, including electronic darts and pinball machines, and always has a great range of videos and music playing till the early hours. If you want live music, go to the Underground Nightclub after 11.00pm. Just around the corner, at Bobo's Bar, you can listen to a good mix of music in a Mexican-style surrounding.

Other activities

There is a toboggan track in St Anton, but it's a long walk up, so go for dinner and, after a few too many, try to toboggan down a dark track with no vision. On the other hand, serious tobogganers should head for Pettneu, 7kms away, where there's a toboggan track with lights and a lift. There's a public 33m swimming-pool in the same village and in Nasserein there's a bowling alley. Ice-climbing courses can be booked through Alpine Faszination (see below).

 Thanks to

Chris Rex from Underground Snowsports.

Essential Contacts

Tourist office

Tel: 05446-226 90   Fax: 05446-2532

Snowboard Shops

•Underground Snowsports

Tel/Fax: 05446-2342 (Ask for Chris Rex).

Board/boots/protection pads hire: Ats330/day

Go no further than The Underground, the only dedicated snowboard shop in St Anton, which will provide contacts, equipment and expertise.

Snowboard schools

•The Arlberg Ski School has half a dozen or so ski instructors, who double up as snowboard instructors when required.

•Alpine Faszination Tel: 05447-5284

A snowboard school, specializing in freestyle teaching. 2.5 hour group lesson: Ats400.

•Alpine Ski School   Tel: 05446-3411

•St Anton Ski School   Tel: 05446-3714

Ischgl

ON THE MOUNTAIN

Ischgl has hosted many ISF world cup events and has always welcomed snowboarders. As a result of this progressive attitude, it has attracted all kinds of boarders, but particularly freestylers, who dig a 1.1km gully called 'Boarder's Paradise', which has all the fun bits and is one of the largest funparks in Europe. The wider Silvretta ski area is vast and efficient, with a capacity of up to 50,000 sun and snow-hungry passengers per hour. All in all, riders are assured of a ball.

Snow conditions

Most of the riding is above 2,000m and north-facing, which means Ischgl is one of the most reliable resorts in the region. The runs back to town are the first to lose snow, but snow-makers soon make up the difference.

Freeriders

There are plenty of runs, but the best follow. Take the Pardatschgratbahn and ride on the black run - go off-piste either side for great hits and jumps (number 4 on the map). Or take the draglift Sassgalun and check out the jumps, including the hair-raising cliff jump, the Hollenkar, on either side. For some great off-piste, head down the Paznauner Taja and ride the area on the right. The trees at Fimbatal, below the Paznauner Taja restaurant, are not only well-spaced, they are a welcome respite when the weather is poor.

Freestylers

Freestylers will be in paradise in Ischgl and mountains wishing to attract snowboarders would do well to model themselves on this one. Ischgl has a halfpipe, open from December till April, which is maintained to a world class standard as it hosts ISF pro tour competitions. Usually over 100 metres long, it is hand dug (cats work on it before it's manually shaped). In the '95/'96 season, Ischgl had one of the largest, and best, funparks in Europe. It was 1,100m long and was divided into a freeride, all-round jump and new school area.

Mountain Information

Mountain chain:

Silvretta Mountains

Vertical metre range:

1,400m - 2,900m

Length of season:

beginning of December - beginning of May

Number of lifts:

5 gondolas, 10 chairlifts, 21 draglifts

Snow-making facilities:

100 machines cover 45kms of piste when needed.

Safety:

Avalanche indicator boards posting daily advice are situated at the three main bottom stations. Off-piste equipment can be hired from the Mountain Guide Association.

Guides:

Snowboard tours are organised by the Ischgl Silvretta Ski School and the Ischgl Mountain Guide Association. For more information, contact Stefan Wolf on - Tel: 05444-5406.

Lift pass prices

swatch access

1 day: Ats350

6 days: Ats1,850

Season: Ats6,479

Lift pass alternatives

The prices quoted are for a VIP pass, which is available to visitors staying in Ischgl, Samnaun or Mathon.

Rider Julian Ettel pic: Richard Walch

Carvers

There are over 200kms of piste in Ischgl and, consequently, endless motorways for all carving abilities. One of the best steep piste areas is the Fimba Nord run from Pardatschgrat down to Ischgl.

GoGo says:

'One of the best resorts ever! Incredible terrain on the backside, towards Switzerland, with windlips, little cliffs and masses of drops, which is the best bombastic area when fresh powder falls. What's more, it's all yours, because the ski geeks don't go off-piste. And it's only two hours from my house.'

pic: Peter Mathis

ABOUT TOWN

Up until 1963, when it installed its first cable car, Ischgl was a typical mountain mining town. Now, it is one of the best serviced mountains in Europe with a vibrant snowboarding community, but it has still managed to maintain much of the traditional Austrian culture.

FREESTYLERS DIG
ONE OF EUROPE'S
LARGEST
FUNPARKS
CALLED THE
'BOARDER'S
PARADISE'

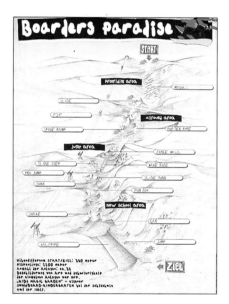

Essential Contacts

Tourist office

Tel: 05444-5266   Fax: 05444-5636

Snowboard shops

• Sport Mathoy   Tel: 05444-5514

Board/boot hire: Ats450/day

• Sport Salner   Tel: 05445 5555

Board/boot hire: Ats450/day

Snowboard schools

• Snowboard School Ischgl

Tel: 05444-5257   Fax: 05444-5752

3 day group lesson: Ats1,200

Probably the best all-round school.

Getting there

By plane: The closest airport is Innsbruck, from where the bus or train transfer takes two hours.

By train: The closest main station is Landeck, from where there is a bus transfer - Tel: 05445-2660.

By car: Head towards Pians and take the turning to Ischgl. If you're coming from Munich, check the Arlberg pass conditions.

Accommodation

The cheapest form of accommodation is either a private room in a Gasthaus or an apartment. Prices range from Ats330 to Ats550. The following come recommended: Irmgard - Tel: 05444-5123, Elisabeth - Tel: 05444-5480 and Bergkristall - Tel: 05444-5297. Otherwise, try the Eggrestüberl - Tel: 05444 5360 from Ats700 per night or the Daniel - Tel: 05444-5356 at around Ats580 per night. For more information, contact the tourist office - Tel: 05444-5266.

Food

For wallet watchers, there is a kiosk serving fast food snacks. For others, the Pizzeria La Nona does the best pizzas and pastas - the price of a meal, with a beer, ranges from Ats140 to Ats200. For typical local food, the Eggerstüberl is recommended, while for a more international, slightly up-market meal, try the Trofaneralm, where dinner costs from Ats180 to Ats300.

Nightlife

Ischgl is reputed to have the best nightlife in the Alps. Before the sun has even had a chance to go down, the après-ride antics can be extremely riotous. Try bars like the Kuhstall, the Treff Punkt, the Kitzloch and the Niki's Stadl, all of which have happy hours and schnapps specialities. For late night dancing, go to the Alte Lobli and the Madlein Wunderbar. The latter, because it plays techno and hip-hop music, is where the young crowd grooves.

Other activities

There are an adventure pool and a sauna, a steam bath, massages, a solarium, a bowling alley, billiards and covered tennis courts. Ask at the tourist office for more details.

Thanks to

Peter Reiner, GoGo, the Ischgl Tourist Office and The Cableways.

GoGo and Friends Boogie pic: Andy Jackson

Kaunertal

ON THE MOUNTAIN

The approach to the mountain is quite spectacular - it's a half hour drive up switchback roads from the valley floor, eventually leaving the tree line behind and heading up towards the glacier. The resort itself, resting at 2,150m, opens into a huge bowl and receives reliable snow conditions year-round. The view from the top station belies a mountain crammed with riding opportunities, if you know where to find them - often taking a guide will assist. Kaunertal has put a lot of effort into snowboarding both in summer and winter - watch out for the test centres and the camps. The Burton team - among others - camped here in '96. The Kaunertal Opening, in October, kicks off the main season with a monster party.

Snow conditions

Conditions at Kaunertal are generally reliable as it lies at high altitude. If conditions on the mountain aren't good, there is always the glacier, open year-round.

Freeriders

As Kaunertal is above the tree line, it lacks in forested areas, but there is plenty of other great stuff. Powder junkies should take the Nederjoch lift for the 'Variante' run, where there's a back area with a half hour powder run and cliff jumps back down to the road (at Fërnergrieß). You will need to get a lift back to the resort, but it's usually not a problem. There are a couple of nice cliff jumps above and to the left of Ochsenalm, the base station. If you are into a bit of a hike (about two hours), head out from the top of Nederjoch and around Weißseespitze. There are some cranking runs from here, however it's important to take someone who knows the terrain. From the top of Dreiländerblick, hike over the back and ride into Italy - a guide and a passport are necessary, but getting back can be a bit of a hassle.

Freestylers

The halfpipe is an ISF standard pipe and is kept in top-notch shape by a local called Mulle - sometimes his walls are over 2.5 metres high. It is located in the Nördersoch 2 area and can be accessed by the Weißsee T-bar, or by hiking. The funpark and boardercross course are also located by the Weißsee T-bar, disembark at the halfway station. Usually there are gap jumps, table tops and various hits, but there were no rail slides in the '96 season.

Carvers

Good carving is found under Nederjoch 1 and 2, and also under the Karles T-bar.

Lifts to avoid

For beginners, the Weißsee T-bar is long and not much fun.

Mountain fare

The only option is the Gletscher Restaurant. It's not very special or cheap, but it serves a range of international cuisines.

Mountain Information

Mountain chain:
Gletscher Region, Kaunertal Fendels

Vertical metre range:
2,150m - 3,160m

Length of season:
All year, thanks to the glacier.

Number of lifts:
3 chairlifts, 4 T-bars

Snow-making facilities:
There is limited snow-making on the bottom lift, but then there's always the glacier!

Safety:
There are warning boards at the base of the mountain and warning lights down the lifts, if conditions are particularly dangerous. The area is avalanche prone - be warned.

Guides:
The ski schools organise guides.

Lift pass prices:
1 day: Ats410
6 days: Ats1,790

Lift pass alternatives:
Other options include a pass that services the whole Kaunertal region, which includes Serfaus, Fiss, Ladis, Fendels, Kaunertaler Glacier, Nauders and Venetberg.

Gletscherregion·Tirol
Kaunertal

pic: Peter Mathis

Funpark pic: Helmut Wahl

Essential Contacts

Tourist office

Tel: 05475-292

Snowboard Shops

•Plankensteiner Tel: 05475-423

(tuition is also available)

Board hire: Ats290/day

Boot hire: Ats120/day

3 days of group lessons:

Ats1,100 without a board

Ats1,350 with a board

1 day trial lesson (with board): Ats550

•Freaks on Snow Tel/Fax: 05475-479

Snowboard schools

•Top Snowboard school Tel: 05475-297

•Freaks on Snow Tel/Fax: 05475-479

Both schools are large with experienced

instructors:

3 day group lesson

(including board/boot hire): Ats1,500

ABOUT TOWN

As it's not actually possible to stay at the resort, accommodation is found in nearby Feichten, a small village which sits at the base of the mountain in a valley that has imposing cliffs on either side. It can be extremely quiet mid-week, but livens up at the weekend.

Getting there

By air: Innsbruck, Munich and Zürich are the nearest airports.

By train: Take the train to Landeck and then the bus to Kaunertal. The bus station is at the train terminal, from where there are regular connections. The earliest bus leaves at 7.30am and the last bus at 5.00pm.

By car: From Munich, take the highway A12 in the direction of Arlberg till the Landeck exit, then follow the signs to Reschen Pass to Prutz and turn left to Kaunertal. From Zürich, head in the direction of Chur till the E64 and then go north to Feldkirch. From there, take the E60 to Landeck, Zams. Travelling through the Arlberg tunnel will cost Ats150.

Accommodation

There are reasonably priced private rooms and pensions, which can be arranged through the tourist office's reservation service. For example, for bed and breakfast, Haus Bergland, Ats180-240 - Tel: 05475 228; Haus Sonnenheim, Ats180-240 - Tel: 05475 266; and Pension Seehof, Ats170-260 - Tel: 05475 216.

Food

There are two shops where self-caterers can buy food, but they are not really supermarkets. For eating out, the Pub Kiwi offers a range of foods and snacks such as pizzas from Ats75 to Ats90. The Sonnenhof has great Tyrolian foods, steaks, salads, meals and beer from Ats200 to Ats270. The Feichtnerhof is a more Tyrolian style restaurant with good sized meals and beer from Ats190 to Ats230.

Nightlife

The weekends see an influx of riders into Feichten and it becomes a party town. Drinking often starts at the glacier's bar at the day's end, getting more serious sd the night progresses. The town itself is small - most people go to the Pub Kiwi and the Zappadello Bar. During weekends, the popular late night spot is the Disco Tenne, which has a great sound system and lightshow; open till 4/5.00am. The local Wieselburger brew is a good drop at Ats38 a 'seitl' (0.3 of a litre).

Other activities

There are skate ramps, for normal use, on the glacier. The Kaunertal Centre has a sauna, whirlpool, waterslide, gym and bowling. During the spring, there is mountain-biking, tennis, hiking and rock-climbing in Feichten.

Thanks to

Pipi and Mulle.

Ötztal/Sölden

ON THE MOUNTAIN

The Ötztal Arena has a vast array of winter terrain to explore, with great tree runs that have natural halfpipes and cliff drops lower down the mountain. Hooking up with the locals is probably the easiest way to locate the best stuff and is essential if your stay is short. An added bonus of the Ötztal area is the year-round glacier, where camps are held in the summer. It's also one of Europe's biggest test centres.

Snow conditions

As the resort has a glacier and is at a reasonably high altitude, the snow is reliable and, as early as the end of October, there is often powder.

Freeriders

For those into powder, when the conditions are right, there are several large open bowls - mostly ungroomed - which provide long open fields under Heidelbahn and long fast runs. There are also some steep runs dropping under the main gondola, Gasilachkogelbahn. Some excellent freeriding and tree runs (if you know where to look) are to be had under the Wasserkar Lift, and, if you don't mind hitch-hiking back, there are more wooded areas from under Gaislachalm down to the road. There are plenty of hits all over Sölden, so we suggest you hook up with a local in the know to ensure that you find the best terrain. For the intermediate, cruising rider, Hochsölden has some good terrain in the Giggijoch area. Good for both intermediates and beginners is the backside, towards Vent, which leads to the Tiefenbach Glacier. During summer, the glacier has a good range of freeriding opportunities.

 Freestylers

The halfpipe and funpark are located together, but they move with the seasons, so in winter they're in Giggijoch (under the Langegg lift) and in summer they're in the Rettenbach glacier region (accessible from the Karleskogellift). The pipe and funpark, with everything including hits, table tops and quarterpipes, are well maintained throughout much of the winter. In the summer, snow conditions mean the hits are a little slushy, but have good landings. For more information about the Billabong Summer Camp in July - Tel: 01532 1152. In the '96/'97 season, Sölden will be hosting the first of the three European legs of the ISF Boardercross World Tour '97.

Carvers

Sölden and Hochsölden are always snow-covered, well-groomed and wicked for carving, but they can get crowded.

Mountain fare

Dishes and drinks vary in price from about Ats50 to Ats150, which is less expensive than the skiing area.

Rider: Tommy Johanssen   pic: Calle Eriksson

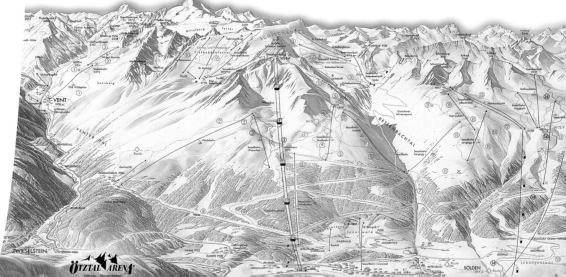

 ÖTZTAL ARENA

pic: Peter Mathis

ÖTZTAL IS A YEAR-ROUND GLACIER, WHERE CAMPS ARE HELD IN THE SUMMER. IT'S ALSO ONE OF EUROPE'S BIGGEST TEST CENTRES

Essential Contacts

Tourist office

Tel: 05254-221 20   Fax: 05254-3131

Snowboard shops

• Intersport Glanzer Tel: 05254-2223

Alpine-oriented, Intersport often has new systems (such as step ins) to test, as well as a good hire fleet.

• Riml Sport Tel: 05254-2223

Snowboard schools

• Ski School Ötztal   Tel: 05452-2203 500

The snowboard school is part of the ski school.

ABOUT TOWN

Sölden, one of the higher Austrian resorts, is located at the end of a river valley and has a long main road running through its centre. Quite isolated from Austria's major centres, it is a mixture of old and new hotels and facilities, which reflectS the fact that it is a relatively modern resort - only about 15 years old. However, it's home to one of the best après-board/nightlife areas in this part of the valley.

Getting there

By air: The closest airports are Munich, Zürich and Innsbruck.

By train: Travel from Innsbruck to Ötztal Bahnhof, then take the bus from the railway station to Sölden. Tel: 0512-717 for train information.

By car: Take the Inntal motorway (A12) and follow the Ötztal exit to Sölden (80kms).

Accommodation

There are a large number of pensions and hotels, ranging in price from Ats350 to Ats2,000 per night, that will suit every budget. Cheaper options include B&Bs such as the Pension Carmen - Tel: 05254-2640, where prices are from Ats335 to Ats370 per night, or the Pension Herta - Tel: 05254-2346, priced from Ats300 to Ats350. A little more expensive is the three star Hotel Alten Mühle, where prices range from Ats590 to Ats640 per night. For more details and options, contact the tourist office - Tel: 05254-221 20 or Fax: 05254-3131.

Food

For a late night feeding frenzy, the Stampear serves meals until 2.30am.

Nightlife

Although there are lots of drinking spots in Sölden, very few have a good vibe for snowboarders. One of the better venues is the Bierhimml, which has live bands and is a good place to start the night. The Amadeus, a disco pub that can get quite lively, is usually the next port of call. For quieter evenings, Le Bistro has four pool tables. The best nightclub in town is the Centre Club, known as CC's, which has a great sound system and is open till late.

Other activities

You can swim in the Sport Centre at the Freizeit Arena, paraglide, cross-country ski, sled, ice-skate, indoor climb, play badminton, bowl, use the fitness centre, take a horse-sleigh ride, or have a sauna, solarium, steam bath or massage.

Thanks to

Klaus Marko and the tourist office.

Rider. Jenny Johnsson   pic: Calle Eriksson

Axamer Lizum

Mountain chain:

Axamer Lizum

Vertical metre range:

1,583m - 2,340m

Length of season:

beginning of December - mid-April

Number of lifts:

1 gondola, 5 chairlifts,

4 T-bars

Snow-making facilities:

The sky.

Safety:

There are indicator boards
at the top and bottom of most
major lifts.

Guides:

The Alpinschule Innsbruck

Tel: 0512-5460

The Schischule Axamer Lizum

Tel: 05234-8868

Lift pass prices:

swatch access

1 day: Ats360

6 days: Ats1,620

Season: Ats3,895

Linked or nearby resorts:

Mutteralhbahn and Glungezer, both
close to Innsbruck.

pic: Richard Walch

ON THE MOUNTAIN

Axamer Lizum is a great mountain for all types of boarders; there are plenty of slopes for beginners right up to extreme terrain for more experienced riders. Alpine riders will find plenty of well-prepared pistes on which to carve, while freestylers have a plethora of natural ground pipes and jumps, cliffs and hits, as well as a halfpipe and funpark. Freeriders also have great off-piste opportunities, if they know where to look. Take note of the avalanche warning lights on the pylons, as the area can sometimes be avalanche prone.

Snow conditions

The snow conditions are generally reliable, as Axamer is a natural snow trap.

Freeriders

Take the train and follow the A17, looking out for a natural halfpipe about 800m long, a couple of windlips and good sized cliffs. If you look at 'X' on the piste map, there is a big cliff on the right side just before the train goes into the station. When there is no avalanche danger, take the same way down and you will first encounter open powder fields. About halfway down, you will come to sections of trees that are great with the right conditions. It's possible to reach the halfpipe through the trees. Much of Axamer Lixum is extreme, so it is wise to hook up with locals who know the area well, but you can be

sure that there is good freeriding all over the mountain. Find your own line!

Freestylers

To get to the halfpipe, take the train to the top and head down A17, which the locals call Damen Abfahrt. Look out for the natural lips and hits on the way down. Shortly after you pass a hut, there is a run off to the right, which leads to the halfpipe. The pipe is usually kept in a reasonable condition throughout the season. The funpark, located in the same area as the pipe, has rail slides and a mixture of different sized hits, quarterpipes and a high jump.

Carvers

There are fantastic alpine conditions for core carvers, especially if you get there early when most of the pistes have been perfectly prepared.

Lifts to avoid

Avoid pistes A22 and A23, as they're boring.

Mountain fare

The Hoadl House at 2,340m has an awesome view and standard fare.

Tommy Unterweger says:

'I've snowboarded at Axams for five years and I love it. I can freeride and I can ride a pipe, so, as long as there is snow, there is no reason for me to go elsewhere, because here you can find everything a snowboarder could possibly want.'

Tourist office

Tel: 05234-8178

Snowboard shops

•Sport Spezial Innsbruck

Tel: 0512-286 404   Fax: 0512-282 701

Stocks a number of speciality boards and

stands out from the crowd.

•Sporthaus Olympia Innsbruck

Tel: 05234-8891

•Wholly Cow, Anich St, Innsbruck

Tel: 0512-570 461

These are the best snowboard shops in

Innsbruck - the staff are informative and they

stock all you need to hire or buy.

Snowboard Schools

•Snowboard School Olympic

Tel 05234-7415

Group lesson: Ats920/3 days

Board/boot hire: Ats420/week

•Snowboard School Axams   Tel: 05234-8868

•Snowboard School Birgitz

Tel: 05234-3238/4

 ABOUT TOWN

The resort sits tucked-in amongst the mountains. To reach it, the road winds around several switchbacks and passes through a town called Gotzens, a time-warp with old Tyrol-style architecture. At the weekends, lots of visitors come down from Innsbruck (40kms away) and the resort can get busy.

 Getting there

By air: Innsbruck airport is super close, but Munich airport is easily accessible too.

By train: From the Innsbruck train station, catch a special bus to Axamer. From Munich, take the train to Innsbruck, then as above.

By car: From the A12, take the Kematen exit and follow the signs to Axams from there.

 Accommodation

There are two choices - either stay in Axams or in Innsbruck, from where a bus goes to the mountain each day. Hotel Central in Innsbruck is recommended, because it does a package that includes rooms, transfers to and from the resort, lift tickets and meals - Tel: 0512-5920. For more information on local accommodation, call the tourist board and pick from their brochure - Tel: 0512-8178.

 Food

There are two supermarkets in Axams. As for restaurants, try the Bürgerstüben for international cuisine and the Freizeitzentrum or the Taverne located at Axams for pizza. There are a whole range of different choices in Innsbruck city, but a couple of the good ones are Chillies (Mexican) and Papa Joes (Mexican, steaks etc.).

 Nightlife

There are a couple of good pubs in Axams - Le Cou, which has darts and pinball is a good place to start the night. Off Limits has pool tables and a cool vibe. For serious nightlife, Innsbruck is the better option - check out Jimmy's, which offers a hard rock vibe till 1.00am. The Blue Chip (downstairs from Jimmy's) goes later into the evening, but can be more expensive. Other alternatives are the Scotch Club, Spectrum and Büro.

 Thanks to

Tommy Unterweger, Christian Hell and Wolfgang Seidel.

Martin Freinademetz   pic: Reinke Weber

A GREAT MOUNTAIN FOR **ALL TYPES** OF BOARDERS; PLENTY OF SLOPES FOR **BEGINNERS** RIGHT UP TO EXTREME TERRAIN FOR THE MORE **EXPERIENCED**

pic: Richard Walch

MATADORCULTURE WEAR

Matador Culturewear, Obanndlweg 9, D-83355 Grabenstätt, Tel. (08661) 1773, Fax (08661) 6023

Rider: Danny Burrows

HEADOFFICE: Matador, Greimelstr. 28, D-83236 Übersee, Tel. (08642) 5335

Eastern Tirol

Zillertal - Mayrhofen, Hintertux
Kitzbühel Alpes - Kirchberg, Kitzbühel
Fieberbrunn
Europa Sport Region - Zell am See, Kaprun

Riders. Seppi and Frank   pic: G Grübl

Zillertal Mayrhofen/Hinterux

Mountain Information

Mountain chain:

Penken - Horberg

Vertical metre range:

1,800m - 2,250m

Length of season:

mid-December - mid-April

Number of lifts:

on the main mountain:

1 cable car, 3 gondolas, 6
chairlifts, 15 T-bars

on the Ziller Valley Glacier:

1 gondola, 2 cable cars, 13
chairlifts, 10 draglifts

Snow-making facilities:

There are several snow cannons,
which patch up small areas when
needed.

Safety:

Avalanche indicator boards are
located at the main lifts.

Guides:

Contact the Ski School Habeler.

Lift pass prices:

1 day: Ats340

6 days: Ats1,550

Season: Ats3,800

Lift pass alternatives:

A 1 to 3 day lift pass only covers
the Penken and Ahorn area. A pass
for 4 days or longer includes the
Ziller Valley lift, the Hintertux
Glacier and local transport.

 ON THE MOUNTAIN

Mayrhofen receives consistently good snowfall,
which enhances great snowboarding conditions
on a range of freeride terrain, including cliff
drops, windlips and vast powder fields. The
Zillertal Pass allows access to 154 lifts in the
Zillertal region, including the glacier of
Hintertux, about 430kms of piste and endless
off-piste.

Snow conditions

Most of Mayrhofen's riding is above 1,550m
and so the snow conditions are generally
reliable. Otherwise the Hintertux Glacier, one
of the most spectacular in the Alps, is a day-
trip from the main resort.

 ### Freeriders

Hintertux and the other mountains in the area
provide grounds for weeks of exploring. Here
are a few good steers. A short half-hour hike
up from the Nordanbahn lift will take you to a
powder face, below which is a permanent
windlip. There is also great freeriding under
the Schafskopflift. For other freeride options,
talk to the riders at Granat or ask at the Total
Snowboard School.

 ### Freestylers

A halfpipe is located at the Penrenlift. It was hand-
shaped for'95/'96 by the Total Snowboard School and,
when it was operational, was first class. However,
there was not enough snow to keep it alive for the
whole season. The funpark is located at the
Tappenalm. It's open all season and there are a couple
of table tops and quarterpipes for all 'stylers from
beginners to pros. There's also a loud sound system
which plays all day - bring your own tapes.
During the summer, the 'Snow Park Camp' is held on
the Hintertux glacier with numerous man-made
objects and reasonable freeriding. Contact Klaus
Marco - Tel: 0644-3080 574.

 ### Carvers

The best area for carving is Tappenalm.

Lifts to avoid

None.

Mountain fare

The best area for snowboarders to meet and hang out
is the Vronis Skialm - it has good music, food and
drink.

"THERE'S A NICE SCENE, WITH GREAT TERRAIN,
NOT TOO MANY PEOPLE, A GREAT TOWN, A GOOD
PLACE TO HANG OUT, AND IT'S CLOSE TO THE
HINTERTUX GLACIER, AND A LOT OF OTHER GOOD
RIDING AREAS, SO YOU KIND OF GET STUCK HERE."
TOMMY EBERHARTER

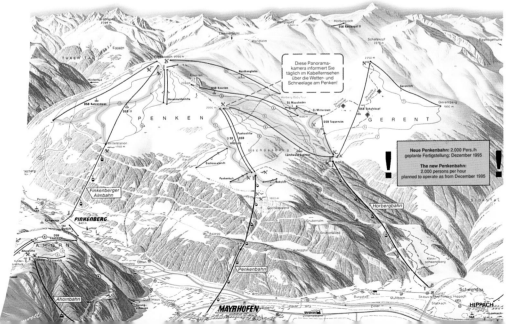

pic: Peter Mathis

By train: The closest station is Jenback, from where there are connecting buses to Mayrhofen.
By car: When travelling from either Innsbruck or Munich, take the Zillertal exit to Mayrhofen.

 Accommodation

There are a number of cheap options for boarders. One of the most popular is the Pension Rosenhof, which is next to the Scotland Yard Pub - Tel: 05285-2252 or 05285-2932. The other option is the Landhaus Carla, a cheap B&B, prices from Ats250-300 - Tel: 05285-2345. The tourist office offers a booking service and further advice - Tel: 05285-2305/2635.

Food

The Pizzeria Mamma Mia has the best pizzas in town, but if cheap traditional food is more to your taste-buds the Restaurant Tirolerstuben and the Wirtshaus Zum Grienahas serve a wide range of local dishes.

Nightlife

For a good chin-wag and a relaxing pint, head for the Scotland Yard Pub or Mo's Bar. Funkmasters can try the Apropos club and the Disco Papageno, both of which close at 3.00am.

Other activities

There is a skateboard mini-ramp next to the police station and the river, good spot! Club Zillertal is the number one address for other winter sports such as tube tobogganing, tandem gliding and snowbobbing - all equipment is on hire. There are also a swimming-pool, fitness studios, tennis, squash, table tennis, bowling and billiards in town.

 Thanks to

Thomas Eberharter and the Baked Beans Snowboard Club.

pics: Mayrhofen Tourist Board

Essential Contacts

Tourist office
Tel: 05285-2305/2635   Fax: 05285-4116
Snowboard shops
• Granat   Tel: 05285-2711   Fax: 05285-2400
The best snowboard store in the area - the staff are more than helpful and quality equipment is for hire.
Snowboard schools
• Snowboard School Total
Tel: 05285-3939   Fax: 05285-2795
3 days of group lessons: Ats980

ABOUT TOWN

Mayrhofen is a large classic town, which has grown very rapidly over the last decade to become the area's liveliest centre. It has the best nightlife in the region and, combined with the fact that it offers access to the various mountains in the Zillertal Valley, Mayrhofen is home to one of the fastest growing snowboarding scenes in Austria.

Getting there

By plane: Innsbruck - a 1.5 hour transfer away - is the closest airport. The other close airports are Salzburg and Munich, from where the transfer takes three hours.

SESSIONS

SANTA CRUZ, CALIFORNIA

Quality Snowear Since 1983

terry Kidwell

Peter Ström

Steve bailey

Jamie Lynn

Jenny Jonsson

Aaron Vincent

DISTRIBUTORS

(A) Quality Products • *tel: 43.512.390040 fax: 43.512.390040.40*
(B) (NL) (LUX) Transind • *tel: 32.2.521.9502 fax: 32.2.521.0841*
(CZ) Mystic Skates • *tel/fax: 42.2.264.675*
(F) Tisseau Bros' Company • *tel: 33.4.76.17.20.10 fax: 33.4.76.17.20.12*
(D) Water Colors • *tel: 49.928.4.4411 fax: 49.928.4.4483*
(GB) (IRL) A4 Distribution • *tel: 44.1925.757.999 fax: 44.1925.757.333*
(GR) Micro Extreme • *tel/fax: 30.31.24.0839*
(IS) Missing Link • *tel: 354.551.0020 fax: 354.551.0012*
(I) Ride On • *tel: 39.30.375.3073 fax: 39.30.29.3276*
(N) Barry Q • *tel: 47.22.11.4550 fax: 47.22.11.4554*
(PL) Megaplast • *tel/fax: 48.22.494245*
(SL) Obsession Sports Marketing • *tel: 386.61.131.5162 fax: 386.61.133.9395*
(S) Pork Distribution • *tel: 46.950.12117 fax: 46.950.26117*
(CH) Beach Company • *tel/fax: 41.1.483.0151*

JAMIE LYNN

Kirchberg/Kitzbühel

ON THE MOUNTAIN

Kirchberg is part of the Kitzbühel Alps ski region and offers 190kms of pisted runs thanks to a regional ski pass that incorporates Kirchberg, Kitzbühel, Jochberg and Pass Thurn. Kirchberg and Kitzbühel even use the same mountain and lift company. However, Kitzbühel is more ski orientated, while Kirchberg has a more relaxed attitude to boarders.

Snow conditions

Kirchberg can suffer snow reliability problems, because (at 1,971m) it is a low altitude resort, but it does have a fair number of snow cannons to make up for the shortfall. Having said that, it's still advisable to check on conditions before you leave home.

Freeriders

Intermediates should try the Maierl 1 (chairlifts one, two and three) or the Red 25 (off the Flackalmbahn Lift), both of which have excellent, wide, open and bumpless pistes, with interesting off-piste areas to the sides. Advanced riders and experts will find a number of long runs, cliff-jumps, windlips and hits. Listed below are some recommended runs.

Steinberkogel: This area is prone to avalanches, but - if deemed safe - has some extreme runs with massive rock jumps and a surf area - 'The Wave' - which is a great windlip. Below, there is a natural halfpipe gully, which becomes smaller and more intense towards the bottom, and from where it is a short walk out back to the lifts. Continue back towards the village and you'll find excellent, wide, fast carving pistes.

The Hochsaukaser: From the D8, there is a 1-2km run with a steep gradient, and a 500m vertical drop. For runs of up to 4kms long, take the Fleckalmbahn gondola to the top and try any number of variations on the way down.

Pengelstein 11: The D3 is a long, slow and often cold chairlift, from where a huge jump 'Doctor Death' is located. As the name suggests, the jump should only be used by extreme riders.

Hieslegg: From the D2, there are forested areas and smooth, open powder runs, but don't drop too low, otherwise it's a long walk out.

Gaisberg: There is a rewarding 1.6km run from the top of a rickety old single chairlift.

Freestylers

Previously a halfpipe was formed at the Kitzbüheler Horn ski region, but this was not properly maintained and was poorly situated. Proposals are being made to incorporate a halfpipe into the planned funpark to be situated under the Kasereck chairlift. The selected area has natural skatepark type terrain and is already a congregation point for freestylers. For a natural funpark try the Pegelstein Bowls (located beneath D7) - a freestyler's heaven with three natural halfpipes and many hits.

Carvers

The main section of Black 23, under the Steinberkogel chair, is excellent for extreme carving as it has a wide flat piste with a good gradient. The Maierl chairs and Pengelstein have well-maintained pistes with wide, relatively flat sections for carving.

Lifts to avoid

The Fleckhochalm T-bar is a steep, long groin-strainer.

Rider. Xaverpic: G. Grübl

ABOUT TOWN

Kirchberg is a typical Tyrolean village with a large resort feel, but it hasn't lost its charm as a picturesque mountain paradise. It possesses all the ingredients of a good holiday resort; the mountain is a winter wonderland and the town has a great ambience and nightlife.

Getting there

By air: The closest airports are Munich (a 138km transfer), Innsbruck (an 86km transfer), and Salzberg (a 169km transfer) - from all three there are regular buses to Kirchberg. Buses can be booked by contacting the station - Tel: 05357-2333.

By train: Trains travel directly to Kirchberg from both Innsbruck and Munich.

By car: From Italy, take the Brennerpass to Innsbruck and then the A12 Autobahn towards Munich. Turn off at Wörgl and follow the Brixental Valley towards Kitzbühel. Kirchberg is 6kms before Kitzbühel.

From Munich in Germany, take the E52 to the Austrian border at Kufstein, then head towards Wörgl, taking the St Johann road at the Kitzbühel Brixental turn-off.

Kirchberg has plenty of cheap car-parks.

KITZBÜHEL IS MORE SKI ORIENTATED, WHILE KIRCHBERG HAS A MORE **RELAXED ATTITUDE** TO BOARDERS

Accommodation

For budget travellers, there are a number of guesthouses, which start from Ats210 per night (i.e. the Christian Haus - Tel: 05357-2505 or the Berghaus Pension - Tel: 05357-2671). There are numerous one and two star hotels; the prices vary from Ats180 for the one star Krimbacher Taxi Haus - Tel: 05357-2404 to Ats360 for the B&B Montana Haus - Tel: 05357-2791. For details and a brochure, contact the reservations department - Tel: 05357-2309 or Fax: 05357-3732.

Food

There are three supermarkets selling standard fare at resort prices. Of the restaurants, Bar La Bamba is the best value for money - prices are from Ats200 (with a beer), try the house speciality spare ribs. For quick pub grub, the Boomerang has decent-sized bar snacks such as toasted sandwiches. For traditional Tyrolean meals, such as gulasch and schnitzel, try the Gasthof Bräuwirt which is reasonably priced. There are a number of pizzerias and a Chinese take-away for fast food. For a quick refresher of coffee and superb pastries, try the Konditorei Lorenzoni.

Nightlife

The major late night attraction is The Londoner, which is usually packed wall-to-wall with Dutch tourists and has a party-hard atmosphere. For house and techno die-hards, The Club offers plenty of entertainment.

Other activities

Paragliding, hangliding, horse drawn-sleigh rides, ice-skating, indoor tennis and the like are on offer. Ask at the tourist office for further details.

pic: Kitzbühel Tourist Board

Thanks to

Chris 'The Kat' Kapma.

Essential Contacts

Tourist office
Tel: 05357-2309   Fax: 05357-3732

Snowboard shops
•Sporthaus Rieser
Tel: 05357-2678 Fax: 05357-3307
Board/boot hire: Ats310/day
•Sport Rudi   Tel: 05357-3413   Fax: 05357-3901
Board/boot hire: Ats310/day
•Sport Ober Tel: 05356-2365
•Sport Etz Tel: 05356-2756

Snowboard schools
•Schischule Kirchberg
Tel: 05357-2209   Fax: 05357-2156
half day group lesson: Ats500
•Ski School Total   Tel/Fax: 05357-3726
Group lesson: Ats650/day

Fieberbrunn

 ON THE MOUNTAIN

Fieberbrunn is a relatively small, but perfect all-round, mountain for all levels of boarder. There are good beginner sections at the mid-station of the main cable car and off the Weissach T-bars; intermediate areas are under the main cable car at Streuböden, Lärchfilzkogel and Doischberg; and the more advanced will find extreme terrain and off-piste areas off the Reckmoos. With good snow-making facilities and reliable fall, this resort rocks.

✳ Snow conditions

Although Fieberbrunn is at reasonably low altitude, it is known to be a snow trap and often has the longest season in the region.

Freeriders

First off, either check with the locals or take a guide when visiting the next two areas. There are great steep and well-spaced tree runs dropping left of the fence under the Lärchfilzkogel - just make sure you don't go too far down before cutting back to the lift. Another good off-piste area is over the top of the avalanche barriers from the top of Lärchfilzkogel - keep following the valley down to the bottom station. Off the right side of Reckmoos, past the avalanche barriers, is a good windlip and tree run.

There is even better off-piste with a bit of hiking, but riders should definitely take a guide with them as the area can be hazardous.

Freestylers

Fieberbrunn is host to one of the two ISF world pro tour competitions 'Lord of the Boards'. Once the monster ice-halfpipe is constructed for the event it is maintained for most of the season, to the delight of punters and practioners. In '95/'96, the ISF competition was a night final, so floodlights were installed and have increased the opening hours of the pipe till 9.00pm. Riders can hike up to the pipe, located at the Streuböden gondola base station, from the car park. The funpark, usually located to the left of the main piste under the Streuböden lift, is only built when good snow conditions prevail. The jumps are also dependent on the snow conditions,

Rider. Sani pic: G. Grübl

which meant that in the lean season of '95/'96 there were none. In previous years, there were table tops and quarterpipes, but - sorry jibbers! - no rail slides.

Carvers

The ISF giant slalom course, located on Doischberg, has aconsistent gradient and is always well-groomed.

✖ Lifts to avoid

If at all possible, avoid the Lärchfilzhochalm T-bar, as it is long and uneven.

Mountain fare

There are three main restaurants, the Alpen Gasthaus at Steuböden, the Wildalpgattal and the Lärchfilzhochalm, which are all fairly expensive, large caféteria style restaurants. The Teehütte at the Rechmoos mid-station and the Lerl over the backside of the Reckmoos offer more traditional foods and services such as sausages, Schnitzels and glühwein at a reasonable price.

ABOUT TOWN

Fieberbrunn is a typical, small Tyrolean village, which is strung-out along a long valley road. It is self-contained, quaint and unspoilt, and is a great place to experience a slice of rustic Austria, as well as to access some of the region's better riding terrain.

Getting there

By plane: The closest airport is Munich, from where it's a two hour journey by bus or train. Groups of up to eight people can order a taxi from Dödlinger. For advance reservations - Tel: (43) 5354-6206.

By train: The journey from Munich (changing at Worgl) takes 90 minutes and costs Ats350.

By car: The route from Munich is clearly marked and always open.

Accommodation

A number of pensions provide B & B services from Ats200-300, while a number of hotels offer half-board from Ats550-700. The tourist office has a brochure (with detailed information and prices) that makes it easy for you to pick your ideal spot. ALso ask at the tourist office for special accommodation, full-board and lift tickets from Ats3,200-4,000 a week. For more information - Tel: 05354 6304 Fax: 05354 2620.

Food

There are a couple of places in town serving cheap, hearty meals at reasonable prices. For pizza, try the Imbis-Kink, the Londoner Bar or the Pizzeria; for a varied menu with traditional Tyrolean dishes and pizza, head for the Alte Post - prices are Ats70-100. The Neue Post has the same sort of fare, plus Tex-Mex, but is more upmarket. For good Chinese food, The Jade is close to the church.

Nightlife

There are four options for a good night out. The Londoner Pub and the River House, located on the other side of the river opposite Imbiss-Kink, both offer pool, bands, food and cheap beer (magic words), in addition to which they both stay open until the last person leaves. The Saloon is a western-style cowboy pub that stays open till late. The only nightclub is the Tenne, which has a great sound system, light show and DJ, Herbie, who plays some interesting tracks that will help you experience the future. It's open till 4.00 -5.00am.

NB: Try out the local potent, the 'jagertee', which is warm, rummy and wine-like. After one, you'll be stylin', after four you'll face plant - be warned.

Other activities

Swim at the Aubad Fieberbrunn pool and sauna complex or try the illuminated toboggan run and snow-rafting that operate on certain nights at Weissach.

Rider. Seppi pic: G. Grübl

Thanks to

Ines, Fieberbrunn tourist office and Drew Stevenson.

Essential Information

Tourist office

Tel: 05354-6304   Fax: 05354-2620

Local snowboard shops

There are four general sports stores, all of which hire out snowboards from Ats280/day.

- Sport Stöckl   Tel: 05354-6345
- Sport Widmann   Tel: 05354-2540
- Sport Kogler   Tel: 05354-2266
- Intersport Günther   Tel: 05354-2620

Snowboard schools

- Ski and Snowboard School (Fieberbrunn)

Tel: 05354-2540

Half day group lesson: Ats350

- Ski and Snowboard School (Rosenegg)

Tel: 05354-2715

Half day group lesson: Ats350

Zell Am See/Kaprun

Mountain Information

Mountain chain:

Europa Sport Region -
Schmittenhöhe (Zell am See) -
Kitzsteinhorn (Kaprun) -

Vertical metre range:

750m - 2,000m (Zell am See)

911m - 3,029m (Kaprun)

Length of season:

Beginning of December to April,
although the glacier at Kaprun is
open all year.

Number of lifts:

6 cable cars, 3 gondolas,
11 chairlifts, 38 T-bars

Snow-making facilities:

On most of the major pistes down
to the village of Zell am See.

Safety: Avalanche indicator boards
are located at most major lifts and
ski patrol checks.

Guides:

Ask at the ski school.

Lift pass prices:

swatch access

1 day: Ats400

6 days: Ats1,930

Season: Ats6,400

Lift pass alternatives:

These passes give you access to
Zell am See, Maiskogelbahn,
Kaprun and Thumersbach. The
Golden Ski Card, in addition to
those areas accessible with a
normal pass, allows you to visit the
Dachstein Tauern Region, the
Dachstein West Ski Region and the
Dolomite Super Area.

 ON THE MOUNTAIN

The Europa Sport Region offers a complete riding holiday, with trees, cliff drops, powder fields, halfpipes, boardercross and much more. It would take at least ten days to explore the main runs, let alone the rest. Add to that the consistent snow conditions, a modern lift system and a welcoming attitude to riders, and the area really does everything for beginners through to advanced boarders. Its commitment to riders, and its understanding of their needs, is proved by the fact that it hosts the Austrian ISF affiliated Cups and ISF Continental Cups.

 Snow conditions

Zell am See is at a moderate altitude, so it can be unreliable during the main months of February and March.

 Freeriders

To the extreme left of Zell am See, under Beiteckbahn, Glocknerbahn and Areitbahn, where the gradient is gentler, are good spots for novices. At the top of Kaprun, there are good beginner slopes in the Magnetköpflifte and Keeslift areas. To find the best titbits, more advanced riders should go with locals. Cliff jumpers will enjoy the drops from the top of Schmittenhöhe (serviced by the Gipfelbahn chairlift). For serious steeps and freeriding terrain, head under the Sonnengratbahn and Sonnkogelbahn, particularly when the conditions are right. Good freeriding and powder opportunities are found to the right of the Langwiedbahn area, under the Alpine Centre. It's up to you to find the various natural obstacles, hits and drops. In the summer, only the top half of Kaprun is open. With a little

GoGo and Seth

hiking, there are a few cliffs of substantial size to be dropped. Once again, go with the locals.

 Freestylers

Zell am See did not have a halfpipe in the '95/'96 season, but the resort's snowboard co-ordinator, Alexander Hollre, says there are plans - as yet unconfirmed - to have one for '96/'97. The funpark in Zell am See is located next to the Schmiedhoflift and is best accessed by riding down from the Sonnkogelbahn cable car. Well-maintained, it has various hits and jumps. During both summer and winter, Kaprun often has a halfpipe, which is usually in reasonable condition, although it could do with a little more work. It also has various jumps set up over the summer, when there is a snowboard camp. Located at the top of the glacier, the camp is serviced by the two short T-bars which start at the base of the Gipfelbahn (the venicular railway from the top restaurant).

 Carvers

The best carving pistes are in the man-made snow areas. To reach them, head from the top of the main cable car or the top of the Hirschkogelbahn back to the village.

Lifts to avoid

The Ebenberglift (a T-bar) is extremely steep and has banned snowboarders. There are some other T-bars (particularly at the top of Kaprun) which are very long, but are just about usable.

Mountain fare

At Zell am See, the restaurant at the top of the Sonnkogelbahn and the Berg Hotel at the top of the cable car are good. However, the Alpine Centre is probably the best option as it has a sit-down cafeteria offering worstle, sausages, fries, Schnitzels and salad from Ats100 to Ats150. Better still, take a packed lunch!

 ## ABOUT TOWN

The old town of Zell am See is set on the shores of the placid Lake Zell, which, combined with a traffic-free centre, makes it a very relaxing place to visit. The still smaller town of nearby Kaprun is quaint and is more of a summer centre, as it services the Kitzsteinhorn glacier. With wide and varied mountain terrain, plus lively nightlife, Zell am See is one of the better places for all-round entertainment.

Getting there

By air: The closest airports are Munich, Salzburg and Innsbruck.

By train: There are direct trains to Zell am See from Innsbruck and Salzburg. From Munich, take the train to Wörgl and change there for Zell am See - Tel: 0662 1717 for train information. From Salzburg, there is a combined ski train/bus service.

By car: Zell am See is a little difficult to find by car - buy a map! From Salzburg, head down the Altenmark Highway in the direction of Graz, till Bischofshofen and then follow the signs. From Munich, head in the direction of Innsbruck, passing Wörgl, St Johann, Fieberbrunn and Saalfelden, then follow the signs.
NB: The roads in this area only have one lane, so traffic can be slow.

 ## Accommodation

There are lots of places to stay in both Kaprun and Zell am See. Some recommendations include the Pension Alpenrose - Tel: 06542-3334, prices from Ats240 per night with breakfast, and Pension Sonnenhein - Tel: 06542-2893, prices from Ats310 per night with breakfast. Alternatively, try the Pension Strasser - Tel: 06542-3161, prices from Ats190 to Ats240 with breakfast, or the Pension Elisabeth - Tel: 06542-3139. Contact the local tourist office for other alternatives.

 ## Food

Probably the easiest, and definitely the cheapest, alternative is to have a pizza delivered - prices start at Ats100. If you'd rather eat out, the Kupferkessel has huge, hearty servings of pizza and steak, with prices from Ats150 to Ats200 including a beer. The Gasthof Steinerwirt serves typical Austrian food, at prices ranging from

Ats120 to Ats180. If you're into Mexican food, the Deli serves large meals until 9.00pm. There are also a couple of Chinese restaurants and a couple of Italian eateries - Guiseppe and the newer Zum Cäsar - which serve top quality food.

 ## Nightlife

For a choice of 33 beers and a typical pub atmosphere, the Beer Keller is a great place to go. If you try all the beers, it'll cost you a thousand schillings and a monster hangover! Prices start at Ats35 for a bottle of beer. The Hirschen Keller is the snowboard hangout - it has decent music and often hosts theme parties. The Crazy Daisy is good after boarding, as it has a young clientele and live music every night during the winter - prices for beer start at Ats29. In Kaprun, the local brew, Schneller, costs from Ats19 and can be found in the Yeti, a typical snowboard watering-hole. One of the best nightclubs in Zell am See is the Viva, a hip hop club, big enough for 300 people, which is open till 4.00 or 5.00am. The Baun Bar in Kaprun is a very commercial (i.e. not a snowboarder's type of scene) disco, but is the only place open late.

 ## Thanks to

Stefan Gimpl, Dieter Steinhardt, Eddie and the rest of the Heavy Tools team.

Essential Contacts

Tourist offices
Zell am See Tel: 06542-260 00
Kaprun Tel: 06547-864 30

Snowboard shops
•Subway Tel: 06547-8335
The best in Kaprun.
•Intersport Brüwold Tel: 06547-8388
Right on the glacier.
•Intersport Scholz Tel: 06542-2606

Snowboard schools
•SBS Tel: 06547-7257
•Rip Star Tel: 06547-8537
•Board Mania Tel: 06547-4123

COMPLETE RIDING, WITH TREES, CLIFF DROPS, POWDER FIELDS, HALFPIPES, BOARDERCROSS AND MORE

DAVID VINCENT

RUSTY EQUIPMENT FOR BOARDING

Eastern Austria

Obertauern
Schladming
Naßfeld
Gerlitzen
Semmering

pic: Peter Mathis

Obertauern

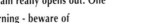

 ON THE MOUNTAIN

Interconnecting lifts allow extensive exploration of the whole Tauernrunde region! While that's heralded as one of the resort's advantages, it can involve a lot of walking on flat cat-tracks. However, when the snow is good, the freeride terrain really opens out. One word of warning - beware of avalanches as most of the riding is above the tree-line.

❋ Snow conditions

Obertauern, thanks to its high altitude and positioning, is snow reliable. However, high winds can cause conditions to change daily.

 Freeriders

As standard procedure, check the stability of landings before attempting what you did the day before, because the area is prone to avalanches. There is an extremely rewarding run a half hour hike from the Gamsleiten Lift, but it is hard to find, so take a guide with you. The front side of the mountain is often full of moguls and best avoided. The north-west side of the mountain (Seekarspitzlift, Panorma, Sessellif) offers some of the best freeriding. Out along the bowl to the right of the Seekarspitzlift, there are windlips and, occasionally, cornices further around. There are also runs under, and to the right of, this run. There are a couple of serious couloirs

 Freestylers

There is a small funpark, usually with a couple of hits and quarterpipes, located at the Plattenkarlift. Obertauern does not have a halfpipe at present, nor are there plans in the offing.

 Carvers

The pistes under Seekarspitzlift are not steep, but they are well-groomed and perfect for carving.

 Lifts to avoid

Although there are no real horror lifts, there are a few T-bars which should be avoided unless the chairs are busy (e.g. the Plattenkarlift T-bar is also serviced by Plattenkarbahn).

 Mountain fare

The Kringsalm is the best self-service restaurant, while the Hochalm is good, but usually crowded.

Mountain Information

Mountain chain:

Radstädter Tauern

Vertical metre range:

1,638m - 2,313m

Length of season:

November - May

Number of lifts:

1 gondola, 10 chairlifts, 15 draglifts

Snow-making facilities:

The resort has 10 snow cannons to help patch the piste when necessary, but the snow is generally good as the resort lies at quite high altitude.

Safety:

There are avalanche indicator boards at every lift station.

Guides:

Contact the snowboard schools (listed on opposite page).

Lift pass prices:

1 day: Ats365

6 days: Ats1,550

Season: Ats5,060

Lift pass alternatives:

When conditions are bad in Obertauern, Zauchensee (half an hour away by car) often has better riding.

pic: Helmut Wahl

Rider. Fred Holdener pic: Helmut Wahl

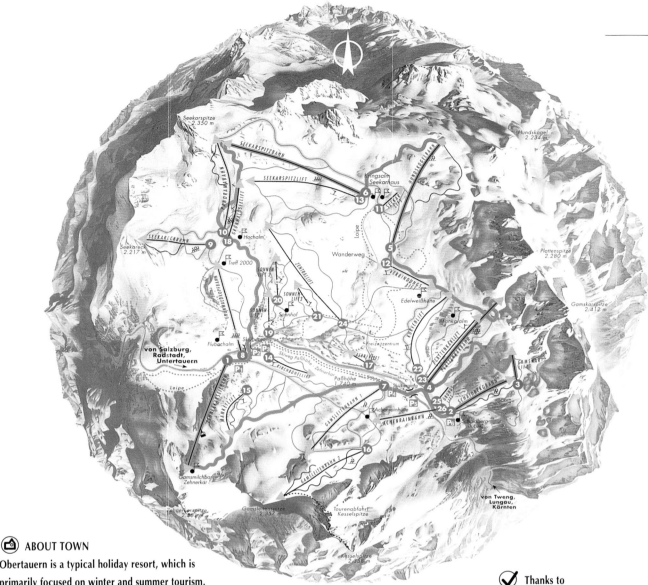

ABOUT TOWN

Obertauern is a typical holiday resort, which is primarily focused on winter and summer tourism. Prices in town are a little more expensive than in other parts of Austria, but the area is visually spectacular.

Getting there

By air: The closest airports are Munich and Salzburg. From the latter, there is a public bus direct to Obertauern four times daily.

By train: The closest station is Radstadt, from where it's a public bus, hitchhike ride or private taxi to Obertauern - Tel: 06621 1717.

By car: From the north exit of Radstadt, take the Altenmarkt (A10) highway until the 'Tauern autobahn' exit at St Michael and travel from Hauterndorf to Obertauern.

Accommodation

It's cheaper to stay in Untertauern or Tweng, both a few kilometres away from Obertauern. In Tweng, room prices at the Martha Santher - Tel: 06471-223 and the Haus Faninger - Tel: 06471-246 start from Ats210, as they do in Untertauern at the Pension

Marchlhof - Tel: 06455 245 and Pension Loitzhof - Tel: 06455 259. The Felseralm - Tel: 6456 203 and the Tauernhof - Tel: 06456 269 are both youth hostel style places.

Food

The supermarket (ADEG) has everything, but at resort prices. There are number of reasonably priced pizzerias and restaurants serving traditional foods, such as Schnitzel, as well as international dishes. Prices are from Ats180 to Ats250 for a meal with a beer. The Taverne is highly recommended for standard pub and Tyrolian grub.

Nightlife

The best starting points for the evening are the Promillo, the American bar and the Polsterzipfl. Later, move on to the Taverne, which will probably be your last stop and where the drinking is priced reasonably. Try the local speciality the Gamsmilchbar, a concoction of milk, cinnamon and rum at the top of the Zehnerkarseilbahn.

Thanks to

Edi Bader and Weiss Andreas (Black).

Essential Contacts

Tourist office

Tel: 06456-7252   Fax: 06456-7515

Snowboard shops

Walk down Obertauern's main street and you will find a number of snowboard outlets. The best, which is more freestyle-oriented, is Blue Tomato.

•Blue Tomato   Tel: 06456-7675

Board/boot hire: Ats300/day

Snowboard schools

•Snowwave Snowboard School   Tel: 06456-6250

Price for a 3 day course: Ats930

•Snowboard Schule Obertauern (the Blue Tomato)

Tel: 06456-7675

LIke its sister shop, freestyle-oriented, it organises a super course class from 2.00pm to 4.00pm daily, costing Ats350.

•Skischule Koch Board Schule

Tel: 06456-7285

Mountain Information

Mountain chain:

Dachstein Tauern Skiparadies

Vertical metre range:

745m - 1,894m

Length of season:

end of November - mid-April

Number of lifts:

4 cable cars, 3 gondolas,

13 chairlifts, 58 T-bars

Snow-making facilities:

Snow cannons cover the pistes when needed, particularly in the Planai and Hochwurzen area.

Safety:

The top of every major station has an avalanche indicator board.

Guides:

Contact the snowboard school (listed opposite) for details.

Lift pass prices:

1 day: Ats375

6 days: Ats1,740

Season: Ats4,900

Lift pass alternatives:

The Dachstein Tauern Region covers 7 mountains and the Dachstein glacier.

pic: Peter Mathis

 ON THE MOUNTAIN

With an all area lift pass, you gain access to seven mountains and the Dachstein glacier, all of which would take several weeks to explore thoroughly. Planai, accessed from Schladming itself, is the main mountain, from where there are plenty of good powder runs in the right conditions, including great drops on to the glacier. The lift system that links this area with the wider region is fast and efficient, and adds to the scope of the resort.

 Snow conditions

As Schladming is mostly north-facing and has an high altitude glacier (2,700m), it is generally snowsure. Most of the major pistes on Hauser Kaibling and Planai have snow cannons, which are used at the beginning and end of the season.

 Freeriders

The best, and the safest, method of exploring Schladming and the surrounding region is to hook up with a local guide - ask at the Blue Tomato Snowboard Shop or at the snowboard school. To start with, however, a few pointers. In good conditions, try the powder runs on the Hitterhausalm areas of Planai, and across the valley under the Gipfellift and Alm lifts. There are some rock hits and cliff jumps on the Dachstein glacier region, as well as under the Mitterstein, conditions prevailing.

 Freestylers

The mountain has two halfpipes - one is located on Planai, under the Larchkogel lift; the other is on the Hitterlam under the Sesselbahn. Both are functional, but could do with better maintenance to keep them in premium condition. For freestylers, the Larchkogel lift is the place to head as there is a pipe, a funpark, a planned permanent boardercross area and trampolines. The funpark has gap jumps and quarterpipes. The Dachstein Schule Tauern (the snowboard school) has its headquarters on site.

 Carvers

As the pistes are smooth and fast, with moderate to steep gradients, they are great for carvers.

Mountain fare

One of the best places to try traditional cuisine in a quaint, wooden hut is at Uncle Willies, where there is often live music. The Kessleralm also serves good food.

pic: courtesy of Schladming Tourist Board

WITH AN AREA
LIFT PASS, YOU
GAIN ACCESS TO
SEVEN
MOUNTAINS AND
THE DACHSTEIN
GLACIER, ALL OF
WHICH TAKE
SEVERAL WEEKS
TO EXPLORE

ABOUT TOWN

Schladming, the largest, and most central town, in
the Datchstein Tauern region, is old and rustic in
appearance. Although there are some modern
developments, these go unnoticed among the
original, narrow streets of the town and the remnants
of the city wall which dates back centuries. Local
residents don't consider Schladming a party centre,
but a visitor will find plenty of entertainment, riding
terrain and Austrian culture.

Getting there

By air: The nearest airports are Salzburg and Munich -
from both it's a couple of hours by train or bus.

By train: Jump on a connection to Schladming's own
station.

By car: Head down the Altenmarkt motorway until the
Schladming turn off, from where the resort is a further
30kms (beware of radar detectors!).

Accommodation

You are advised to book before you arrive, as the
resort tends to get full. The tourist office offers a
booking service, whereby you detail your budget and
requirements, and they organise a reservation - Tel:
03687-22268 for more details. Other options include
the local Youth Hostel, located near the centre of
town, priced from Ats80-90 per night. Pensions
located near the lifts include the Penna, the Wehrhof
and the Fischbacher, all priced from Ats2,500-2,700.

Food

For a cheap, quick fast food option, try the Bosna
Stuberi, where the best burgers in town are served.
There are a couple of great pizzerias, the Giovanne
and the Siedergasse, which serve large portions of
pasta. For even larger, grilled meals, the
Talbachschenke offers a varied menu. There are
plenty of other restaurants offering meals from Ats180
to Ats230 with a beer, but the ones we've named are
the budget choices.

Nightlife

For après-riding and relaxing, the Siglu is one of the
best places to sup a little schnapps or relish a pint.
The main local hang-out is a small bar, Raudis,
located in a side street off the main square. It has
random drink specials and, although pokey, can be
hilarious fun. The Sport Café is the place to shoot pool
and drink beers. La Porta is the place to fuel up before
heading for Sonderbar, which is the best disco in town
and has good music, but is expensive and operates a
somewhat random cover charge.

Other activities

The Sport Hotel has swimming, tennis and squash
facilities.

Thanks to

Eric, Blue Tomato Snowboard Shop and
Snowboard Dachstein Tauern.

Naßfeld

ON THE MOUNTAIN

Naßfeld, located on the Italian border, is a small, picturesque resort. Beginners are best off on the Sonnenalpe, where it's flat and there is a private lift from the ski school. Intermediates will enjoy the Zweierlift. Advanced riders should head to Rudnigtal. Those who just want to bronze themselves will love the Gartnerkofel sun trap. The resort management are in the process of installing a gondola from the village of Tröpolach up to Madritschen (1,919m), which will make the resort more accessible, by eliminating the long drive up to the resort.

Snow conditions

Although good for southern Austria, the resort still has to use its 80-odd snow cannons to keep certain areas in good nick.

Freeriders

The best place to ride is Runigtal, where the runs, some of them steep, are rarely crowded and there's lots of shade, so the powder stays. At Trogkofel, there are some cliff jumps and good powder areas. For another wicked run, hike up to Roßkofel from Madritschen and ride down the little valley. Alternatively, take the FIS lift, hike to Gartnerkofeland and follow the line to the right side of the Gartnerkofel-Vierersesslebahn - there are tree runs lower down the slope.

pic: G. Grubl

Freestylers

There was`a pipe in the '95/'96 season, but its future is uncertain. The funpark is at Sonleitnbahn, where there is a high jump, quarterpipe, rail slides and lots more jumps, so it's almost like a small boardercross. Sonleitnbahn is a little tricky to find, so ask for directions.

Carvers

Take the Sonleitnlift and exit down the right side of the Kanonenrohr lift for some good carving on slope No 51.

Lifts to avoid

The FIS T-bar is tricky.

Mountain fare

The Schlanitzeralm and The Watschigeralm are old Austrian huts serving large portions of traditional food at good prices.

Mountain Information

Mountain chain:

Karnische Region

Vertical metre range:

1,300m - 2,004m

Length of season:

November - April

Number of lifts:

3 quad chairlifts, 20 T-bars

Snow-making facilities:

80 snow cannons have all the slopes covered.

Safety:

There are avalanche indicators boards at the top and bottom of the mountain. The ski school has off-piste rental equipment.

Guides:

Ask at the Sölle snowboard school.

Lift pass prices:

1 day: Ats375

6 days: Ats1,785

Season: Ats4,950

Lift pass alternatives:

A Naßfeld pass includes Weissensee and Kötschach-Mauthen, which are both about 20 minutes away by car.

Essential Contacts

Tourist office

Hermagor

Tel: 04282-2043   Fax: 04282-2043 50

Sonnenalpe Naßfeld

Tel: 04285-8241   Fax: 04285-8242

Snowboard shops

• Sport Sölle   Tel: 04285-8285

Tel: 04282-206 852 (in Hermagor)

• Alpensport Schwarzenländer

Tel: 04285-8165

Snowboard schools

• Snowboard School Sölle

Tel: 04285 8281 or 824-710

Board hire: Ats290/day

Boot hire: Ats120/day

3 days of group lessons:

Ats1,100 without a board

Ats1,350 with a board

pic: F. Witmer

ABOUT TOWN

Hermagor is a small, newish town, where most of the shops, restaurants and supermarkets are spread out along the main road. There are a few bars and pubs for evening drinks, but nearby Villach has more to offer in the way of nightlife.

Getting there

By air: Vienna is the closest airport, from where train and bus transfers run regularly to Villach.

By train: Take a train to Villach and then head in the direction of Kötschach-Mauthen to Hermagor (the trains run from 6.00am - 8.15pm).

By car: Head for Villach and take the 111 to Hermagor.

Accommodation

It's more expensive, but more convenient (as no bus transfers are necessary), to stay in one of Naßfeld's hotels. The cheaper option is to stay in a pension in Hermagor, where having your own car will make life easier. Recommended are the Frühstückpension Enzi in Jenig, where prices range from Ats230 to Ats250; the Oberjörg's Ferienhäuser in Rattendorf, Ats230 to Ats250 - Tel: 04285-227 5527; the Haus Guggenberger in Hermagor, from Ats170 - Tel: 04282-2851; and Haus Jost in Hermagor from Ats170 - Tel: 04282-4080. For more options, contact the tourist office in Hermagor or Sonnenalpe Naßfeld.

Food

Hermagor's main road houses a Chinese restaurant, with meals costing from Ats100 to Ats140. Similarly priced options are available at the pizzerias, where meals are priced between Ats100 and Ats150. More traditional food is on offer at the Gasthot Barenwirt (Ats120-160) and the Lärchenwirt (Ats130-170). In Villach, the Brauhof has typical Austrian food and excellent beer - prices range from Ats80 to Ats120. The India King in the Gerbergasse has meals for Ats120, while the Greek restaurant in the Lederergasse has delicious food from Ats150 to Ats200. The Goldener Löwe serves a wide range of international dishes for Ats120 to Ats180.

Nightlife

For a beer after a day on the mountain in Naßfeld, try the Alpenhof Plattner, the Schneemannbar, the Woldistuben or the Watchigerlam, old ski huts with a great ambiance. For a real party, head for Villach. Go get pissed at the Brachof, where the beer, and the prices, are good. However, the cheapest places for a beer (Ats28) are either the Bistro or the Hutab. The B2 stays open till about 2.00 - 3.00am, as does the Black and White Bar, which is a great place to get loose. Alternatively, try the Walasco, a disco that stays open until 4.00am, or the Fun/Filou, which is usually full of tossers, but can be amusing.

Other activities

Try the gyms, tennis, swimming or ice-skating.

Thanks to

Horst from Sport Sölle and Scharti (Christian Schartner).

Gerlitzen

 ON THE MOUNTAIN

Gerlitzen is neither very steep, nor very big by resort standards, but it is perfect for freestylers and intermediate to advanced freeriders. Look out for the few entertaining off-piste runs to be found, particularly after a good snowfall.

 Snow conditions

There area is at low altitude and therefore conditions can be unreliable, hence the number of snow cannons.

 Freeriding

Take the Gerlitzen - Gipfelbahn for most of the good freeriding. On both sides of the lift, there are plenty of off-piste options, with lots of tree runs. Try Klösterle 1 and 2 for speed.

 Freestylers

There's a great halfpipe at the Pöllingerlift - the Austrian Cup was held there in the '95/'96 season. There is a funpark at the same location with a high-jump, rail slides, quarterpipes and other jumps. Jibbers should take the Neugarten-Abfahrt for good hits, tricks and spins.

 Carving

There is a permanent slalom course, which is always at its best in the morning.

Mountain fare

There are more than ten restaurants, but the pick of the bunch are Restaurant Prince and the Pacheiner Hütte, which both serve good cheap food.

Mountain Information

Mountain chain:

Wintersportregion Villach

Vertical metre range:

900m - 1,911m

Length of season:

December - end of March

Number of lifts:

1 gondola, 6 chairlifts,

6 T-bars

Snow-making facilities:

Lots of snow cannons, which are used extensively.

Safety:

There's minimal avalanche risk, bu there's an avalanche indicator board at the bottom of the gondola. Or, ring the slope hotline: Tel: 04248-2400.

Guides:

Ask at the ski school.

Lift pass prices:

1 day: Ats300

6 days: Ats1,510

Season: Ats3,600

Lift pass alternatives:

Gerlitzenalpe/Kanzelhöhe, Villache Alpe, Debratsch, Oreiländereche and Verditz, as well as to Italy and Slovenia.

pic: Søren Egeberg

Essential Contacts

Tourist office

Tel: 04248-236   Fax: 04248-3295

Snowboard shop

•Sports Unlimited   Tel: 04242-26958

Ask for Markus - he's the man in the know.

Snowboard Schools

•Ski School Kanzechöhg-Gerlitzen

Tel: 04248-3222/4   Fax: 04248-3222

2 hours of lessons for 4 days: Ats900 or

Ats1,500 (inclusive of equipment hire)

 ABOUT TOWN

Annenheim, located beside the picturesque Ossiacher See, is the town servicing Gerlitzen. With only 500 inhabitants, it's one of the smaller villages in the greater Treffen area. Villach is 6kms away and is a better place for entertainment.

➔ **Getting there**

By air: The closest airport is in Vienna.

By train: Take the train to Villach and then take a train or bus in the direction of Feldkirchen, getting off at Annenheim or Sattendorf (from where you can take a bus).

By car: Follow the signs to Villach and then head along the Osstachersee (94) to Annenheim.

 Accommodation

There are a number of small townships dotted around the area where accommodation can be found. A list of recommendations, which start from Ats250, follows: the Gästehaur Martinschitz in Jattendorf - Tel: 04248-2325; the Gästehaus Nagele in Annenheim - Tel: 04248-2734; the Adofine Unterberger in Bodensdorf Tel: 04248-36124; and the Landahus Raimund in Jattendorf - Tel: 04248-2777. For further information, contact the tourist office.

 Food

In Annenheim, there are only two restaurants. The Kanzelstüberl, serving pizzas and sandwiches from Ats90, is located down by the lift station. The Al Castello is a pizzeria charging normal restaurant prices (Ats110-160).

😵 **Nightlife**

For a beer after a day's riding, go either to the Restaurant Price or the Pacheiner Hütte to hang-out with the boarding community. Otherwise, go to Villach (as described in the Naßfeld section).

Someone says

'It's a small resort from where you can ride into Slovenia and Italy on the same ticket. The terrain is not steep, but you can have good fun here!'

Other facilities

A sauna, swimming-pool, solarium, gyms, tennis, ice-skating, ice-hockey, indoor horse-riding, bowling, massage and cinema are all on offer.

✓ **Thanks to**

Friedl Kolar and the tourist office.

PERFECT FOR FREESTYLERS, INTERMEDIATE AND ADVANCED FREERIDERS. ENTERTAINING OFF-PISTE AFTER A GOOD SNOWFALL

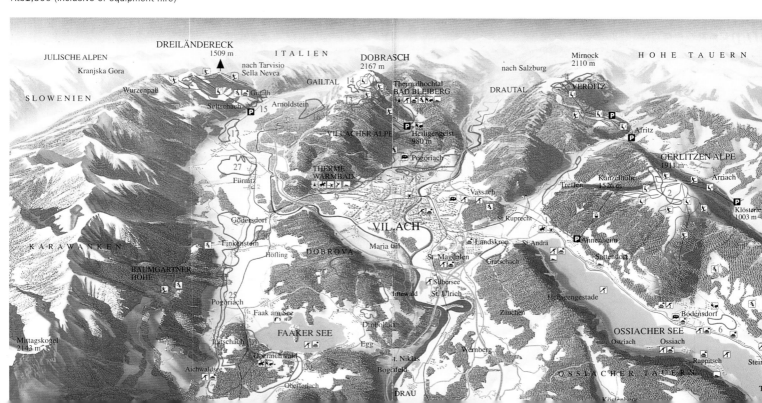

Semmering

 ON THE MOUNTAIN

Semmering does not compare with some of the other resorts, which have more extensive terrain. Most riders will cover the area in a week, but that does not mean that Semmering does not have some enjoyable places for all styles of riding. Freestylers, in particular, will have endless fun on the halfpipe and the soon to be completed funpark. One of the better scenes for snowboarding in this part of Austria, the resort is at the centre of the Eastern scene.

 Snow conditions

It's at low altitude and, consequently, snow conditions suffer.

Freeriders

Stay on the more enjoyable terrain at Hirschenkogel, where there are often two great hits to be found: one is past the halfpipe, the other is halfway down the Kogelabfahrt run. Although not officially allowed, the toboggan run can be a fun, simulated boardercross course and there's an old ski jump close to the end. If there is a lot of snow, there are good tree runs under Doppelesselbahn east. Most of Stuhleck is good for cruising and is, therefore, better for alpine riders. However, those looking for a little back-country should hike from the top of the Berg station towards Stuhleck. The T-bars to either side of the Komfort Vierer-Sesselbahn, at the base of Stuhleck, can be good for beginners.

To make any of these runs more enjoyable, hook up with either a local person who knows the area well or one of the many weekend boarders from Vienna.

Freestylers

The halfpipe is located on the Hirschenkogel and is maintained in reasonable condition by the locals. It is usually built by Christmas and is touted as the best pipe in Europe. Take the West lift up, followed by the Kogelschlepp lift. In '95/'96, Semmering did not have a funpark, but there are plans for a park in the '96/'97 season.

Carving

Most of the Stuhleck is good. When there is new snow, Hirschenkogel is fantastic, because it's too steep to piste, but otherwise it suffers from moguls.

 Lifts to avoid

Unless you're a beginner, the T-bars on Sonnendstein don't give access to anything worthwhile. A lot of the T-bars on Stuhleck are long - avoid the longest ones i.e. Schlepplift and Kaltenbarch.

Mountain fare

Liechtensteinhaus, on the top of Hirschenkogel, has a good range of food such as sausages, Schnitzels and fries, plus more; price for lunch and beer Ats150-180. This is where most of the snowboarders hang out.

Mountain Information

Mountain chain:
Ski Region Semmering

Vertical metre range:
800m - 1,640m

Length of season:
beginning of December - April

Number of lifts:
4 chairlifts, 9 T-bars, 1 baby lift

Snow-making facilities:
Out of the whole region, 10kms are covered by snow-making facilities. Stuhleck has cannons on its main runs up to 1,200m. Hirschen Kogel has snow cannons on three of its major pistes.

Safety:
Semmering doesn't usually suffer from avalanches, but always check with the ski patrol.

Guides:
The mountain is small, so there isn't any great need for guides.

Lift pass prices:
1 day: Ats300
6 days: Ats1,440
Season: Ats4,465

Lift pass alternatives:
The lift pass gives you access to three mountains in the area - Hirschen Kogel, Stuhleck and Sondwendstein.

ONE OF THE BETTER SCENES IN THIS PART OF AUSTRIA, IT IS AT THE CENTRE OF THE EASTERN SCENE

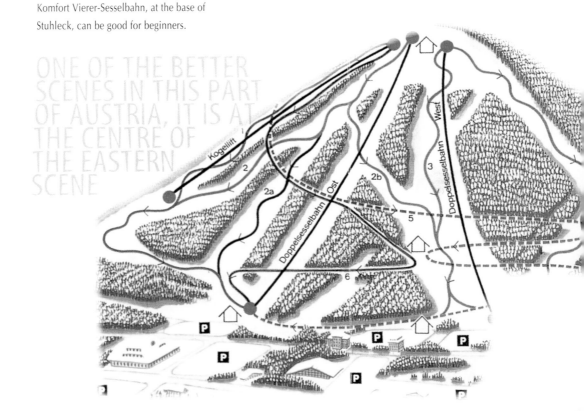

ABOUT TOWN

Semmering appears out of nowhere in the Austrian countryside, with large Victorian style hotels and clandestine rustic buildings atop rocky outcrops. At the turn of the century, Semmering was used by the rich and famous (such as Sigmund Freud and Stefan Zweig) as a mountain retreat, because the air purity was purported to be the best in Europe. Today, it's a small, well-serviced mountain town, which has become a focal point for the Easter snowboard scene. It is the best, and easiest, mountain for visitors from Vienna and the surrounding areas to access, so it can be busy during the day (particularly weekends) and quiet at night.

➜ Getting there

By air: The closest airport is Vienna, a 90km journey away.

By train: There are hourly train services to Semmering from Vienna and Graz.

By car: From Vienna, head down the Sud autobahn A1 and follow the signs to Semmering.

Accommodation

For those with cash to blow on a lover, the four star Hotel Panhans is the place to impress; the price for one night's accommodation is Ats800-1,000 - Tel: 02664-2264. The more economy minded should head for the Pension Haus Ton, priced from Ats270-300 - Tel: 02664-8181; the Berghof Latzlesperge, priced from Ats350-420 - Tel: 02664-2320; and the Pension Edelweiss, priced from Ats395-560 - Tel: 02664-2284. For more information, call the tourist office.

Food

At the base of the Kogel, there are several restaurants (the Gasthof Sonnblick, the Berghoff and the Erzherzog Johann) serving reasonable food at fair prices. There's also a pizzeria on the main road.

Nightlife

There are a number of cafés and restaurants at the base of the mountain, which are reasonable for après-boarding. However, as most people come to Semmering on day trips, the nightlife is limited. The best place for a few drinks is the Pinguin (or the glass igloo dome), close to the main road, and the Gasthaus Sonnblick, on the

pic: Rob Reichenseld

left just before the corner to Hotel Panhans. The only thing which resembles 'nightlife' is the Tanz Café at the Hotel Panhans - good at weekends and holidays, it is even better when the Swedish girls from the hotel school are out to play.

Other activities

Tennis is available at the base station in the winter. There is a swimming pool at the Hotel Panhans which is available to the public. There is also sledding and ice bowling.

Thanks to

Dieter Steinhardt.

Dieter Steinhardt says

'For me it's good to come because the whole freestyle snowboard scene of Vienna and the east stays at Semmering at the weekends. It's the only place near Vienna where you can see a little progression of freestyle snowboarding.'

Essential Contacts

Tourist office

Tel: 02664-2539   Fax: 02664-2335

Snowboard shops

•Puschi Tel: 02664-2471

Board/boot hire: Ats2,500

Board service: Ats300-400

Snowboard schools

•Zentra Sport Puschi Tel: 02664-2471

2 hour private lesson: Ats280

Germany

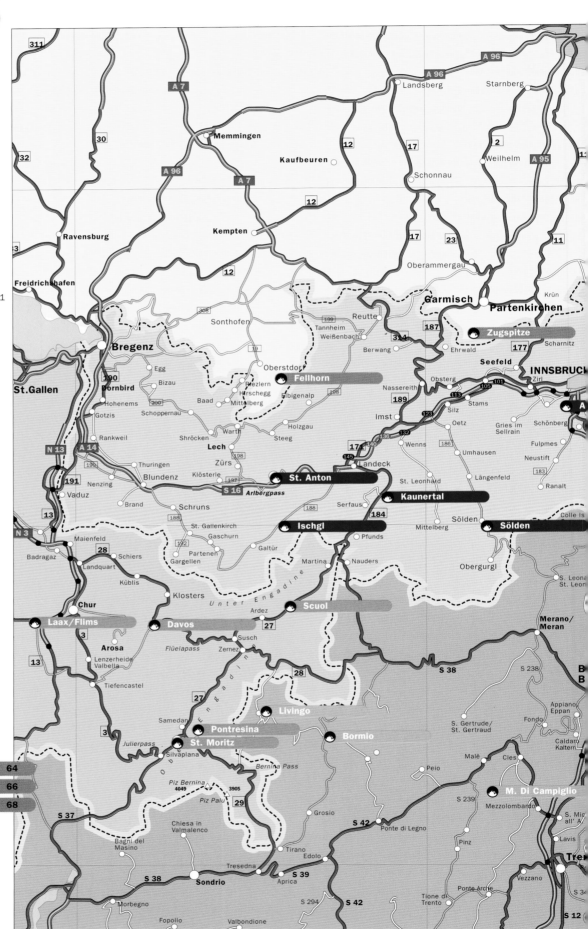

NITROSNOWBOARDS
seth neary
photo by dano pendygrasse

thespiritofperforma
the spirit of performan

Fellhorn pic: Richard Walch

Zugspitze

Mountain Information

Mountain chain:

Zugspitze

Vertical metre range:

710m - 2,964m

Length of season:

November - May

Number of lifts:

27

Snow-making facilities:

The Gods.

Safety:

There is an avalanche indicator board at the base station.

Guides:

The Ski und Snowboard Center Zugspitzplatt.

Lift pass prices:

1 day: 58Dm

6 days: 248Dm

Season: 590-720Dm

Lift pass alternatives:

A 720Dm season pass gives you access to Zugspitze, Alpstitze, Kaprun, Engelburg, Schnalstal and Tignes.

pic: Helmut Wahl

ON THE MOUNTAIN

Zugspitze is the mountain with the longest season in Germany, as it boasts a glacier which is the recipient of early November snow that lasts until late May. As it's only 65kms from Munich, it's popular with the city's snowboard community. The resort itself is not the most challenging, but it gives beginners and intermediates a good grounding on most terrains.

Freeriders

The lifts on the Zugspitzplatt are not very challenging, but are perfect for beginners and intermediates. The runs to the side of the pistes are fun, when there is fresh snow. The Talabfahrt also has interesting terrain for freeriding. There are some windlips at Zugspitzplatt and there are tree areas further down the mountain.

Freestylers

There is a halfpipe.

Carvers

The Zugspitze is the best place for carving.

Mountain fare

There are a couple of restaurants, but neither is especially cheap. Our advice - take a packed lunch.

IT'S ONLY 65KMS FROM MUNICH, AND IS POPULAR WITH THE CITY'S SNOWBOARD COMMUNITY

pic: Uli

Rider. Peter Bauer pic: Richard Walch

ABOUT TOWN

Garmisch-Partenkirchen is a small town with a long history of winter sports. It hosted the Winter Olympics in 1936 and still has a wide variety of facilities available, while retaining the atmosphere of a rural Barvarian village. Situated close to the Austrian border, an hour's drive from St Anton and other larger resorts, it is a great place to visit en route to another destination.

Getting there

By plane: The nearest airports are Innsbruck and Munich, from where Garmisch-Partenkirchen is an hour's ride in a train or bus.

By train: There are trains from Munich to Garmisch-Partenkirchen every hour.

By car: Take the Autobahn from Munich to Garmisch-Partenkirchen, travelling south for 60kms.

Accommodation

Room prices start at 35Dm per night. B&Bs are available in Farchant, a village 10 kilometres from Garmisch-Partenkirchen. For more information, contact the local tourist office.

Food

Tip No.1 - don't eat in the hotels, because they are expensive! There are various Gasthausers serving mostly cheap Bavarian food, some great Italian restaurants in the centre of the village and a MacDonalds, plus several supermarkets.

Nightlife

The only place to drink - and pick up local beauties - is the Music Café. It's not the most progressive place on earth, but it does have sounds and stays open till 3.00am at the weekend.

Other activities

Garmisch-Partenkirchen offers a wide variety of sports facilities, such as a public swimming-pool with a spa and sauna, an ice-skating rink and several places for sled-riding.

Thanks to

Sumo.

Essential Contacts

Tourist office

Tel: 08821-18 06

Local snowboard shops

•Ski und Snowboard Center Zugspitzplatt

Tel: 08821-79 11

Snowboard hire: 40Dm/day

Snowboard School

•Ski und Snowboard Center Zugspitzplatt

Tel: 08821-79 11

2 days of lessons, including boards: 200Dm

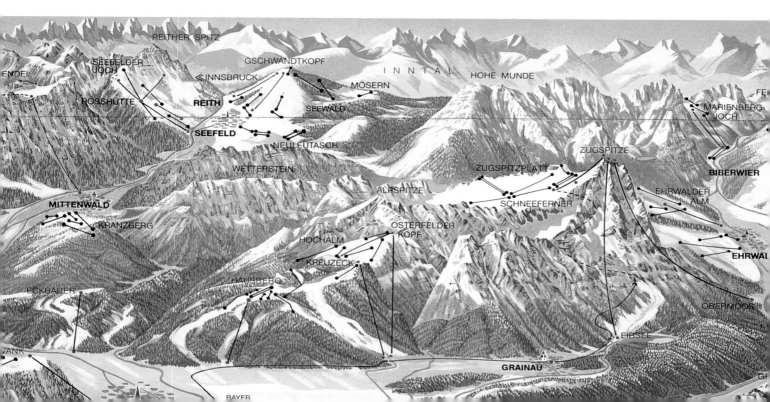

Fellhorn

Mountain chain:

Fellhorn

Vertical metre range:

920m - 1,967m

Length of season:

December - April

Number of lifts:

15 draglifts

Snow-making facilities:

Everywhere.

Safety:

There is an avalanche indicator board at the base station.

Guides:

Ask at the tourist office or Out of Bounds.

Lift prices:

1 day: 52Dm

6 days: 250Dm

Season: 650Dm

Lift pass alternatives:

None

ON THE MOUNTAIN

The Fellhorn warmly welcomes riders of all levels, so the scene is big and friendly. Locals and visitors alike look after one another, and, consequently, it's a great place to learn or improve. Freestylers, however, are particularly well catered for. If you have any queries or problems, Lars or Sven - the local experts at the Out of Bounds Snowboard Shop - will be happy to help out.

Snow conditions

With low altitudes and south-facing slopes, the Fellhorn isn't particularly snow reliable. However, the slopes are protected by trees and there are plenty of snow-making facilities to compensate.

Freeriders

There are a couple of fat jumps off the Wanklift. The Kanzelwand Lift has great powder, but be aware of the avalanche danger. When there is enough snow, the forested area above the village has some great riding.

Freestylers

Freestyle Riders will enjoy the halfpipe, which hosts ISF Pro Tour competitions and is, therefore, always well looked after. It's steep enough to get speed up for big air jumps. The funpark, the best parts of which are the very high tables, is near the pipe.

Carvers

Take the Scheidtoblelift, from the top of which the pistes are perfect for carving.

Lifts to avoid

Some of the lifts can get crowded at peak times.

Mountain fare

The restaurant at the Fellhorn has great food and is a good place to hook up with other riders.

ONE OF THE FIRST RESORTS IN GERMANY TO ACCEPT SNOWBOARDING

pic: Richard Walch

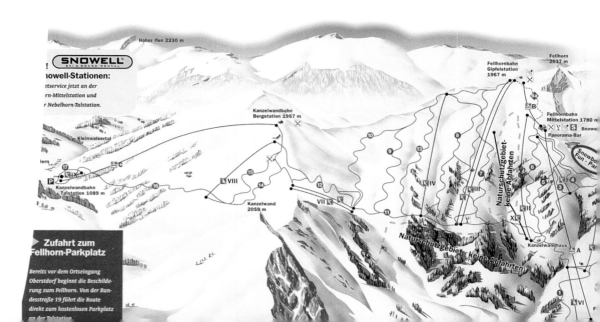

ABOUT TOWN

Obersdorf, where German figure skaters and long distance ski jumpers prepare for international competition, is one of Germany's most important winter sports centres. It was also one of the first resorts in Germany to accept snowboarding, so it is popular with riders, particularly those from nearby Stuttgart. From Obersdorf, Fellhorn is a 15 minutes by car.

Getting there

By plane: The closest airports are Munich and Stuttgart - from both it is a 1 to 2 hour bus ride.
By train: From Munich or Hamburg, catch a train to Kempten, from there take a train to Obersdorf.
By car: From Stuttgart or Munich, head to Kempten and then take the A980 to Waltenhofen, followed by the B19 to Obersdorf.

Accommodation

The cheapest place to stay is the Youth Hostel in Obersdorf. Otherwise, there are cheap pensions and hotels in the centre of Obersdorf. For groups, the cheapest option is to rent an apartment (often part of an old farmhouse) outside Obersdorf for 30Dm per night. For more information - Tel: 08322-805 44.

Food

The Costa Esmeralda serves good, cheap Italian food. Upstairs, there is a Chinese restaurant.

Nightlife

The most fun club in Obersdorf is the Walk In, where the best drink is a huge, sumptuous and frozen strawberry margarita. Often the crew from CPS or H-Blockx hang out here.

Other activities

In Obersdorf, there's a giant public pool with an artificial wave machine, an ice-skating rink and a 12 metre wall for free climbing.

Thanks to

Uli, Lars and Sven.

pic: Richard Walch

pic: Uli

Essential Contacts

Tourist office
Tel: 08322-805 44
Local snowboard shops
• Out of Bounds
Contact: Lars or Sven
Tel: 08322-455/4
Snowboard schools
• Out of Bounds
Tel: 08322-455/4
2 hour group lesson: 130Dm

Sudelfeld

pic: Søren Egeberg

Mountain Information

Mountain chain:

Sudelfeld

Vertical metre range:

800m - 1,624m

Length of season:

December - April

Number of lifts:

20

Snow-making facilities:

None

Safety:

No avalanche problems.

Guides:

Not necessary.

Lift pass prices:

1 day: 38Dm

6 days: 174Dm

Season: 360Dm

Lift pass alternatives:

None.

ON THE MOUNTAIN

Sudelfeld is a favourite spot among Munich's snowboarders. About 20Dm cheaper per day than a comparable resort in Austria, it has great places for both freeriders and carvers. Although not the world's most challenging resort, as most of the slopes are not very steep, it is perfect for beginners and intermediates.

✳ Snow conditions

Although Sudelfeld isn't a high altitude resort, it seems to be a snow trap, harbouring large amounts of the white stuff.

Freeriders

Off lift 10, there is great riding terrain, including a natural halfpipe. If there has been a recent dump of snow, take Lift 9 and walk 300 metres to the left, where there's a brilliant spot that catches, and keeps, powder.

Freestylers

In the '95/'96 season, the halfpipe wasn't in use due to lack of snow. A new pipe is being built at Wallerlift.

Carvers

From the Waldkopf Lifts, there are steep pistes which are perfect for practising carving turns.

🍲 Mountain fare

Great food at reasonable prices at the Sonnenalm, which is also a good place to hang out with the local boarders.

Essential Contacts

Tourist office

Tel: 08033-301 20

Local snowboard shops

Knott & Stadler Sporthaus

•Oberaudorf   Tel: 08033 1467

Board hire: 30Dm/day

Snowboard schools

There are plans to open a snowboard school in Sonnenalm for the '96/'97 season.

Rider Helmut Boxenriter pic: Wolly Rooster

ALTHOUGH SUDELFELD ISN'T A HIGH ALTITUDE RESORT, IT SEEMS TO BE A **SNOW TRAP** HARBOURING **LARGE** AMOUNTS OF THE **WHITE STUFF**

ABOUT TOWN

Oberaudorf, 10kms away from Sudelfeld, is a small town close to the Austrian border that has been built in typical Bavarian style. A handy one hour drive from Munich and Innsbruck, it is also close to some large Austrian resorts. Due to its location, Sudelfeld has a regular influx of city weekenders and holidaymakers, so it can get crowded at peak periods.

Getting there

By plane: The closest airports are Munich or Innsbruck, which are both an hour's drive away.

By train: Take the Innsbruck train from Munich, disembark at Brannenburg and, from there, take a bus.

By car: Take the motorway from Munich to Rosenheim or from Innsbruck to Brannenburg.

Accommodation

The best budget option is the youth hostel at the base of Sudelfeld. The disadvantage, however, is that there are no pubs, so don't forget to bring your own alcohol. Other options are the Pension Wallerlift - Tel: 08033-2381, where prices start at 37Dm, and the Sporthotle Wilder Kaiser - Tel: 08033-4025, which has a swimming-pool and sauna, and where rooms cost from 55Dm per night.

Food

Brannenburg has two brilliant Italian restaurants and the Gasthof Waller in Niederaudorf serves genuine, traditional Bavarian food.

Nightlife

At the Gasthof Waller, every week an old man brews his own beer, which is unbeatable and one of the area's best kept secrets. There are a couple of pubs, but neither is outstanding. For late night entertainment, there is a nightclub called Zoo, which is appropriately named. If you visit in March, go to the smart and stylish Seecafe in Kiefersfelden, as it is located beside a little lake and you can sit outside when it's warm enough.

Other activities

In Oberaudorf, rent sleds from the bottom station for a night-time joy ride.

Thanks to

Sumo.

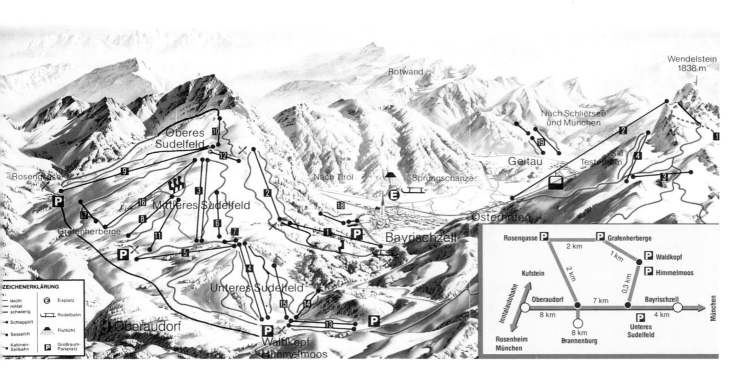

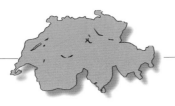

Switzerland

CountryInformation

Capital: Bern

Population: 6,000,000

Time: GMT + 1

Currency : Swiss Francs = Sf

UK £1.00 = 1.94Sf

US $1.00 = 1.28Sf

Telephone information

ISD Code: 41

Local directories: 111

International directories: 191

Police: 117

Tourist information: 120

Winter snow report: 162

Swiss Snowboard Association:

Tel: 1 388 5070 Fax: 1 388 5075

Main Travel Routes:

By road: Access to all the main resorts are easy when driving from the north, though the main east and west passes are closed in winter.

By air: Geneva and Zürich are the two main airports with rail connections to all resorts avaliable from there.

Swiss Air: 0041-1-258 3400

By train: Swiss trains are incredibly efficient and bus connections where necessary are easy. For main travel lines - Tel: 120

Snowboard magazines:

Flat Magazine, Zone Magazine 7th Sky, Boarder Generation, On Board

Besançon · esoul · D 437 · D 461 · N 57 · D 437 · Neuchâtel · Pontarlier · N 57 · LAUSANNE · Thonon · GENÈVE · Lake Geneva · Bonneville · Samoens · Cluses · N 205 · Flaine · Sallanches · la Clusaz · Megève · St. Gervais · les Houches · Argentière · N 506 · les Contamines · N 212 · Albertville · Bourg-St. Maurice · la Rosière · Chamonix · Martigny · Col de la Forclaz · Vallorcine · Grd. Combin 4314 · MONT BLANC/ MONTE BIANCO 4808 · N 90 · Valgrisench · Parco Valsavarenche

BASEL · 3 · 317 · 34 · N 3 · 18 · 12 · 5 · N 2 · N 1 · N 2 · Solothurn · 6 · 5 · 2 · Biel/Bienne · N 1 · 1 · 20 · 10 · BERN · 10 · Belp · 6 · Fribourg · Thun · N 12 · 12 · 11 · Interlaken · Wengen · Lauterbrunnen · Mürren · Jung 4158 · N 9 · Gstaad · Kandersteg · Lenk · Montreux · Leukerbad · Leysin · Goppenstein · Les Diablerets 3210 · Crans Montana · Brig · Sierre · 9 · Visp · Sion · St. Luc · St. Niklaus · Avoriaz/Morzine · Zinal · Evolène · Täsch · Saas · Verbier · Zermatt · M. CERVINO MATTERHORN 4478 · MONTE ROSA 4634 · Cervinia · Bionaz · Valtournenche · Champoluc · Gressoney-la-Trinite · Gressoney-St. Jean · S 26 · Brusson · Aosta/Aoste · Verrès · S 507 · Cogne · Champorcher · S 505 · Pont St. Marti

LIVING LARGE
DANI **KIWI** MEIER

RAD AIR
SNOWBOARDS

Meiringen, Bidmi: Kilian Ralbas

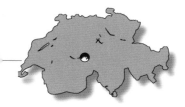

Meiringen/Hasliberg

Mountain Information

Mountain chain:

Berner Oberland

Vertical metre range:

1,061m - 2,433m

Length of season:

beginning of December - end of April

Number of lifts:

1 express gondola, 2 gondolas,

6 chairlifts, 3 draglifts.

Snow-making facilities:

5 moveable snow cannons.

Safety:

No avalanche indicator board, but

follow all signs and avoid roped off

areas.

Guides:

Contact the snowboard school (see

opposite page for details).

Lift pass prices:

1 day: 46Sf

6 days: 191Sf

Season: 610Sf

Lift pass alternatives:

Holders of a Swiss Rail pass get a

50 percent reduction on lift

passes. Alternatively, if you only

want to ride the park, a limited

access, one day pass costs 28Sf.

ON THE MOUNTAIN

Snowboarding first started in the Tschuggi gullies in Meiringen in '86 and the resort has now had a halfpipe for three years. The mountain has terrain to please all types of rider, with gullies, cliff jumps, natural half and quarterpipes, plus heaps of wide, open space. There are a couple of wide bowls with limited pisting, located above Mägisalp, where the snow is reliable. The tree runs, however, are lower down and suffer frequent snow shortages.

✱ Snow conditions

These are variable, as the mountain is only moderately high and much of the rideable area is south-facing.

Freeriders

The Mägisalp and Häägen chairlifts access most of the freeride terrain, where there's a wide choice of gullies, hits and a few cliffs. Other good off-piste areas are found close to the Hinder Tschuggi T-bar and the Planplatten chair.

Freestylers

Normally there's a halfpipe in the funpark, but in the '95/'96 season the snowfall was lean and the pipe didn't operate. To avoid this happening again, the resort management is committed to developing a rideable earthpipe and may invest in a pipe dragon to keep it in good shape. The funpark, with numerous hits, rail slides and benches, is maintained all season. Located above the learner slopes at Mägisalp, the funpark sound system blasts music all day.

Carvers

The best pistes for carvers are the long, red, looping run down from Hochstrass and the FIS Stecke from Planplatten.

Mountain fare

The Maggis Restaurant has great outdoor drinks and snacks, as does the more traditional and cosy Häägen-Stubli Restaurant.

The view from Häägen pic: Tim Rainger

MEIRINGEN HAS A LIVED-IN, LAID-BACK ATMOSPHERE AND IS GENERALLY VERY FRIENDLY TOWARDS SNOWBOARDERS

rider: Reto pic: Tim Rainger

ABOUT TOWN

Famous as the setting for the fictional death of the intrepid Sherlock Holmes, Meiringen has a lived-in, laid-back atmosphere and is generally very friendly towards snowboarders. As a rule, it's a bit of a one-horse town - there's one ski store, one snowboard store and only a couple of bars. All the shops, restaurants and hotels are located in the village, but the self-catering accommodation for hire is mostly at Hasliberg, 5kms up the mountain, which is linked to Meiringen by bus and gondola.

Getting there

By plane: Bern and Zürich are one hour away by train.

By train: Hourly trains run from most main cities.

By car: Take the highway from Bern, via Interlaken, and likewise from Lucerne over the Brunig pass. Chains aren't required and the pass is always open.

Accommodation

There is not much available in Meiringen - the cheapest place to stay is the Youth Hostel, opposite the tennis hall. The centrally located Hotel Victoria is good value, with prices starting from 40Sf per night - Tel: 033 - 971 1033. For those capable of wading through German language catalogues, the tourist board has a huge range of chalets in its accommodation brochure - Tel: 033 - 972 5161 for reservations.

Food

There are several good supermarkets selling all sorts of food at resort prices. For a cheap burger, try the van on the parking square. A delicious local speciality is chás bråtel (melted raclette cheese on bread). If you are staying in a hotel, half-board is probably the easiest way to deal with the food problem. The food at the Hotel Victoria is good!

Nightlife

The Alpen club and the Sherlock Holmes bar are excellent pubs, serving up loud music and a healthy injection of snowboard mentality. The Lion Pub has pool tables, billiards and an easy-going ambiance. Late night action happens at the Disco Sunset in the Hotel Sherpa - entry is free, but the drinks are far from cheap.

Other activities

Indoor tennis, a heated swimming-pool and good sled runs are all available in times of bad weather. Contact the tourist office for more details.

Thanks to

Reto and Heinz Neiger, Daniel from Eiszeit, Florian Dubendorfe, Hotel Victoria and the Meiringen/Hasliberg Tourist Board.

Essential Contacts

Tourist office

Hasliberg   Tel: 033- 972 5151 Fax: 033- 972 5150

Meiringen   Tel: 033- 972 5050

Snowboard shops

•Eiszeit Tel: 033- 971 5141

Board/boot hire: 38Sf/day

The centre of the snowboard scene, offering good equipment and back-up services, with loads of local knowledge.

Snowboard schools

•Bidmi (located on the mountain)

Tel: 033- 972 5141   Fax: 033- 972 5150

Group lesson: 40Sf/day

The boys pic: Tim Rainger

Shirlock - what's in your pipe pic: Tim Rainger

Gstaad

Mountain chain:

Berner Oberland

Vertical metre range:

948m - 3,000m

Length of season:

November - mid-May

Number of lifts:

14 gondolas, 3 cable cars,
38 draglifts, 11 chairlifts,
3 singlelifts

Snow-making facilities:

Surprisingly, none.

Safety:

There are avalanche indicator boards at every main station.

Guides:

The snowboard schools have guides, otherwise contact Kusi Fahrni at 1001 Sport in Zweisimmen - Tel: 033- 722 2018

Lift pass prices:

swatch access

1 day: 46Sf

6 days: 233Sf

Season: 890Sf

The Gstaad Super-Ski region includes 250kms of piste and 69 lifts in the various valleys surrounding the town, including Les Diablerets (see separate review). A lift pass gives you access to the buses and trains, plus free entry (until 5.00pm) to the heated indoor swimming-pool in Gstaad.

Lift pass alternatives:

A season pass is also valid in Andorra (Ordino), Alpe Vaudoises, St. Moritz, Kitzbühel and Adelboden-Lenk.

 ON THE MOUNTAIN

The Gstaad Super-Ski Region, at the head of three valleys, includes 11 separate lift operations offering access to 250kms of piste and untold off-piste areas. All the stations are linked by free buses and, due to the huge size of the area, there is a general lack of crowds.

 Snow conditions

The vast majority of the area is not extremely high and, given it's southerly orientation, snow conditions (except on the glacier at Diablerets) are inconsistent. The season isn't long, but in deepest winter, after a fresh dump, it's a great place to ride.

 Freeriders

Zweisimmen, Saanenmöser and Schönried are the three linked mountain areas most popular with the snowboard fraternity. The liftees were friendly and encouraged snowboarding from the beginning, so the riders have stayed. A new lift, built during the summer of '96, links Rinderberg and Sannerslochgrat, finally uniting Zweissimmen completely. There are a series of tree-lined, open snow-covered fields, and it's a good all-round intermediate area with jumps, freestyle slopes and a funpark. Below Rinderberg, there are some good tree runs and often great powder. Head in the direction of St Stephan, from Saanerslochgrat, and you'll find some nice windlips. The Hühnerspiel has some small cliffs. Here's a brief breakdown of what the various areas have to offer.

Lauenen: More intermediate terrain is accessible from the Wasserngrat top station. The mountain is open - it's not too steep, is particularly good with fresh powder

(it's north-facing) and is only crowded at weekends, especially around Christmas and in February.

Wisplile: Two stage telecabins and a couple of T-bars service a small area directly accessible from Gstaad - this is easy riding.

Saanen and Rougemont: Both offer access to the Videmanette area, where there is very little piste, but great freeriding - take a guide. Above Eggli, there are several descents, which, while not as steep as Diablerets, are none the less intense and hold powder well.

Chateaux d'Oex and Les Moulins: Two small fields, accessed by bus, offering intermediate freeriding.

 Freestylers

The centre of the freestyle scene is Sannenmöser, with the funpark at Sannerslochgrat being the nucleus.

 Carvers

250kms of piste - not many super steeps, but some nicely groomed runs. Les Diablerets is the big blast for adrenaline junkies.

Lots of lovely terrain in which to do lots of lovely turns pic: Tim Rainger

Town panorama pic: Courtesy of Gstaad Tourist Board

Essential Contacts

Tourist office

Tel: 033- 748 8181   Fax: 033-748 8183

Snowboard shops

•1001 Sport Zweisimmen   Tel: 030-220 18

1 day board/boot hire: 45Sf

6 day board/boot hire: 135Sf

Full board service: 40Sf

(amazingly low considering the quality)

Wax: 5Sf to 10Sf

(depending on how polite you are)

This is the hard-core store which has everything - sales, rentals, advice and repairs. Ask to speak to Kusi, he's been around since the beginning, and knows both the sport and the area extremely well.

•Fun - 4 - you Gstaad   Tel: 033-744 9540

Located near the supermarket and train station in Gstaad, the shop sells/hires boards and clothing.

Snowboard schools

•Swiss Snowboard School Tel: 033 744 8040

1 day half day group lesson: 27Sf

(minimum 4 people)

In '96, there were various snowboard schools, but they are planning to amalgamate for the '96/'97 season in order to offer a better service.

ABOUT TOWN

Gstaad has a jet set reputation. Roger Moore, Liz Taylor and a number of other glitterati have wintered in the town, attracted by a combination of inviting location and rustic charm. A number of stunning chalets line the hills, but the atmosphere in town is unpretentious, and the underground snowboard scene is alive and kicking. Gstaad is the main shopping area, but the surrounding villages of Schönried, Saanenmöser and Zweisimmen are better, and cheaper, places to stay. The only catch: if you don't have a car, it's difficult to get between villages late at night, as buses and trains only run during the day, though hitching blind drunk does work.

Getting there

By plane: The closest airports are Geneva, a 2.5 hour transfer away, and Bern (Belp), from where it's a one hour transfer by train.

By train: The connection from Geneva airport goes via Lausanne. Change at Vevey for Gstaad.

By car: Head from Geneva to Aigle along the highway, then wind up into the mountains via Diablerets or Châteaux d'Oeux to Gstaad.

Accommodation

The Snoeb and Sleep is a specialist snowboard hotel on the piste, a five minute walk from the station to Schrönried. It's an old, traditional Swiss-style 30-bed chalet, simply decorated and reasonably priced with ride-to-the-door convenience. There's a bar, with snowboard videos constantly playing, a stereo and satellite TV, plus a small terrace. Prices start at 39.95Sf per night, with additional supplements for bedding and towels. B&B and half-board deals are also available - Tel: 033 744 7034. Other options are staying in a local home (look for the 'Zimmer' sign), which costs from 25Sf per night, or a three star hotel, such as the Hotel Bahnhof next to the station in Schönried - Tel: 033-7444 242 or the Gasthof Derby,

one hundred metres from the station and cable car at Zweissimmmen - Tel: 033-722 1428, which costs around 80Sf per night.

Food

The cheapest place to sit down and eat is the restaurant above the Co-op supermarket in Gstaad. At the Arc-en-Ciel, you'll get a 12Sf pizza and Wally's snack bar serves 5Sf burgers.

Nightlife

Lots of options, but the most popular haunts are Ricki's in Gstaad and Boo in Saanen. Bellerive (between Gstaad and Saanen) has various DJs and loads of game machines. Grotte (Schönried) plays jungle, techno and dance music. Chesery is a live jazz bar in Gstaad.

Other activities

Befitting a world class resort, Gstaad has a range of recreational options, including ice-skating, ice hockey, sleigh rides and ballroom dancing. Your lift pass gives you free access to a swimming-pool in Gstaad until 5.00pm.

Thanks to

Martina Reiter (a legend!), Steve, Kusi, Greg Holt, Sam and Vanessa, and Hotel Bahnhof.

GSTAAD
DAS ELEGANTE SCHWIMMBAD IM BERNER OBERLAND

GSTAAD HAS A JET SET REPUTATION BUT THE **UNDERGROUND** SNOWBOARD SCENE IS **ALIVE AND KICKING**

Soul

fx 900

NIDECKER SNOWBOARDS

AUSTRIA-SAIL & SURF GMBH-PHONE ++43 61 32 25 450 - FAX ++43 61 32 25 435 · GERMANY-MAKO SPORT-PHONE ++49 89 89 42 540 - FAX ++49 89 84 04 937
SUISSE-NIDECKER SNOWBOARDS-PHONE# ++41 21 822 33 33 - FAX# ++41 21 822 33 31
www.nidecker.ch - info@nidecker.ch

Red Bull, European extremes - March 96, Verbier pic: Tim Rainger

Johnny Eisenhurt having fun in Leysin pic: Helmut Wahl

Les Diablerets

Mountain range

Vaud Alpes

Vertical metre range

1,160m - 2,970m

Length of season

December - May,

plus summer camps in late

June and early July

Number of lifts:

4 cable cars, 4 gondola,

9 chairlifts, 30 draglifts

Safety:

There are avalanche

indicator boards at the cable

car stations.

Guides:

Ask for Pierre-Alain Werro at the

tourist office. An exceptional

mountaineer, he teaches

snowboarding and skiing.

Lift pass prices:

swatch access

There are two ticket options:

1: Diablerets, Villars and Gryon

1 day: 42Sf

7 days: 236SF

2. Full Alpes Vaudoises pass,

including Les Diablerets, Isenau,

Leysin, Les Mosses, Villars and

Gryon

1 day: 46Sf

6 days: 263SF

Lift pass alternatives:

All tickets of four days or more are

valid on the Gstaad Super Ski

region and at Adelboden-Lenk.

Col du Pillon - some of the sexiest freeride terrain in the Alps   pic: Tim Rainger

ON THE MOUNTAIN

Diablerets is a big, steep mountain renowned for its great powder and extreme off-piste terrain. There are a few pistes of good quality, but the main attraction for snowboarders will be either the deep powder or the legendary summer freestyle snow camp on the glacier.

Snow conditions

Due to the high altitude, the northern aspect of some crucial parts of the mountain and the glacier, conditions are reliable.

Freeriders

The whole mountain rips. There are only a couple of red pistes, with tons of rideable terrain in between. The Combe d'Audon gives access to a few easy, near-piste bowls, with lots of hits and some small cliffs. Pierre-Pointes, accessed from the first stage of the Col du Pillon gondola, is a massive natural freeride park, with some of the sexiest terrain in the Alps, ranging from open bowls to lightly spaced tree runs, with little cliffs, hits and chutes everywhere. It also holds the powder really well. A good place when there's a white-out is Le Meilleret, which has a large forested area and a little anti-clinal valley. There are two or three hairy off-piste descents from the Scex-Rouge, but these should not be attempted without a guide. A young rider died the day we rode there, attemping to find a line down an unrideable face. No guide, no life.

Freestylers

The winter halfpipe and funpark are located just above the Isenau top gondola station. The lift company purchased a pipe dragon in summer '96 to ensure a perfect transition for the 7th annual summer camp, which has three halfpipes, a boardercross, gap stadium and snow park. Prices: 420Sf (without accommodation) or 740Sf (with accommodation), including a lift pass, skate park, bungee assisted tramp training, wake boarding and sounds. Contact the James B. organisation at Bruno Morini, Route du Jorat 39A, 1000 Lausanne 27 - Tel/Fax: 021-784 4075. Alternatively, get details from the tourist office.

Carvers

The Combe d'Audon and Run 5, under the Oldenegg-Cabane gondola, are the smoothest and longest.

❌ Lifts to avoid

The three stage Col du Pillon gondola can be hideously slow on crowded days. However, there's a rumour that a new system is to be installed imminently.

Mountain fare

There's a restaurant at the summit of Scex-Rouge where you can get standard fare at high prices, but beware the hamburgers as they're a hoax. The terrace café under the Col du Pillon bottom station is where the locals hang out, especially at the end of the day.

Any excuse for air - Alain showing his fear of heights pic: Tim Rainger

Essential Contacts

Tourist office

Tel: 024-492 3358   Fax: 024-492 2348

Snowboard shops

• Jacky Sports is run by hard-core boarders.

Tel: 024-492 3218   Fax: 024-493 11 64

Board/boot hire: 45Sf/day

• Holiday Sports   Tel: 024-492 3717

Board/boot hire: 45Sf/day

• Savino Sports   Tel: 025-531 573

Snowboard schools

• Swiss Ski School (at the tourist office)

Tel: 024-492 2002   Fax: 024-492 2348

Group lesson: 45Sf/day

 ABOUT TOWN

Diablerets is a small town, with restricted accommodation and social opportunities. There are a couple of restaurants and a few hotels, bars, ski and snowboard stores, but that's it, so it's not the place for party animals. The real action is up on the glacier, which is a free bus ride from the town centre.

Getting there

By plane: Geneva airport is the nearest.

By train: Take the train to Aigle and change for Diablerets - in total a 2.5 hour transfer.

By car: There are no road problems, either from Gstaad or Aigle.

Accommodation

Most boarders stay at les Diablotins, which costs 39Sf to 56Sf a night - Tel: 024-492 3633 or Fax: 024-492 2355. You can also stay on the mountain at Isenau (1,800m) for 34Sf a night - Tel: 024-492 3293 or in a 30 bed dormitory for 30Sf a night at Cabane - Tel: 024-492 2102. For self-catering options and a full list of accommodation possibilities, phone the tourist office - Tel: 024-492 3358.

Food

The Locnada Livia pizzeria and the Poste restaurant are the cheap spots to eat out.

Nightlife

Get drunk somewhere else. Diablerets is a small family resort, which has no nightlife of any significance. Most of the locals go either to Leysin or to Gstaad to get loose. If you haven't got the energy to go anywhere else, the MT-Bar and Ormonan are relaxing for a beer or more. La Pote Saloon disco is the only late night spot.

Other activities

Walking, chess, cooking, curling, parapenting, mid-biking and snow-mobiling.

Thanks to

Alain, Mickey, Cookie, Mitch, Pierre-Alain Werro, Sven Mermod, the tourist office and Jacky Sports for the well-timed loan of a 165cm.

High up in a bubble pic: Tim Rainger

A BIG, STEEP MOUNTAIN RENOWNED FOR ITS FAT POWDER AND EXTREME OFF-PISTE TERRAIN

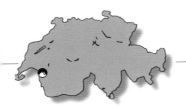

Leysin

Mountain Information

Mountain chain:

Alpes Vaudoises

Vertical metre range:

1,300m - 2,200m

Length of season:

early December - mid-April

Number of lifts:

2 gondolas,

8 chairlifts, 3 T-bars

Snow-making facilities:

Limited snow cannons service

the Berneuse chair.

Safety:

No real avalanche danger,

but keep an eye on the

indicator boards.

Guides:

There's not a huge

amount of serious off-piste to

explore, but guides from the

ski school are available.

Lift pass prices:

1 day: 38Sf

6 days: 189Sf

Season: 580Sf

Lift pass alternatives:

Full Alpes Vaudoises pass

(as for Les Diablerets)

1 day: 46Sf

6 days: 263Sf

Essential Contacts

Tourist office

Tel: 024-494 2244/5

Fax: 024-494 1616/1364

Snowboard shops

•Hefti Sports

(directly opposite the base station)

Tel: 024-494 1677

Fax: 024-494 1744

Board/boot hire: 57Sf/day

Board/boot hire: 230Sf/7 days

An extensive snowboard fleet,

a good repair service and

spot-on staff.

 ON THE MOUNTAIN

Leysin is a small, but interesting, mountain serviced by two main gondolas, which connect with a network of T-bars and chairlifts, all of which are well-maintained and run at high speed. It's a sunny, south-facing resort with many small shaded areas which harbour the best powder. The very varied and fun terrain between the pistes, plus the resort's welcoming attitude to snowboarders, makes it a cool place to visit.

 Snow conditions

As the resort is south-facing and at a low altitude - the highest point is only 2,200m - it is obviously at its best in deepest winter (January/February).

 Freestylers

Leysin has had a halfpipe, built for competition, for the last four years. Sadly, it isn't maintained all season, but, snow conditions permitting, the halfpipe will be perennial. A local rider, Nicolas Vaudroz, kept a neat funpark in the '95/'96 season, giving Leysin the fat thumbs up.

Carvers

Most of the piste offers carving potential, with the steepest terrain off the Chaux de Mont (where the ISF slalom course is built).

Freeriders

With good snow conditions, Leysin is a cool place to ride. There's no super huge or terrifying terrain, but the combination of gullies, tree patches and small powder areas near the piste can keep you searching for a while. If you don't mind a bit of walking, there are a couple of good off-piste runs between the Tours, down to Mayens and Crête du Fer.

 Lifts to avoid

The T-bar to the Chaux de Mont peak is radically steep at the top, lifting even big guys into space - a bit of a challenge.

pic: Courtesey of the Leysin Tourist Board

NO SUPER HUGE OR TERRIFYING TERRAIN, BUT THERE'S A COMBINATION OF GULLIES, TREE PATCHES AND SMALL POWDER AREAS

 Mountain fare

At the top of the Berneuse, there is a revolving restaurant with awesome views, but it's expensive. The cheap option is the snack bar downstairs, which is an excellent place to chill out at the end of the day and watch the hang-gliders.

Checking out '96 World cup in the Funpark pic: Tim Rainger

ABOUT TOWN

Leysin is a typical Swiss mountain village, with spectacular views south over the Dents du Midi. The town snakes upwards, around several S-bends, from the old village at the lowest funicular exit. The closest exit to the Berneuse gondola, where most of the rented accommodation (Club Vagabond and Le Feydey) and the supermarket are found, is the Leysin Feydey.

pic: Tim Rainger

Getting there

By air: Geneva has the nearest international airport.
By train: From Geneva, take the Lausanne/Aigle train and change at Aigle on to the funicular for Leysin. Train and funicular timetables are linked, and the whole journey takes exactly two hours. The cost of a Geneva/Leysin return is 40Sf.
By car: First off, chains are required. From Geneva, follow the N1 and then the N9 to Aigle, from where it's a 15 minute drive up the mountain. The whole journey takes about an hour and a half. Coming from the north, take the N12 south from Bern and then the N9 from Montreux.

Accommodation

Club Vagabond is the obvious choice. It's a soulful old hotel, snowboarder friendly, with good rooms and showers at a reasonable rate; B&B costs 27Sf per night - Tel: 024-494 1321. The Feydey is the other budget choice (which is next door to The Vag), but it doesn't have a bar, so it is much quieter; the price for a B&B is 30Sf - Tel: 024-494 1147.

Food

Club Vagabond is the only place in town offering low price meals, starting at 8Sf for a burger and chips. The Fromagerie is a traditional Swiss-style restaurant with a varied, but pricey, menu. Check out its roaring fires, and off-the-wall wood and stone interiors. There's another good restaurant and bar, L'Horizon, up the hill from Club Vagabond.

Nightlife

There are two main venues: Club Vagabond (aka The Vag) is usually free, and plays music ranging from rock and blues to house and hip-hop. If Euro-pop and ski-bunnies are more your style, try Club 94, where the entry charge is 5Sf.

Other activities

The excellent sports centre at the tourist board office includes squash courts, indoor tennis courts, a sauna, swimming-pool, massage facilities and a café/restaurant. You can rent rackets and balls if necessary, but the centre has no towels or swimming costumes, so take your own. The entry fee is 5Sf.

Thanks to

Bernedette, Pierre and all the girls at the tourist board, Dominic, Big Loose, Ken, Terri and the club Vag team, all the Kiwi crew and Nicholas from Hefti Sports.

Further essential Contacts

Snowboard schools

• Swiss Ski School

Tel: 024-494 1202   Fax: 024-494 3249

Nicholas Vaudroz pic: Tim Rainger

Group lesson (4 people only): 26Sf - There is a 10 percent reduction for a 2 hour lesson.
• The snowboard school within the ski school offers a small number of lessons.

Verbier

Mountain chain:

Valais Alpes, Four Vallées

Vertical metre range:

1,500m - 3,300m

Season duration:

November - May,

glacier in the summer

Number of lifts:

100 - the list goes on forever

Snow-making facilities:

Mainly on the bottom slopes nearer the town, to keep access ways open and beginner trails covered.

Safety:

There are avalanche indicator boards on the top and at the bottom of the Les Ruinettes gondola. The Swiss ski school hires off-piste equipment.

Guides:

Contact the Swiss Ski School or the Fantastique.

Lift pass prices:

1 day: 57Sf

6 days: 297Sf

Season: 1,066Sf

Heliboarding:

Ask at the Swiss Ski School for details and prices.

 ## ON THE MOUNTAIN

Verbier is huge, with over 400kms of piste and seemingly limitless off-piste. In fact, there's so much to it that the Verbier area is almost worthy of a guide book in itself. There seems to be a different lift, a new mountain, and another run everywhere you look, and besides what you see, there's the back-country to explore! Ski guru John Falkiner, who has lived in the area for 22 years, says he still finds new runs. As it is so well-known internationally, it often gets crowded in the high season. If this is the case, go over the valley to Brusson or over to the Super Saint Bernard and ride into Italy.

✳ Snow Conditions

As the resort is at 1,500m and the highest altitude is 3,300m, it normally doesn't lack snow, which falls frequently between November and April. Unfortunately, it can suffer badly from the effects of the 'föehn', a hot wind from northern Africa which gets trapped in the valley. When this phenomenon occurs, there are numerous snow slides and it's advisable not to go off-piste.

Freeriding

Verbier is a mega-freeride mountain. The terrain is among the most spectacular and varied in the Alps, and the runs seem endless. The area, as stated above, can be prone to avalanches and kills a number of careless or unlucky people every season. Never ride without a transceiver if you are going off-piste and either take a guide or befriend one of the locals. It's almost impossible to describe all the options because there are so many, but listed here are a few tasters.

For excellent tree runs, go across the valley to Bruson - you'll find trees, trees, trees!

If you want to do some cliff jumps, take the 116, 117 or 118 lifts. There are cliffs all over the place, but check out the landings first. Bec des Rosses was the site of the Red Bull European extremes in '96. The competitors hiked for about two hours and then went straight down the front/north face. It's strictly for experienced riders with guides and definitely not for the faint-hearted. For a long run, ride 'round' the mountain down to Fionnay. Mont Gelé has some excellent riding off both the front and back side.

Kiwi finding his own snow pic: Tim Rainger

Pick your line with care. Another good run starts from the Col des Mines and heads down the Vallon d'Arbi, which turns to forest at the bottom.

Freestylers

Both in summer and winter, the pipe and the park are on the Mont-Fort. In winter, the pipe and park are at the bottom station of 'Le Jumbo'; in summer, they're moved near the top. The lift which services the area (114 - La Chaux 2) has its own natural hits all the way!

Carvers

112 'Attelas 3' is a great run for carving, as it is steep and impeccably manicured. 117 Lac des Vaux is a great place to learn how to carve. 108 is, at times, really steep and always well-groomed. We could go on for ever. Explore!

ABOUT TOWN

Verbier is one of the most prestigious resorts in Switzerland and it's easy to see why. Built up the mountain at an altitude of 1,500m, it has some of the best views in the world. The town has also been kept reasonably tasteful. For these and other obvious reasons, it attracts some of Europe's more pretentious clientele, and bursts at the seams with yuppies and posers. But beneath this veneer, there are committed core boarders, skiers and mountain folk who live here because the mountain has some of the most radical territory in the Alps. Plus there's everything else here that you could want - all you need is cash!

Accommodation

Verbier is not a cheap place to lay your head. The best bets are self-catering apartments (phone the tourist board), friends or tour operator packages. When we were there, we met a guy who was charged about 40 bucks for a broom cupboard by a hotelier who knew there were no beds in town. Go Vic! There is no Youth Hostel in Verbier. Other cheaper options include private rooms costing between 25-35Sf. If you stay in a hotel, try Les Ruinettes - it has accommodation and a restaurant attached which serves good local fare. Another cheap option is Les Touristes, a B&B from 50Sf a night. Contact the tourist office for more alternatives.

pic: Tim Rainger

Food

The Off-shore, handy for the lifts, is a good place to feed before or during the day, as it serves good breakfasts and lunches at a fair price - but be warned, it stocks no alcohol. Harold's Hamburgers is the only place in town producing exceptional burgers, but at a cost of 8Sf. Going up the price ladder, the Borsalino has some of the best pizzas and pastas in town for around 20Sf, and there is a Tex Mex which serves dinners from 20Sf. The Bouchon Gourmand offers great French cuisine from 35Sf a meal. The Feracheval is the local hang-out, particularly in summer, where a variety of different meals (pizza, fondue) are served for about 25Sf. However, the cheapest way to get by in Verbier is self-catering and there are an abundance of reasonable supermarkets.

Nightlife

Most tourists pay a visit to the pub Mont-Fort, a huge drinking establishment which stays open till 2.ooam and is owned by an Englishman - beers cost from 5Sf. The Nelson is a similar venue, with pool tables, which is also open till 2.00am. If you prefer a cosier atmosphere with live music, the Croquignole is a popular hang-out, particularly among the locals; beer is from 3Sf. For a bar/disco type atmosphere, try Marshalls/Aristo which always has a different DJ. Later on in the evening, the Tara Club is the place to dance.

Other activities

Check out the skate park, tennis, golf, pool, a whirl pool, sauna, gym, paragliding, climbing, ice-climbing, mountain-biking (downhill), squash and much more.

Thanks to

David Zimmerman,
Verbier tourist board and press office, and Scharti.

Essential Contacts

Tourist office

Tel: 026 -316 666 Fax: 026 - 313 272

Snowboard Shops

• Xtreme Tel: 026-317 810

An all round snowboard shop specialising in an extreme, off-piste approach. For detailed local advice ask for Christophe Gregoire.

• No Bounds Tel: 027-771 5556

Mainstream snowboard store with specialist snowboard school.

Snowboard schools

• No Bounds Snowboard School

Tel: 027-771 5556

Prices for 2 hour group lesson: 27Sf

• Swiss Snowboard School

Tel: 026-315 556 Fax: 027-771 4449

They have special lessons for freestylers.

Price for 4 day group course: 85Sf

• Fantastique Snowboard School

Tel: 026-312 212 Fax: 026-317 233

Price for 3 hour lesson for 2 people: 160Sf

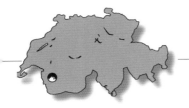

Crans-Montana

 ON THE MOUNTAIN

Crans-Montana, with a summit at 3,000m, is no dwarf. There's lots of varied terrain and some superb views, but high sunshine hours can be a problem in a bad season.

Mountain Information

Mountain chain:

Valais Alpes

Vertical metre range:

1,500m - 3,000m

Length of season:

beginning of December - mid-April

Number of lifts:

1 funitel, 1 aerial cableway, 5 gondola, 8 chairlifts, 23 J-bars, 3 T-bars

Snow-making facilities:

There are 60 snow cannons covering 3kms of piste, when needed.

Safety:

The pistes stay closed and off-piste riding is not permitted, if there is avalanche danger.

Guides:

Contact the guide office for details.
Tel: 027-480 8888   Fax: 027-480 8899.

Lift pass prices:

1 day: 56Sf

6 days: 255Sf

Season: 874Sf

Covers all lifts in Crans-Montana and Aminona, as well as the bus.

 Snow conditions

Due to its sunny, south-facing aspect, the powder doesn't tend to last, but at least this means that the slopes are rarely icy. The only place that is snowsure is the run down from the Plaine Morte glacier.

Freeriders

Most of the lifts are between 1,700m and 2,400m, but there are some alternative descents from the 3,000m Plaine Morte summit (for example, both sides of Mont Bonvin can be ridden, though with caution). On the west side, Cry d'er - Chetzeron, you can ride through trees, which is cool when there's fresh snow. On the east side, there are cliff bands with some great jumps, but be wary of avalanche danger. For good, up-to-date, local advice, take the red gondola to Cry d'Er and ask Dave at the Altitude Surf Shop.

Freestylers

The halfpipe, located at Pas de Loup, is reasonably well-maintained, but, because it's a surface pipe, suffers in times of poor snow. Even though there are a chairlift and a button lift nearby, most people walk to it. The funpark, with seven or eight hits and an old car to bonk, is at Aminona, where there's also another halfpipe. Again, there's a chairlift nearby.

Carvers

Carvers will especially enjoy the Piste Nationale from Bella-Luiy to Les Barzettes.

Mountain fare

There are five restaurants dotted around the mountain, but the rule of higher altitudes and higher prices applies, so it's advisable to eat at the bottom of the slopes. If you are up there and you're famished, Des Voilettes is a popular self-service restaurant, and there's a panoramic restaurant with a small bar at the summit that sells burgers and other snacks.

rider: Fabien Rohrer pic: Katja Delago

CRANS AND MONTANA BETWEEN THEM HAVE MORE HOTEL BEDS THAN ANY OTHER RESORT IN SWITZERLAND

Jean Daniel admiring heaven pic: Tim Rainger

 **ABOUT TOWN**

Crans and Montana between them have more hotel beds than any other resort in Switzerland, which can mean traffic on the snow. Located on the north side of Crans-Montana are the two officially separate towns, which have grown together with years of development. They are quite similar and have equally easy access to the mountain. The commercial areas, roughly 20 minutes walk from end to end, are scattered along the base of the mountain.

 Getting there

By air: The closest airport is Geneva, 190kms away.

By train: Travel from Geneva airport to either Sion or Sierre and then catch the PTT bus from Sion or the SML bus from Sierre.

By car: Follow the signs! You'd have to be a bit of a div to miss it!

 Accommodation

The Hotel Olympic in Montana is a good place to stay, prices from 80Sf per night - Tel: 027-481 2985 or Fax: 027-481 2953. Another option is the Hôtel de al Forêt, which has a hot pool and sauna - Tel: 027-480 2131 or Fax: 027-481 3120. La Moubra is a cheap dormitory with beds priced from 21Sf per night, in the campsite next to the lake - Tel: 027-412 851. For an extensive list of alternatives, contact the tourist board - Tel: 027-481 2132 or Tel: 027-485 0404.

Food

The San Nick, a pub/restaurant serving good food, in Bluche (3kms from Montana) is a popular meeting point for the younger generation. If you like Tex-Mex, the Embassy, near the police station, does large meals, washed down with Coronas. Otherwise, there are pizzas and crêpes at various restaurants for approximately 12Sf each.

 Nightlife

Alternatives in Montana are No. 1, (next to the Hotel Olympic), and the Amadeus bar, (below the Hotel Olympic), which closes about 2.00am and is usually rammed before the clubs. The young crew in Crans tend to hang out in the Constellation Bar, playing mini-foot and pinball. During the day, it's also a good place to have a coffee in the sun. The Absolut nightclub, also in Crans, is open till 4.00am or 5.00am, but you have to be reasonably respectable to gain entry.

Other activities

If you want to try parapenting bi-planes, contact Johnny - Tel: 077-286 249 or the Ski School Montana. Other options are skating, sledding and ski-bobbing.

 Thanks to

Jean-Daniel (Avalanche Surf Shop), Eric Hosp (Pacific Surf Shop), Bruno Huggler (tourist office Crans-Montana) and Jean Daniel's Mum at the Hotel Olympic.

Essential Contacts

Tourist board

Montana

Tel: 027-485 0404   Fax: 027-485 0460

Snowboard schools

•Ski School of Montana

Tel: 027-481 1480   Fax: 027-481 6338

Snowboard Shops

•Avalanche Shop (Montana)

Tel: 027-480 2424

Board/boot hire: 53Sf/day

Board/boot hire: 182Sf/6 days

Sells boards, boots, clothing and accessories, and has a full service and repair workshop, plus a large rental fleet.

•Pacific Surf Shop (Crans) Tel: 027-481 1320

Sells and rents boards, boots, clothing and accessories.

•Altitude Surf Shop Tel: 027-481 0222

At the Pas du Loup station on the mountain, it rents and sells boards and accessories.

Central Switzerland

Engelberg
Andermatt
Saas-Fee (Valaise Alpes)

View from the Titlis viewing platfrom pic: Tim Rainger

Locals rule Saas-Fee pic: Tim Rainger

Engelberg

Mountain Information

Mountain chain:

Berner Oberland

Vertical metre range:

1,050m - 3,020m

Length of season:

December - May

Number of lifts:

1 funicular railway, 6 gondolas,
4 chairlifts, 13 draglifts

Snow-making facilities:

There are no permanent snow
cannons, but they can be brought
in if snow cover is light.

Safety:

There are avalanche indicator
boards at the bottom station and
at the Trübsee gondola exit. Safety
equipment can be hired from any
one of the ski schools or from Bike
'n' Roll in town.

Guides:

Available through the snowboard
schools - prices are the same as
for an individual lesson.

Lift pass prices:

1 day: Mon-Fri 47Sf
       Sat & Sun 54Sf

6 days: 214Sf

Season: 760Sf

Lift pass alternatives:

The resort sometimes has a late
season - dependent on snow - from
the middle of April for two or three
weeks. Passes cost 150Sf.

Linked or nearby resorts:

A season ticket allows you to
ride free of charge at:
Tignes/Grand Motte (France),
Garmish-Partenkirchen (Germany),
Kaprun (Austria) and
Val Senales (Italy).

ON THE MOUNTAIN

Engelberg is a low key, but surprisingly,
impressive mountain, offering a handful of the
longest vertical drops in the Swiss Alps. The
main area, Titlis, which is 2,000m above the
village, has terrain to suit all abilities and types
of riders, but it's not extensive for those just
starting out. Beginners could head for
Gerschnialp, a flat area with rope tows - cheap
passes are available to riders only using this
area. For intermediates, there is a wide variety
of terrain for improvement. For experienced
riders, Engelberg offers some long, extreme
runs and steep-as-you like off-piste, which
requires a guide and safety equipment.

Snow conditions

The Titlis area, with its high, north-west facing
slopes, keeps reliable snow cover until May.

Freeriders

The Laubersgrat face, which is visible from the
Gerschnialp-Trübsee gondola, offers one of the
longest, most challenging runs. It is also one of the
most dangerous and an avalanche killed a rider in '96,
so be warned. The Jochstock T-bar has access to great
off-piste terrain on both sides, especially down the
north face to Alpstublii, and the Engstlenalp Lift, while
slow, has a great freestyle run through a long gully.

Freestylers

A halfpipe was built for the Swiss Cup in '96, but it
hasn't been maintained. The local riders were
lobbying the mountain to prepare a pipe for '97.

Carvers

For excellent carving flats, try the Jockpass and the
Rotegg. All the pistes, predominantly red and black,
are kept in tip-top condition. The short black descent
from the Titlis (the Bucklipiste) is also a good burn.

Mountain fare

El Burro Loco, a Mexican restaurant (below the sun
terrace at the base of the Rotair gondola), has
excellent, filling food such as tostadas from 13Sf. It's
particularly popular with the snowboard scene.

WITHOUT THE GLITZ AND
HYPE OF SOME OF THE MORE
FASHIONABLE SWISS
RESORTS, BUT THE
MOUNTAIN ITSELF HAS SOME
SERIOUS ATTITUDE

pic: Tim Rainger

pic: Tim Rainger

ABOUT TOWN

Engelberg is a busy, well-established resort, with surprisingly few modern developments to destroy the quaint feel of the village, which is famous for its huge, and still beautiful, 12th century monastery. The town ticks over without the glitz and hype of some of the more fashionable Swiss resorts, but the mountain itself has some serious attitude and is definitely worth a visit for that reason alone.

Getting there

By plane: Zürich airport is closest, a 1.5 to 2 hour transfer away.

By train: The closest major station is Lucerne, from where Engelberg is a further 50 minutes.

By car: Travel along the N2 motorway (via Lucerne) and take the Stans Sud exit. The road is always open.

Accommodation

Hotel Engel is the obvious place for snowboarders,

it's a big old hotel with a huge dining room. There is a youth hostel, but it's a little way out of town and an early curfew makes it restrictive. Self-catering options and other details can be sourced from the tourist board - Tel: 041-637 3737.

Food

There are several supermarkets and a few cheap restaurants. For a large, tasty pizza, try the pizzeria at the Alpen Club. For filling Mexican fare, the Yucatan Restaurant is a good place to eat when really hungry.

Nightlife

The Sporthalle has an excellent afternoon drinking session, with live bands from 4.00pm onwards. The bar at Hotel Engel has a pool table and pub atmosphere. Club Spindle is the late night spot, which can get quite hectic even at off-peak times - it's free during the week, but has an entry fee at the weekend. Besides a number of cod-ordinary drinks, sample the local delicacies - 'haldro' (a mint tea with prune schnapps) or 'café chruitar' (with a mountain flower liqueur).

Other activities

There's a swimming-pool with a spa and sauna at the Sport Hotel, just out of town. It's a free bus ride (which stops about 6.30pm) or a 20 minute walk away. You have to wear a funny little hat, which they rent you and makes you feel a bit dorky, but it's worth it as it's cool playing on the water slide with the kids. Engelberg also has a small casino for all you fruit machine or roulette junkies.

Thanks to

Charles Christen at the tourist board, Hotel Engel and Christoph Frick.

Essential Contacts

Tourist office
Tel: 041-637 3737   Fax: 041-637 4156

Snowboard shops
•The OK Snowboard Shop
Tel: 077-437 075
There are several ski shops, but OK is the hardcore, independent outlet.
1 day board/boot hire: 34Sf

Snowboard schools
•The Swiss Snowboard School
Tel: 041-637 4050   Fax: 041-637 2770
4 hour group lesson: 84Sf (including day pass)

ENGELBERG

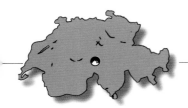

Andermatt

 ON THE MOUNTAIN

Andermatt is famous for its thick, inviting powder, which dumps in big time on the steep, north-facing slopes. It's favoured by extreme riders, as it has an abundance of easily accessible off-piste terrain, with a sheer gradient and a correspondingly high adrenaline factor.

 Snow conditions

The snow falls in abundance. And, because the slopes are north-facing and at high altitude, once it arrives, it stays.

Freeriders

There are three separate lift areas, which are nicely graded according to ability. For beginners, the Nätschen and Stöckli chairlifts (accessible from the town) lead to smooth and flat south-facing terrain. Intermediates will enjoy the **Winterhorn**, located above the village of Hospental, where a long chairlift and T-bar give access to mid-range and safe off-piste terrain. Not too steep, this area holds the powder well and many of the runs lead back to the village. **Gemsstock** is a real charge. A two stage gondola rises 1,600m above the valley floor, giving access to three excellent long black runs, from which pockets of powder, hits, jumps and couloirs can be reached. The options are endless, but the main runs are the Gletscher, the Gurschenstock and the Sonnen. Across the other side of the glacier is the

Felsental ('Cliff Valley'), the best known off-piste area in the valley, but - you have been warned - it is suicidal without a guide.

 Freestylers

There was a half-made halfpipe in the '95/'96 season, but it wasn't functional. For '96/'97, the resort is planning an earthpipe, which - if it comes to fruition - will be located beneath the Gurschen T-bar. The funpark had the same feel as the halfpipe; a few fun boxes were scattered around, but not in any cohesive order. Andermatt is better for freeriders and serious off-piste riders.

 Carvers

There are three long red runs which are excellent for carving. Alpine boards are used in abundance here.

 Lifts to avoid

The Gemsstock gondola can be as slow as a wet week and leaves spasmodically when the resort's not crowded (which is exactly when you want it to leave on time).

Mountain fare

Only a couple of mountain restaurants, nothing super interesting or cheap. Who needs lunch when there's so much powder?

FAMOUS FOR ITS **THICK** INVITING **POWDER**, WHICH DUMPS IN ABUNDANCE ON THE STEEP, **NORTH-FACING SLOPES**

Mountain Information

Mountain chain:

Central Alps (Uris)

Vertical metre range:

1,447m - 2,963m

Length of season:

November - May

Number of lifts:

2 cable cars, 6 draglifts,
4 chairlifts

Snow-making facilities:

There is little need, as there is usually too much snow!

Safety:

Andermatt probably receives more snow than any other part of Switzerland. For this reason, and the steepness of the slopes, it's extremely avalanche prone. There are indicator boards at the mountain base and middle station, with warning lights which should be heeded.

Guides: Contact the local snowboard shop, Snow Limit (listed on the opposite page).

Lift pass prices:

6 days: 187Sf

Season: 555Sf

A Region Urstenal Pass includes Realp, Winterhorn, Nätschen-Gütsch and Gemsstock.

A weekly ticket for the whole of the Oberalp region, i.e. Andermatt-Gemsstock, Andermatt-Nätschen-Gütsch, Hospental-Winterhorn, Oberlappass-Calmut, Sedrun-Reuras and Disentis, is slightly more expensive.

Tourist office

Tel: 041-887 1454   Fax: 041-887 0185

Snowboard shops

• Snow Limit Tel/Fax: 041-887 0614

Board/boot hire: 45Sf/day

Excellent guides and a wide range
of hire equipment.

• Snow Virus Tel: 041- 887 0866

Board/Boot hire: 35Sf.

The Lutersee drag lift pic: Tim Rainger

 ABOUT TOWN

Situated in the Usern Valley, at the crossroads
of central Switzerland between the Oberalp
Pass, Saint Gotthard Pass and the Furka Pass,
Andermatt is a slightly dilapidated old town,
which was one of the pioneering ski resorts,
popular with the Brits at the turn of the
century. It is now the domain of riders from
Bern and Lucerne, and small numbers of serious
skiers. The town is located at the base of the Piz
Gemsstock and over the years has witnessed
many avalanches, testament to the steep terrain
and heavy snowfall in the area. The town's
compact nature means everything is accessible
by foot.

Getting there

By plane: The closest main airport is Zürich,
130kms away.

By train: It's a three hour train transfer from
Zürich to Andermatt. Coming from St Moritz
(east) or Brig (west), the Glacier Express cruises
through some of the most spectacular snow
scenery for several hours.

By car: The easy drive from Zürich takes 1.5 hours -
there are no problems with road closure. It's a few
kilometres from Gäschen, which is accessible from
the main motorway.

Accommodation

The Hotel Kronen has excellent half-board with
sumptuous, filling food; price for one night 70-115Sf
(depending on season) - Tel: 041-887 0088 or Fax:
041-887 1838. Another half-board option (on
request), which caters for groups, is the Haus Bonetti;
priced from 36Sf (with breakfast) - Tel: 044-674 40.
For further choices, contact the tourist office.

Food

Open till midnight, and with an outdoor patio for the
late afternoon sun, the café-style Spycher serves
cheap, light snacks such as pizzas, toasted
sandwiches and salads; prices range from 7Sf for a
bowl of soup and crusty roll. For the same sort of
atmosphere and food, the Postillion, just opposite, is
also recommended. The Hotel Kronen offers a hearty,
mid-priced menu.

Nightlife

The Spycher has a lively evening atmosphere, though
it's not really a snowboard bar. For late night dancing
and more drinking, there are two places, the
Downhill and the Gotthard, which are similar -
they're free to enter and, although they open at
9.00pm, nothing really starts to happen until
midnight, once everyone is well-oiled.

Other activities

Andermatt is a great place to learn more about
mountain craft. Ask at Snow Limit.

Thanks to

Bernado at Snow Limit, the tourist board and
Hotel Kronen.

Snowing in town, a fresh dump on the mountain pic: Tim Rainger

Andermatt - view of the town from the St. Bernard Express pic: Tim Rainger

Saas-Fee

 ## ON THE MOUNTAIN

Saas-Fee is famous for its height, long season and glacier, which usually sees consistent snow throughout the year. The accessible terrain is divided by the glacier, which is riddled with crevasses and should never be ridden without a good guide. Saas-Fee offers a complete choice of riding on one mountain, with a healthy freestyle scene and some all-time off-piste to seek out.

 ### Snow conditions

Most of the riding is among the highest in Europe, between 2,500m and 3,500m, and much of it is north-facing. These two factors mean Saas-Fee is extremely snow reliable.

Freeriders

There is a wide variety of terrain to explore and many of the pistes offer easy access to short off-piste runs such as those which follow. The area either side of the Kamel button lift is steep at the top, becoming gentler near the bottom and often holds fat snow.

Kiwi Wall is a well-known adrenaline rush located just below the Gletscher-promenade. The Gletscher Band, below the Feechatz draglift, is a semi-safe route through the glacier. However, do not attempt it without a guide, because huge crevasses await your errant footfall. The Morain, accessible from the base of the Längfluh chairlift, is another good off-piste area, but it should be tackled with prudence. The pick of the couloirs lies under the Alpine Express (near the top) and is accessible from the Plattjen, where there are also some fantastic tree runs. For an excellent day's outing, there is an off-piste excursion from the 'traverse Britannia hut'. Once again, don't go without a guide. Heliboarding can be arranged with nearby Zermatt Helicopters.

Freestylers

In winter, there is a halfpipe and a small funpark (above Maste 4), which are serviced by the Mittaghorn draglift and Felskinn gondola. In summer, the halfpipe and funpark are located just below the top station.

Carvers

All the pistes are well-maintained, with many choices from blue to black runs.

Mountain Information

Mountain chain:

Valais Alps

Vertical metre range:

1,800m - 3,500m

Length of season:

Open all year round.

Number of lifts:

1 mountain railway, 4 cable cars, 3 gondolas, 2 chairlifts, 17 draglifts

Snow-making facilities:

Snow cannons cover 2kms of piste on the lower slopes.

Safety:

All cable car stations have avalanche indicator boards and off-piste equipment can be rented at the lift station.

Guides:

Mark Derivas, the best local snowboard guide, is contactable through the ski school or on Tel: 027-957 4464 (winter) or Tel: 027-957 2268 (summer).

Lift pass prices:

swatch access

1 day: 56Sf

6 days: 260Sf

Season: 850Sf

Lift pass alternatives:

The Saas-Grund and the Saas-Almagell fields can be accessed with a more expensive ticket - two days (the minimum) costs 108Sf, 6 days costs 278Sf. It's a worthwhile option in January or February, when these resorts get the sun that Saas-Fee doesn't.

Local air pic: Tim Rainger

Luftseilbahnen Saas-Fee AG

Im Vorwinter können nicht alle Anlagen garantiert werden

Lifts to avoid

The poma lift up the Piz Kamel, on the far left, is steep and difficult for beginners. Expect crowds and queue delays - said to be better than they were - at the bottom station of the Alpine Express when snow conditions are bad elsewhere.

Mountain fare

The bar and terrace at Maste 4, at the top of the Alpine Express is where the young crew tend to hang-out and enjoy a few beers (as we did - thanks to the generous barman).

Essential Contacts

Tourist office

Tel: 027-957 1457   Fax: 027 957 1860

Snowboard shops

•Popcorn

Tel: 027-958 1914   Fax: 027-957 2300

One of the best snowboard stores in Switzerland, with sales, a huge rental fleet and friendly, helpful staff.

Snowboard schools

•The Paradise Snowboard School

Tel: 027-958 1914

Well-versed in the fine art of snowboard teaching, Paradise organises all kinds of tuition for all ages, including group packages, press assistance and training camps. Contact: Olivier Schmidt.

ABOUT TOWN

Saas-Fee is known as the 'pearl of the Alps', as the village is surrounded by mountains in the same way that an oyster shell encircles a pearl. A picturesque Alpine resort, Saas-Fee is car-free (except for electric cars acting as taxis and trade vehicles) and drivers face hefty car park fees for the duration of their stay. It is compact, with most of the club and restaurant action taking place along a few hundred metres of the main shopping street and all the lift stations just a few minutes walk from the centre of town.

Most of the visitors are German, although the snowboard scene is international - in autumn 80 percent of the mountain users are riders.

Getting there

By plane: Geneva, Zürich and Bern are all 2-3 hours away.

By train: The closest stations are Brig or Visp, from where there are hourly bus connections.

By car: Chains are not required and the road is only closed in exceptional circumstances.

Accommodation

Saas-Fee has a snowboard hotel standards scheme, which requires premises to offer certain basic facilities for riders, including an area to service boards. The Hotel Garni Imseng is a good place to stay, one night's accommodation costs 80Sf - Tel: 028-581 258. The details and telephone numbers of others are available from the tourist office.

Food

There are over 60 restaurants, some with incredible reputations and prices to match. The pizza parlours and the set menus at the hotels offer some of the best price options. The Lavern has a delicious tomato fondue - one of the best we tasted. For self-caterers, there are several good supermarkets where lunch snacks and cheap beers can be bought.

Nightlife

The Popcorn Snowboard Shop has a bar with pool tables - there is no admission fee and, as it's open till 3.00am, there's a kicking party atmosphere with all kinds of hard-core music - getting legless is going to cost you! If you're going to be around for a few nights, you might want to purchase your own bottle of whisky and leave it above the bar. It'll only cost you 100 bucks! The Go-Inn is another thumping bar. Again entry is free, but the music can be pretty dire.

Other activities

Skating and curling.

Thanks to

Judith Schaad and the Saas-Fee tourist office, Hotel Garni Imseng and The Paradise Snowboard Crew: Olivier, Alex and David.

pic: Tim Rainger

Saas-Fee pic: Tim Rainger

TEMPLE
CUMMINS

Palmer

PALMER PERFORMANCE

Advanced Sandwich Prepreg Technology
Exclusive Palmer Channel™ Design
New Generation of Multifunctional Board Shapes

www.PalmerUSA.com
©1996 Palmer

rider: Reto pic: Peter Mathis

Flims/Laax

Vision ISF Boardercross '96 pic: Richard Walch

Mountain Information

Mountain range:

Bünder Alpes

Vertical metre range:

1,100m - 3,020m

Season duration:

beginning of October -

beginning of May

Number of lifts:

12 draglifts, 10 chairlifts,

6 shuttle cars, 4 cable cars

Snow-making facilities:

Extensive and regularly used for

the funpark, halfpipes and trails.

Safety:

The avalanche indicator board at

the bottom gondola is updated

daily. Mountain Fantasy

(a specialist trekking store in

Flims, Waldhaus) has avalanche

gear and snow shoes.

Tel: 081-936 7077.

Guides:

Ask at the Snowboard Garage.

Tel: 081-9216969

Fax: 081-921 6454

Lift pass prices:

swatch access

1 day: 45-55Sf

6 days: 270Sf

Lift pass alternatives

The season pass includes

unlimited riding in Davos, Klosters

and St Mortiz.

rider: Marco Lutz pic: Richard Walch

ON THE MOUNTAIN

Laax is a high altitude, glacial mountain with a long history of snowboarding. In '96, it was host to a multitude of competitions and parties, including an ISF boardercross and halfpipe event. Laax is one of the most enlightened resorts in Switzerland; it is 100 percent behind snowboarding and was ahead of its time in investing in Europe's first pipe dragon. In '96, the boardercross competition was held in late April and was probably the most talked about snowboard event held in Europe. People rode, partied and slept on the mountain - the vibe was special. Riders visit from all over Europe and the freestyle scene, in particular, is thriving. Great live music and raging parties accompany all events.

17, and on to Plaun. The Plaun and Curnius chairlifts both offer easy-going freeride terrain with tree runs in-between. The area between Vorab and Crap Masegan often harbours a few choice windlips. To get the most out of the area, as for anywhere else, we suggest hiring a guide for at least one full day.

Freestylers

There are two pipes at Laax; an earthpipe located at Crap Sogn Gion and a surface pipe on the Vorab glacier. Both are kept in good order by a pipe dragon. Local pros Reto Poltera and Erich Bartschi have designed and maintained a legendary snowpark; it's long with about 30 mega-hits, table-tops, jumps and pipes, plus a load of other launch ramps of various kinds that defy description.

A HIGH ALTITUDE, GLACIAL MOUNTAIN WITH A LONG HISTORY IN SNOWBOARDING

Snow conditions

Laax generally enjoys good snow cover and an extended season. In '96, when the last event of the European calender was held here in late April, the snow conditions were fine.

Freeriders

There are a number of killer runs - go right from the top of the Vorab Pign and follow the Sattel. A long gully runs out from the bottom beside the Alp Ruschein. Another long run takes you down from La Siala between the bottom stations of runs 16 and

Carvers

The Bill Kid run on the Alp Dado is the favoured carving piste, though most of the mountain offers good, but not ultra steep, carving terrain.

Mountain fare

At Crap Sogn Gion, close to the halfpipe, there is a full-on snowboard bar and club, playing pumping tunes. There are several excellent places to eat and drink at various points on the mountain; the Crap bar at the bottom station is a good place to meet people for breakfast or at the end of the day.

rider: Sven Werner pic: Richard Walch

pic: Richard Walch

Essential Contacts

Tourist office

Tel: 081- 921 4343   Fax 081-921 6565

Internet http:www . laax. ch/

Snowboard shops

•The Snowboard garage

Tel 081-921 6969 Fax: 081-921 6454

Board/boot hire: 55Sf/day

Snowboard schools

•The Snowboard garage

Tel 081-921 6969 Fax: 081-921 6454

Half day lesson (three people) 40Sf.

Reto from the snowboard shop also organises summer camps

ABOUT TOWN

The area is divided into the two villages of Flims and Laax, which are five kilometres apart. Strung-out over some distance, with no particular focus point, free buses connect the two. Laax is a tranquil farming village, which has kept its original rural charm, although Murschetg, a purpose-built complex, a short bus ride away, has much of the accommodation.

Getting there

By plane: Zürich is the closest airport.

By train: Take the train from Zürich to Chur, then change to a PTT for the 40 minute bus ride to Laax.

By car: From Zürich, take the Chur motorway (N3) and exit for Flims via Disentis and Oberalp. From the west, travel via the Furka pass and Andermatt. This pass is closed to cars in winter, but it's possible to put your car on the train for 60Sf.

Accommodation

Hotel Ventira - Tel: 081-920 8080 and Hotel Cathoumen - Tel: 081-921 4545 offer bed and breakfast from 40-50Sf a night. The best value for money is the town's backpacking joint; Gliders Paradise, in Flims, priced from 25Sf per night - Tel: 081 911 2903.

Food

You can eat fine soups, snacks and drink beer at the Crap bar at the base station till midnight. At the same location, the Plazza serves Swiss cuisine, with prices ranging from 13-20Sf. In Flims, the Pizzeria Pomodoro does good pizzas (13-20Sf).

Nightlife

In Flims, the Albana Pub is an English-style pub, with a good juke box and party atmosphere. For more late night action, try the Chatswood playing Euro-disco till 1.30am. In Laax, have a drink and a surf on the Internet at the Crap bar at the valley station - it's open till midnight. The place to dance till 4.00am is the Casa Veglia Disco, although the choice of music is marginal.

NB: Keep an eye out for concerts at the base of the mountain and in Laax - you're guaranteed a good time.

Other activities

There is a trampoline at the valley station outside the 'Snowboard Garage'. The pool complex nearby has a counter current, sauna, massage and more. The Grava public pool in Laax has a sauna, whirlpool etc. - Tel: 081-921 4610.

Thanks to

John the Guide, Ahriane Ehrat at Crap Sogn Gion, Mountain Railways and the tourist office.

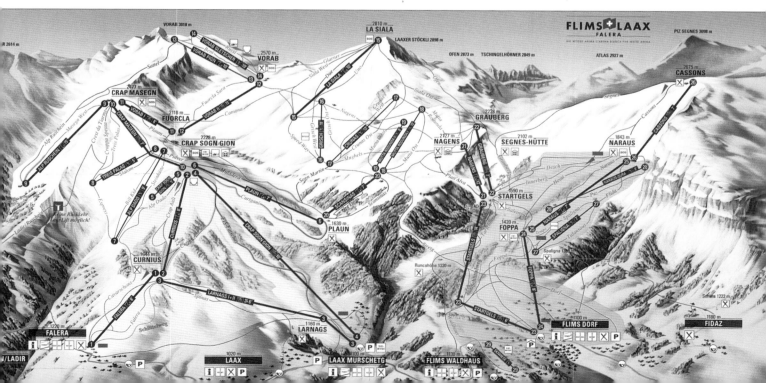

Davos/Klosters

pic: Courtesey of Davos Tourist Board

Mountain Information

Mountain chain:

Bündner Alpes

Vertical metre range:

1,540m - 2,845m

Length of season:

end of November -
end of April

Number of lifts:

3 gondolas, 3 cable cars,
10 cable airways,
36 draglifts, 7 chairlifts

Snow-making facilities:

Areas are covered, when necessary

Safety:

There are avalanche indicator
boards at the bottom stations. If
you're interested, Davos is home
to the Institute of Avalanche
Studies
Tel: 081-417 0222

Guides:

Available through the
snowboard schools.

Lift pass prices:

1 day: 52Sf
6 days: 259Sf
Season: 900Sf
The season pass includes access
to Flims, Laax, Oberengadin, Arosa
and Kitzbühel.

Lift pass alternatives:

The REGA pass includes the
Klosters area.

 ## ON THE MOUNTAIN

Five main mountain areas accessible on one lift pass constitute Switzerland's biggest winter resort, moving up to 55,000 people an hour. Jakobshorn was home to the '95 world championships and the final event in the Ballantine's ISF world series '96. The others offer excellent riding for all levels and huge off-piste potential.

 ### Snow conditions

Snow reliability is fair, through neither of the mountains are of glacial height, and not much of the slope is north-facing.

Freeriders

The freeride terrain is too huge to really do justice to individual runs, but a brief description of each of the main mountains follows.

Pischa (2,483m): A small area on one side of the Fluelatal Valley, with good freeriding and a variety of terrain. The main attractions are a long natural halfpipe down the Grat run and the wide open terrain below the Meder run. Pick a line and head for the Davoser See.

If you're prepared to walk, there are some good off-piste areas accessible, but the main reason for riding in Pischa is the lack of crowds.

Jakobshorn (2,590m): One of the mountain's best known by the European snowboard community. Jakobshorn towers above Davos Platz with the bottom station a stone's throw from the railway station. It's an all-ability mountain with good intermediate freeriding off all the lifts. The tree lines which cover the bottom third of the mountain can hold some of the best snow, although the forest is dense in places.

For extreme riders, Jakobshorn north is very steep and easy to reach. The north-facing area from Bramabuel to Teufi, though extremely avalanche prone, holds great powder. Catch the bus from Teufi back to Davos village. For intermediate riders, safer and more open freeride areas can be found either side of run 13 down to the village of Muhle. The trees at the bottom are variable and you can get stuck sometimes. The Bräma Rotte runs, with open terrain that's not too steep, are also fun. Jakobshorn is also home to wild monthly full moon parties - it's radical riding down in the moonlight after a few bottles of wine.

The Rinerhorn: The big open powder fields off the backside of the Juonli and the valleys running down to Glaris (accessed by walking from Nullisch Grat) are the main features of the Rinerhorn. Run number 10 on the piste map is the longest trail.

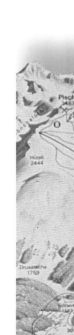

Shcatzalp/Strela: The whole valley, which includes the Guggerbachtäll run down to Schatzalp, has good freeriding with rollers, little cliffs and cornices. It's also a good mountain to head with a guide and some snowshoes. There's even a toboggan run open till 10.00pm that's loads of fun. There are no lights but people light fires, party and ride the wooden sleds all night. The area is usually uncrowded.

Parsenn: The Parsennbahn offers access to a lot of terrain. At the top of the WeisSfluh (2,844m), you'll find the highest snow in the region and some of the most extreme areas, which are strictly for advanced riders. Go any way off the top station. From WeisSfluhjoch, ride to Grotschnagrat. Further down the mountain, the freeriding is more suited to intermediates, the easiest being accessed from the Höhenweg Station down to Davos Dorf. Below the Meierhofer Tälli, you can ride down to Wolfgang, enjoying good snow and lots of little steep chutes before the tree line. This area is also home to the famous 10km run down to Serneus (above Klosters). It's a flat on the top, but fun, with a long tree run at the bottom. From Serneus, catch the train back to Davos or Klosters.

Gotschna: Most famous for its intense north-facing terrain and also as the place where Prince Charles's guide died in a well publicised ski avalanche. The off-piste is extreme, with cliffs and chutes, and is strictly a danger zone - we never told you about this spot. See the disclaimer at the front of the book!

Madrisa: Facing south, above Klosters Dorf, the Madrisa has some good open freeride terrain, including a long ride all the way down the Chuecalanda (run 12) and through the trees to Klosters Dorf. There is also good riding if you hike for half an hour to the left from Rätechenjoch (2,602m). The Madrisa piste (Run 8) leads to Schlappin and the entire area offers interesting options.

 Freestylers
Strangely, the facilities for freestyle riders at Davos are sub-standard. A permanent halfpipe at the top of Jakobshorn is not well maintained and the competition halfpipe by the base of the mountain is only maintained during ISF competitions. There was no real funpark to speak of in the '95/'96 season. Ain't that a shame!

 Carvers
There are 88 pistes totalling over 270kms in length - carve on!

⊗ Lifts to avoid
The very long T-bars and the Hauptertallibahn, which is ancient, and a bit of a nightmare - doors occasionally fall off and it is often closed.

 Mountain fare
The Restaurant Jalzhut, just below the top Jakobshorn gondola station and beside the halfpipe, has loud sound, cheap food and drinks (10Sf for a coke and a plate of pasta). It rages with people dancing on table tops to booming music of a questionable nature. You're better off with a packed lunch!

THE FREERIDE TERRAIN IS TOO HUGE TO REALLY DO JUSTICE TO INDIVIDUAL RUNS

ABOUT TOWN

Davos is supposedly Europe's highest town and it is very much a town, not just a village, with a long winter sports history. The various suburbs stretch from Klosters via Davos Dorf to Davos Platz and, in truth, the sprawl is ugly. However, the advantage of being a bigger town is that it is packed with amentities and has the liveliest nightlife in the Graubunden. Davos Platz, the biggest part of the town, is where most of the snowboarders tend to stay.

Getting there

By air: The closest international airport is Zürich, from where Davos is a three hour transfer by bus or train.

By train: From Zürich, there is a connection every hour to Davos via Zürich central and Landquart; the price of a one way ticket is 54Sf.

By car: Take the highway from Zürich airport to Landquart, then head for Davos. Chains may be required to get over the Wolfgang pass to Klosters.

Essential Contacts

Tourist office

Tel: 081-415 2121

Fax: 081-415 2131

Snowboard shops

•Top Secret (located at the gondola station at the base of Jakobshorn) - Tel: 081-413 7374 A large shop with sales/rentals.

•Rude Dude   Tel: 081-413 2701 A small shop, specialising in trekking and an off-piste approach, a hundred metres up the road from the Spielsalon.

•Paarsenn   Tel: 081-410 1014

* For a specialist repair service, try Helmi's snowboard and ski service, just around the corner from Rude Dude - he's the best guy in Davos.

Snowboard schools

Both Top Secret and Paarsenn (telephone numbers above) have snowboard schools.

Bird eye view of the Pareller slalam course '95 pic: Sang Tan

rider: Ingrmar Backman pic: Sang Tan

 Accommodation

In Davos Platz, the Bolgenschanze is the obvious choice and one of Europe's first specialist snowboard hotels. It has a roaring bar downstairs and basic bunkroom accommodation upstairs. It's within walking distance of the train station at Davos Platz, near the mountain station. You can also stay on the mountain at Jakobshorn in a guesthouse with six bedrooms, half-board is available and is cheaper with a ski pass. Self-catering accommodation can be booked through the tourist office's brochures. For more information and contact numbers, call Davos Direct Reservations Line - Tel: 081-415 2121.

 Food

The big news for fast food junkies is the Burger King in Davos Platz! The Steinhof is a Thai restaurant, with excellent food at good prices (for Davos Platz). The Spielsalon, located near the railway station, has the cheapest snack food in town. You can play video games and pinball, while eating burgers for 6Sf, fries for 5Sf and kebabs 8Sf. Hotel Face (Davos Dorf) and Hotel Europe (Promenade Platz) both do good pizzas. Other cheap eats include the Dischma (Davos Dorf), which offers local specialities, and the Red Dragon at the Hotel Terminus serving reasonably priced Chinese food. The restaurant above the Spa supermarket in Davos Dorf has main meals for 12-15Sf.

 Nightlife

The Bolgenshanze is the place where most of the snowboarding crew hang-out. It offers live bands, DJs and theme parties, and is open till 2.00am; beer is priced from 4Sf a pint. The Schuetzen pub has cheap beers at happy hour. Later in the evening, the Red Light is a small bar/club with no admission fee, but outrageous drink prices (a large vodka mix is 18Sf) and music ranging from good to atrocious.

Other activities

There is a public swimming-pool, fitness centre, tennis courts, an artificial skating rink, a sauna, cinema, museums and more.

 Thanks to

Pepe Shouen, Mischa Kaeser at Rude Dude, the Bolgenschanze Hotel and the tourist office.

Scuol (lower Engadine)

 ON THE MOUNTAIN

A curiously uncrowded resort area that's always been a big part of the Swiss and European snowboard scenes. As the majority of the terrain isn't super steep, it's perfect for freeriders. The lift system gives access to several snowfields, most of which are on top of a grass base, so even with minimum snow levels there are no rocks! As a bonus, Scuol is renowned for sunshine hours, which, when it's not snowing, are an impressive 86 percent of winter days.

 Snow conditions

Scuol's high sunshine hours and southerly aspect can mean low snow levels in bad seasons, but this does not usually cause too many problems as the snow is almost always dry-packed groomed or powder.

Freeriders

Beginners will find the undulating, groomed slopes perfect for learning, while intermediate freeriders will have great fun on the low-angled rolling hills. Lift accessible off-piste is endless, with runs up to 11kms long and a variety of terrain such as windlips, ravines, chutes and cliff jumps, but you'll only find the best stuff with local knowledge. For a great windlip hit, try the Tit, accessed off the Salaniva chair. The Rock Stein is a pretty nice leap accessed off Mot da Ri, from where you can also find an exciting couloir. Again, off the Mot de Ri is the Riverbed, which has hits, hips and lips.

The tree runs are further down the mountain, but look out for 'green areas' and respect the forest. When the snow levels are good, you can ride all the way into the village of Scuol, clocking up at least 8,000 vertical metres of tree-covered powder runs, all with gondola access. Off-piste runs lead into the neighbouring villages of Ftan and Sent. Scuol is not the most extreme of steep resorts, but it always has guaranteed snow and fast freeriding fun.

 Freestylers

There is an earthpipe and pre-formed earth park, guaranteeing excellent park terrain even during low snow seasons. There is a permanent halfpipe, shaped by a transition tool and connected to the funpark, where table tops, large kickers and quarterpipes are permanently built into natural terrain. However, there's only a minimum amount of hardware for die-hard jibbers. The park, serviced weekly by the resort management and The School, is easily accessed by lift and there's a restaurant, Alpetta Hütte, nearby.

 Carvers

The 'Autobahn' is a favourite carving piste. Beginners should head for the 'Schlivera runs', which have a snowboard only area that is perfect for learning. Those who wish to ride fast should take the Champatsch chairlift, from where there are plenty of choices.

Mountain fare

The Alpette Hütte is the place to hang - it's close to the pipe, has cranking sounds, good food and a terrace bar. The self-service option for a quick, cheap bite is the Chapena.

A BEAUTIFULLY PRESERVED, 12TH CENTURY ROMANSCH SPA TOWN AT THE NORTHERN END OF THE ENGADINE VALLEY, A STONE'S THROW FROM THE AUSTRIAN AND ITALIAN BORDERS

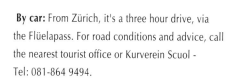
rider: Marco Bruni pic: T.K.O.

 ABOUT TOWN

Scuol is a beautifully preserved, 12th century Romansch spa town at the northern end of the Engadine Valley, a stone's throw from the Austrian and Italian borders. The town's mineral waters are famed for their therapeutic qualities and, together with the incredible new spa complex, draw visitors seeking healing and relaxation. There are only a few accommodation and eating choices, and a limited, yet spirited, nightlife.

 Getting there

By plane: It's a three hour transfer by train from Zürich airport.

By train: From Zürich, take the express train to Chur and change there for the Rhätische Bahn to Scuol. Alternatively, there is a direct train from St Moritz.

pic: Tim Rainger

By car: From Zürich, it's a three hour drive, via the Flüelapass. For road conditions and advice, call the nearest tourist office or Kurverein Scuol - Tel: 081-864 9494.

 Accommodation

There is not a lot of choice. The Hotel Quellenhof, in the centre of town, is one of the best bets with good half-board deals i.e. accommodation for one night and two meals costs 58Sf - Tel: 081-864 1215 or Fax: 081-864 0234. Prices at the Holiday Hostel Gurlaina range from 13Sf to 15Sf per night per person for groups - Tel: 081-864 1422/23. Chamanna Naluns is a B&B style option with one night's accommodation from 37Sf - Tel: 081-864 1601 or 081-864 1412. For ride to the door convenience, the Chasa Alpina is a good place to stay and gives discounts for group bookings - Tel: 081-864 9339.

 Food

The Co-op, located on the main road, is the biggest supermarket in the village and sells a wide range of cheap food. Restaurants include the Trü pizzeria, La Terrassa (a family restaurant serving generous, well-priced portions), the Italian Giovanni's (which serves great pasta) and a Chinese restaurant in the Bad Scuol complex. High class cuisine, at an affordable price, is recommended at Hotel Filli in the lower part of town.

 Nightlife

The nightlife revolves around private parties and the bar at La Terrassa, where people congregate to drink beer, have a snack and play billiards. Above La Terrassa, there is a nightclub, Galaria Milo, that gets

so overcrowded in the season that most people forego it for outside or back home activities. A totally individual bar is Trais Portas, run by a local boarding couple, where classical music is played and the best cocktails in town served. Very mysterioso!

Other activities

Chess.

 Thanks to

Dani 'Kiwi' Meier,

pic: Tim Ranger

Markus and Ute Kobelt, the local tourist board and The School.

 Essential Contacts

Tourist office

Tel: 081-864 9494   Fax: 081-864 9939

Snowboard shops

There are no specialist stores, but the ski stores sell some snowboard equipment. The School hires boards and boots of all kinds, and sells some small goods.

Snowboard schools:

The School   Tel: 081-864 8220

The first snowboard school in Switzerland, The School has been around for over a decade. It offers excellent instruction on all levels and also has a large fleet of quality hire equipment.

Camps

The 'Mosca Brothers' hold a race camp in early April for carvers of all levels. A freestyle/freeride camp is also run by The School in April. For details of both, call The School.

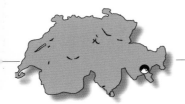

Upper Engadine
St Moritz

 ON THE MOUNTAIN

The Upper Engadine region encompasses a number of excellent riding areas, centred around the main towns of St Moritz and Pontresina. All are connected by one pass, though strangely public transport between them is not included in the price. The geography of the valley floor and the differing aspects of the serviced areas can mean varied conditions in each area on the same day. To check what's going on, monitors showing live video links of local conditions are located at all the gondola stations and at the tourist office. Despite fairly dire expectations, there is a neat snowboard scene in the valley, focusing on the Playground in Paradise snowboard store in St Moritz and The Workshop in Pontresina.

 Snow conditions

The valley and its surrounding areas have a reputation for consistent, but moderate, levels of snow. Though it can come in from all directions, the Engadine is primarily exposed to snow from the south, which means that if there is a low pressure system moving from the Med over Italy, it's going to be dump time in St Moritz.

Freeriders

The three main areas accessed from St Moritz are Suvretta, Marguns and Corviglia. Suvretta extends west to the adjoining billionaire's village of Champfer, while Marguns stretches east to the village of Celerrina. Both are tops for off-piste, with Marguns offering the more challenging hits and speed.

Corviglia, the resort's main mountain, is a playground for freak riders. Piz Nair offers long, fast chutes and bowls for advanced riders, while the area around Très Fluors has long fluffy runs. However, check their safety first as both areas are prone to some occasional slippage. For those who prefer air over speed, head for Lach Tal, 500 metres west of Corviglia station, which is a sick natural halfpipe that is ungroomed, except for hits built by local pilots.

At Silvaplana, five minutes west of Corviglia by car, the combined resorts of Corvatsch and Furtschellas offer heaps of intermediate difficulty tree and stone riding, as well as steep chutes for the more

One of the hottest grommets in Europe - Michi Albin, St. Mo. half pipe - check the lines pic: Richard Walch

disciplined. Also great fun, at the far east point of Corvatsch, is the Hahnensee run, which quickly throws you back to St Mortiz Bad, through a rush of trees and scree, plus nice staircase drops. Then it's just a two minute walk out to the nearest bus stop. However, this run is only open when there is enough snow.

 Freestylers

St Moritz offers some of the best training facilities available to jibbers. An epic 90m halfpipe shaped by a pipe dragon tops the list, but a huge quarterpipe, a four metre gap jump and loads of beginner friendly hits await the jib-ophiles. This combination, plus a T-bar back to the start, where a blaring sound system is in operation, make St Moritz a favourite training ground for Swiss Champions and World Cuppers at large. Slowly but surely, St Moritz is shedding its diamonds and fur coat image by hosting a large number of local, national and international boarding events, with the guidance of the PIP crew. If you watch MTV, you probably saw the snowball special from Corviglia, when the Canadian funk core group Sunun Bonm played underneath a gap jump with riders going big, right over their heads. At Corvatsch, a hit park of intermediate level and a boardercross course round up the man-made stuff, but follow the fall-line and you'll find many natural hits worn in for you by the local crew.

 Carvers

There are many well-groomed pistes of all levels for carvers to enjoy. At Corviglia, try Très Fluors's red run, or take the Grisch lift to Plateau Nair, then ride all the way down to Marguns for an interrupted speed rush on a smooth, wide piste.

 Mountain fare

Pack your own lunch, but don't lug it around - leave it in the lockers in Corviglia station. If you would prefer a hot meal, but don't want to spend 25-100Sf for lunch, try one of the cafés at Corviglia or Marguns where a half roasted chicken and fries will set you back 15Sf. At Corvatsch, the mid-station restaurant has killer pizzas, made to order, for 14Sf.

pic: Peter Mathis

FAVOURITE TRAINING GROUND **FOR SWISS** CHAMPIONS AND **WORLD CUPPERS** AT LARGE

 ABOUT TOWN

St Moritz is what it is because the town lies amid stunningly beautiful scenery and has a fascinating cultural mix. While it is well known as the glitzy centre of a super snobbish resort, is surrounded by village, such as Pontresina (15 minutes by bus or train) and Celerina (5 minutes by bus or train), which are more relaxed, (though still not particularly cheap). St Moritz itself is split into two distinct parts - St. Moritz Dorf (the old town overlooking the lake) has shops, expensive hotels, restaurants and bars, while St Moritz Bad is a '70s blot on the landscape with cheaper accommodation. Buses connect the two villages, but the walk only takes twenty minutes.

 Getting there

By air: The nearest connections are Milan and Zürich, both about four hours away by train.
By train: The station is near the Dorf at the bottom of the hill. Taxis from the station to St Moritz Bad cost 18Sf for a two kilometre transfer! During the day, it is serviced by buses.

Accommodation

Most of the affordable accommodation is in St Moritz Bad. The Sport Hotel Stille serves wholesome half-board food, and has a bar and pool tables, but connections to the lifts and town aren't good. The youth hostel, the most expensive in Switzerland, is right next door.

 Food

One of the few cheap places to eat out in St Moritz is the Hotel Laudinella, where a family size pizza costs 35Sf and feeds four to six people. They're huge! Another cheap alternative is the traditional Swiss fondue, found at most of the local restaurants, which costs about 30Sf per person. Benni says 'eat at home!' There are good supermarkets in town.

Nightlife

In St Moritz, the Stubli and the Müli bar in Hotel Schweizerhoff are the best drinking holes, a beer will set you back 6Sf. The Cava Bar is an OK night club that does not charge an admission fee and plays loud music. There's also a pretty spaced-out strip club, where there's no admission fee, for late night desperados.

Other activities

St Moritz is home to the Cresta Run, an upper class British sledding institution, and quite a few other novel events, such as a race where competing horses tow skiers and, so far, one snowboarder, G.P.Schmidt across the famous frozen lake.

G.P.Schmidt - First ever Snowboarder allowed in the coverted horse drawn Ski race on the lake pic: TKO

Essential Contacts

Tourist office
Tel: 081-864 9494   Fax: 081-864 9939
Snowboard shops
•Playground in Paradise (St Moritz)
Tel/Fax: 081-832 2363
A cool shop, run by core local riders G.P.Schmidt and Benni Sacks, which dispenses good gear, private lessons (in several languages) and guides (they rip).
•The Wave (St Moritz)
Tel: 081-833 8090   Fax: 081-837 3377
The Wave Snowboard School Division
Tel/Fax: 081-833 4490

Essential Contacts

Tourist office

Pontresina   Tel: 081-842 6488

Fax. 081-842 7996

Snowboard shops

The Workshop (Pontresina)

Tel/Fax: 081-842 6502

This is Reto Lamm's Shop, which
is mostly freestyle-oriented. Aside
from board and boot rentals,
freeride guides and board services,
such as edge and base grinds,
waxing and base fixing are
available. Prices vary from 20Sf to-
60Sf.

Snowboard schools

Snowboard School Pontresina

Tel: 081-842 7610

Fax: 081-842 6071

A Swiss licensed school, based at
The Workshop and at the Ski
School Pontresina. Excellent tuition
is available in several languages.

Summer Camps

Flag summer camps, held at
Diavolezza in June and July, are
organised by Mickey Fruh and Reto
Lamm. It's a freestyle/freeride
scene for people who just want to
ride in a nice park and pipe, and
spend the afternoons hanging out
with their friends. A lot of world cup
riders train here, without coaching
pressure and stress. For all
enquiries contact The Workshop or
Fax: 00 41-81-842 7560.

pic: Tim Ranger

ON THE MOUNTAIN

Pontresina consists of the village run known as
Alp Languard, the bottom section of which
houses Reto Lamm's 'fun garden'. Muottas
Muragl is considered by many to be one of the
most beautiful views in the world, as is the
Lagalb, which lies right across the road from
the big bad, super-rad resort of Diavolezza.

Freeriders

Feast on the daily meals served up in
Diavolezza and Lagalb. Carry your speed from
the glacier on high and exit the piste to the
right. The rest is up to you, as there are tons of
natural quarterpipes, windlips, bowls, trees,
decent sized cliffs and a huge natural halfpipe
under the gondola. This is where local pros
Reto Lamm and Mich Albin can usually be
found when not in the pipe at St Moritz.
NB - If you can afford a four minute heli-flight
and a guide, treat yourself to Piz Palu, the
majestic glacial runs made famous by James
Bond and the white magic crew.

Freestylers

The fun garden in Pontresina, open until
10.00pm on Friday nights, is a great place to
do six or seven quick hits, especially on foggy
days. In the summer, try the Diavolezza
halfpipe with Reto. The Flag Snowboard Camp
is held here in July.

At Corvatsch, a hit park of intermediate level and a
boardercross course round up the man-made stuff,
but follow the fall-line and you'll find many natural
hits worn in for you by the local crew.

Carvers

Muotta Muragl offers wide, sparsely populated, but
rather short, runs. Go up for the tree valley, five lakes,
two glaciers view and a beer, anyhow! Lagalb is
awesome for trench warfare. It mellows only slightly
from a black to a red run, but then it's full speed
ahead to the end-to-edge city. Diavolezza's pistes are
a carver's nirvana from top to bottom, with smooth
vast flats and steeps rolling nicely into one another.

Mountain fare

Similar to St Moritz, but, in addition, there's good
pizzocheri and hearty soups to be had. At the top
station, you'll enjoy a brilliant view over the glacier
while you warm up. Alp Languards top Hutte is a great
place for lovers to enjoy grilled meat at reasonable
prices, considering the regional average. It's also a
great place for naturalists to spot giant capricorns,
golden eagles and cross-billed finches, so bring your
cameras or field glasses while you lunch on the sunny
terraces.

Rider. Reto   pic:Peter Mathis

Rider Reto pic: Peter Mathis

RETO LAMM LIKES
FUR COAT FREE
PONTRESINA FOR
ITS MELLOW,
MOUNTAIN-
CLIMBING
AMBIANCE

ABOUT TOWN

Reto likes fur coat free Pontresina for its mellow, mountain-climbing ambiance, plus it only has around 1,400 locals and it's five minutes from St Moritz, but holds unique charm all of its own, and is ideally situated amongst some of the coolest mountains in Switzerland.

Nightlife

In Pontresina, the boys and girls drink at the Postli, the Cento bar and at the Hotel Saratz.

Getting there

By train: The train station at Pontresina is close enough to walk to many of the accommodation options with a lightish bag
By Car : The roads are easy

Food

In Pontresina, there's a good pizzeria next to the tennis courts and a bistro attached to the swimming-pool. Everything else is expensive.
There are good supermarkets in town.

Accommodation

The Youth Hostel is next to the railway station and is probably the best deal in town, with a bargain-priced restaurant to boot. Other recommendations include the Hotel Alvetern, an old wooden chalet with a communal kitchen that is run by a young couple, prices are 55-100Sf per night - Tel: 081-842 64 67.

The mid range Hotel Hauser, the affordable Hotel Saratz and the Hotel National are priced from 110Sf to 230Sf, while the Hotel Sonne is priced from 130Sf to 180Sf. For more information and details, contact the tourist office.

✅ Thanks to

Tim King at TKO Productions,
Reto Lamm at the Workshop,
J.P.Schmidt and Benni Sacks at
Playground in Paradise,
Anina from the Tourist Board, and
Marco Bruni.

pic: Tim Rainger

Italy

Country Information

Capital: Rome

Population: 56,778,000

Time: GMT + one hour
(central European time)

Currency: Lira

UK £1.00 = 2,378 lira

US $1.00 = 1,585 lira

Telephone information:

ISD Code: 39

Local directory enquires: 12

Int directory enquiries: 176-170

Italian Snow report: 162 (in Italy)

Emergency services: 113

Snow conditions: 44-66 1906

Main Tourist Board Details

Italian State Tourist Board

Via Marghera 2, Rome 00185

Tel: 39-6 -49711

National Airline:

Air Italia Tel: 6-656 22151

Weather reports:

On T.V. Rai Uno: before news

Newspapers: In all dailys

La Republica, La Nazione

National Snowboard Magazines:

Onboard Italia

National Snowboard Associations:

Tel: 39 45 59 01 70

Fax: 39 45 59 0797

Connect...

Standing or coasting, Switch offers a natural step-in motion and quick one finger release. An open channel frame combined with the Switch Active Closure™ latch deliver faultless connection in the worst conditions. Openings exhaust snow and ice as you step in, while the patented multi-position latch continually tightens your boot to the board even with snow in-between.

Autolock 100 & 500 Series Step-In Bindings

Switch Manufacturing   **www.switch-sf.com**

A4 Phone 01925 757999 Fax 01925 757333

Italy

Cervinia
Livingo
Bormio
Madonna di Campiglio
Val Gardena

Cervinia

ON THE MOUNTAIN

Cervinia has Italy's highest riding and some of its longest runs - up to 13kms! Most of the riding is in a huge, wide, usually sunny bowl, which makes it an enjoyable place to spend a lengthy holiday. The riding is extensive and the scenery is among the most impressive in the area.

pic: Jeff Webb

Snow Conditions

Due to its height, the snow conditions are generally excellent. In the summer, it's possible to board on the glacier at Plateau Rosa (3,000m), which is connected to the resort of Zermatt in Switzerland.

Freeriders

The piste covered by the Pancheron cable-car offers some good on and off-piste runs. Other magical areas are the Plateau Rosa and La Cima Bianche Laghi. On these runs it is better to be taken by a guide, as the glacier can be dangerous due to the number of crevasses, which can be death traps. From Cervinia, it is possible to reach Valtourneche through to Colle Superiore and Inferiore of Cime Bianche.

Rider. Jerome pic: Jeff Webb

Freestylers

There is a halfpipe located close to the centre of Cervinia, in the Bontadini area.

Carving

The most well-known, panoramic and exhilarating piste is the Ventina. Pistes No.5 and No.6 are also challenging. For beginners, and for riders who want fun, the ideal piste is that of Rocce Nere.

Mountain fare

The Chalet Etoile on the Rocce Nere is the spot where all the boarders in Cervinia hang-out. At the hut you will find a large terrace, solarium, a bar and self-service foods. One kilometre down the mountain is Plan Torrette, another hut popular because of it's sun-exposed terrace.

Mountain Information

Mountain chain:

Aosta Valley

Vertical metre range:

2,050 - 3,400m

Length of season:

November - May,

on the glacier May - October

Number of lifts:

6 cable ways, 2 gondolas,

10 chairlifts, 17 draglifts

Guides:

For heliboarding itineraries, contact La Cadure, which is run by Nicola Corradi and Marco Bramese, two alpine guides, and ski and snowboard teachers.

Prices: L60,000 to L70,000

Tel: 0166 949267.

Lift pass prices:

1 day: L50,000

6 days: L250,000

swatch access

Linked resorts:

A six day pass covers Cervinia and Valtourneche; Zermatt is just the other side of the Matterhorn.

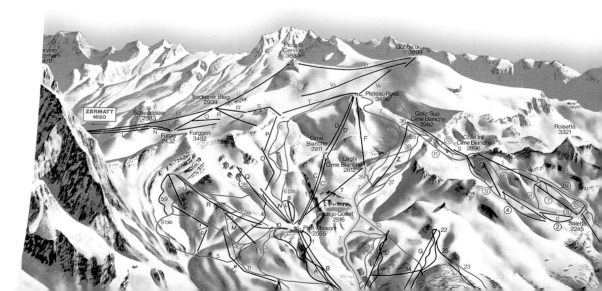

Tourist office

Tel: 0166-949 136/086

Snowboard shop

•GDL Sport Tel: 0166-948 713

Board/boot hire: L47,000/day

Board/boot hire: L143,000/6 days

•Sport Cristallo - Tel: 0166-948 077

Board/boot hire: L45,000/day

Board/boot hire: L143,000/6 days

•Snowboard Club Delire Fun Club Cervinia,

Carrel-Breuil Cervinia - Tel: 0166-948 077

Contact: Angelo Vallet.

Snowboard school

•Cervino - Tel: 0166-949 034.

1 hour lesson: L47,000

6 days of lessons: L180,000

 ABOUT TOWN

Cervinia, although an ugly mish-mash of architecture, is set in some of the area's most stunning scenery, which is dominated by the beautiful Matterhorn. The town centre has a very tranquil atmosphere due to the fact that it's traffic-free.

Getting there

By air: Turin, the closest airport, is a 1.5 hour transfer away by car.

By rail: The nearest station is Chatillion, from where there are regular bus tranfers.

By car : Cervinia is 1001kms from Calais and 150kms from Milan. Join the Milano -Torino motorway at Samthia and head towards Valle D'Aosta

Accommodation

There are over 44 hotels and 400 chalets/apartments in Cervinia. The cheapest option is the self-catering Critallino apartments. For more information, contact the tourist office which will provide a list of places, prices and locations - Tel: 0166-949 136, Fax: 0166-949 731.

 Food

The Pania is the place to sample local specialities. The Casse Croute has the biggest, best pizzas in the world.

 Nightlife

The best places to drink, dance and be merry are the Chimera, Blow up and Princess.

Other facilities

There's bowling, public pools, three paragliding centres, toboganning, ice hockey and ice skating.

Thanks to

Angelo Vallet.

pic: Jeff Webb

ITALY'S HIGHEST RIDING AND SOME OF ITS LONGEST RUNS - UP TO 13KMS! MOST OF THE RIDING IS IN A HUGE, WIDE, USUALLY SUNNY BOWL

Minne, Jesse, Tommy, Sergio and Marco pic: Jeff Webb

Livigno

Mountain Information

Mountain chain:

Engadina (north)

Alta Valtellina (south)

Vertical metre range:

1,816m - 2,797m

Length of season:

early November - May

Number of lifts:

3 gondolas, 10 chairlifts, 17 draglifts

Snow-making facilities:

There are 24 snow cannons covering 12kms, when needed.

Safety:

There are avalanche indicator boards located outside the main lift entrances.

Guides:

Contact the ski school for guides and rates.

Lift pass prices:

1 day: L45,000

6 days: L240,000

Season: L720,000*

(* These are high season prices.)

Lift pass alternatives:

swatch access

A pass for 6 days or more covers Bormio, Santa Caterina, Valdisotto and one day in St Moritz. A year long Four Season Card costs L950,000.

 ON THE MOUNTAIN

The Italians call Livigno 'La Piccola Tibet' (or little Tibet), as it has a congenial atmosphere that is much enjoyed by those who visit this mountain sanctuary. The bottom of the mountain has huge wide pistes, which are perfect for beginners and carvers. Freeriders will find a vast area for boarding with terrain, cliffs and gullies all accessible from the lifts.

✳ Snow conditions

Livigno is at high altitude area - most of the boarding is above the 2,500m mark - and, consequently, has an extended season.

 Freeriding

The best areas - M. Della Neve, M. Sponda, Il Mottolino and, on the other side, the eastern most Salin run - combine steeps and hits. All these areas have rideable off-piste lips, small cliffs and tree-riding. When the powder falls, many of these areas are also often left untouched.

Freestylers

The halfpipe, located by the Pemonte T-bar, is about 45m long, is hand made and is suitable for beginners to intermediates. There are a few hits by the halfpipe, but nothing formerly organised.

Carvers

Most of the pistes are well-groomed, fast and fun, and there are over 100kms of them!

✕ Lifts to avoid

The lower lifts are extremely slow.

Mountain fare

There are some gems up on the mountains, as the Italians love their food. The cheapest options are the stand up snack bars, but for something a little different try Tea del Plan or the Mottolino.

DUTY FREE SHOPPING STATUS, SO STOCK UP ON ALCOHOL

pic: Roby Trabucchi

ABOUT TOWN

Livigno is made up of four communities - Santa Maria, San Antonio, San Rocco and Trepallo - which are all strung out along the valley floor. As it's right on the border with Switzerland, it has duty free shopping status, so shredding shoppers can stock up on alcohol, perfumes and the like. As Livigno can be reached by car from Milan or Zurich in roughly five hours, lots of Europeans visit to have a blast, spending what they haven't blown shopping on a good night out.

Getting there

By air: There are several airports in the vicinity - Zurich's 230kms away, Innsbruck's 190kms away and Milan is 230kms away.

By train: Take the train to Tirano, from where it's a 2.5 hour bus transfer.

By car: If travelling from Switzerland, note the tolls at the Zernz tunnel: L6,000 per car and L2,000 per person. On the southern approach, the pass is quite steep and chains are mandatory in times of heavy snow.

Accommodation

There are a wide range of choices, including a grand total of 94 hotels and 292 chalets and apartments. One of the cheapest options is to stay in a private home; prices for one night's B&B start at L22,000. Otherwise, book an apartment though the Associanzione Albergatori agency - Tel: 0342-997 140. Prices at hotels such as the Piccolo Tibet (2 star) - Tel: 0342-970 092, Fax: 0342-970 108 and Hotel La Montanina (2 star) - Tel: 0342-996 060, Fax: 0342-997 056 start from L46,000 a night . For more information, contact the Azienda Promozione Turistica.

Food

There are a number of restaurants offering an appetising range of food, but the best are in the hotels. Make sure you try the local dish known as 'pizzocheri', wholewheat noodles, vegetables and tons of garlic, baked with cheese, which sells for about L7,000. Another cheap option is a pizza, which costs from about L6,500 for an ample portion; try Bait dal Ghet or the Toilasor. Marco's Video Pub has a wide range of food, including full English breakfasts and great hot 'caldo' sandwiches.

pic: Roby Trabucchi

Nightlife

The best bar is Marco's Video Bar, where English is spoken and MTV plays on a big screen. For some late night strutting, there are quite a number of discos including the Discoteca Il Cielo and the Classic Dance bar, which is where the locals and tourists get together. For a bit of salsa, there is the Latin Music Disco and the Kokodi, where the more serious shakers and movers get down.

Other activities

Rent snowmobiles for a laugh or try the paraglide club for some serious air - Tel: 03373-386 693.

Thanks to

The Zinermann sporting crew and the tourist office.

Bormio

Mountain chain

Lombardy

Vertical metre range:

1,225m - 3,010m

Length of season:

early December - mid-April

Number of lifts:

Bormio: 2 gondolas,

6 chairlifts, 4 tow bars

Santa Caterina: 2 chairlifts,

7 T-bars

Snow-making facilities:

Portable and fixed snow cannons cover 13kms of pistes.

Safety:

There is are avalanche warning lights at the main top and bottom stations. For more information, call the Centro Nivometeorologico Regione Lombardia - Tel: 0342-905 030, Fax: 342-905 133.

Guides:

The Guide Alpine in Bormio have guides.

L280,000 - L350,000/day

Tel/Fax: 0342-910 991

Lift prices:

1 day: L46,000

6 days: L220,000

Season: L720,000-L950,000

(including Stelvio)

Lift pass alternatives:

The Alta Valtelina pass covers Livigno, Santa Caterina (12kms away) Valdisotto and Valdidentro, plus one free day in St Moritz.

 ON THE MOUNTAIN

Due to their proximity to the Austrian and Swiss borders, Bormio and Santa Caterina see a wide and varied crowd filter in over weekends and holidays. At Bormio, the terrain is quite steep and more suitable for intermediate to advanced riders. Santa Caterina, 12kms away by bus, is flatter, but has more hits and tree-riding possibilities, and often has no crowds.

 Snow Conditions

Both Bormio and Santa Caterina have high, north-facing slopes, which are usually snowsure. Santa Caterina is the better place to find fresh, uncluttered runs after a snowfall.

Freeriders

Bormio: A steep wall, the Cima Bianca, situated below the top gondola is excellent when conditions permit; there are huge windlips and jumps near the bottom of the run. Most of the gondolas at the top are good for long runs, while the lower T-bars are better for short runs with hits, particularly through the wooded areas on the lower slopes.

Santa Caterina: For a good view of the three valleys that meet in Bormio village, take the Costa Sobretta Lift and follow the D'Ell Alpe signs back to Malga Plaghera. For a wooded run, head to the Edelweise. For a long leg-burner, continue up the spine of the Monte Sobretta from the highest lift and drop into the face, but check on safety first.

pic: Roby Trabucchi

 Freestylers

There were no halfpipes or funparks in Bormio or Santa Caterina, but the resort management does have plans for the '96/'97 season. The nearest pipe and funpark is in Livigno.

 Lifts to avoid

None.

Mountain fare

There are seven mountain restaurants, ranging from self- to silver-service. Highly recommended are those at Bormio 2000 and Rocca - they are snack-food oriented and reasonably priced. Baita da Mario at Ciuk offers excellent food and an inviting ambience.

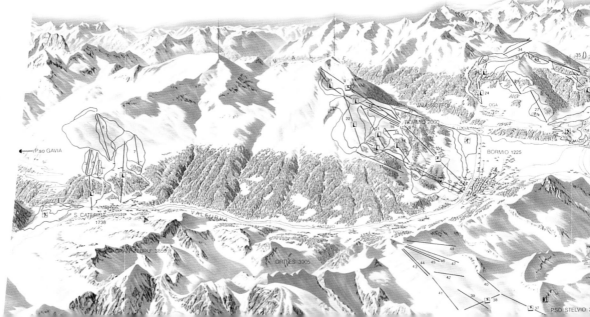

BORMIO IS LOCATED IN A SUNNY, SHELTERED BOWL AT THE MEETING POINT OF THREE VALLEYS

Rider. Thierry Kunz pic: Jeff Webb

 ABOUT TOWN

The town of Bormio is located in a sunny, sheltered bowl at the foot of the Stelvio Pass, at the meeting point of three valleys. Originally a Roman Spa town, the thermal baths still provide a soothing treatment after a hard day's boarding and burning. The town centre is a well-preserved example of 17th century architecture complete with cobbled streets and washing troughs (the hard up, take note!). It's a 10 minute drive to nearby Santa Caterina, a small town nestled in the forest.

Getting there

By air: The closest airports are Milan and Bergamo, both a two to three hour transfer away.
By train: The main train station is at Tirano, from where it's a 40km transfer by train or bus.
By car: From Milan, the journey takes 2 hours or more by car. The roads are reasonable, but chains are necessary after fresh snow and you should watch out for wandering deer.

Accommodation

Some of the best deals are in private homes. If you're with a group, a cheap option is to hire an apartment; prices start from L460,000 for a week (for four people). Otherwise, two star hotels with breakfast vary from L37,000 to L50,000.
If you have your own car, even better deals are to be had between Bormio and Santa Caterina. For example, there's a cosy hotel/restaurant, Al Taula, run by a snowboarding family - Tel: 0342-910 105, Fax: 0342-905 090.
For more information about private homes, apartments and hotels, contact the reservations agency Ufficio di Bormio - Tel: 0342-903 300, Fax: 0342-904 696, or the Ufficio di Santa Caterina Tel/Fax: 0342-935 598.

Food

Eating in Italy has always been an art form and the restaurants in Bormio are no exception. For lunch, the Crai grocery store is a good place to buy a selection of cheeses, meats and crusty ciabatta bread for L7-10,000. In the evenings, most of the restaurants advertise a 'menu turistico' - expect to find a pasta entree, salad, fish and desert, with bread and a glass of house wine from L17,000 to L 25,000. Recommended restaurants include the Taulá, the Piccolo Mondo and the Vecchia Combo. For pizzas, try the Jap or La Stua.

Nightlife

In Bormio, the Clem Pub has a great happy hour with free finger-food snacks, billiards, darts and the world's biggest olives. For those snowboarders with a phobia of skiers, avoid the King's Club disco on Friday nights as the ski schools have their meetings there. At other times, it's a popular place to go.
In Santa Caterina, the Camino pub has live music and a popular après-ski drinking session. Later at night Snoopy's is the place to listen to live music, play pinball and shoot darts. Spot the Gods at the Zeus Disco, where the entry fee is L10,000.

Other activities

One of the most invigorating and relaxing activities has to be a visit to the hot baths and saunas of the Bagna Vecchi Terme, 3kms out of town. There is also a big indoor skating rink.

 Thanks to

The tourist office, Hotel S. Lorenzo, the Zeta Shop Alexandro, Lui Stronzo, Marco Bruni, the crew at the Al Taula Restaurant, Mirella, Andrea, Claudio and Fausto.

Rider. Thiery Kunz pic: Jeff Webb

Essential Information

Tourist office
Tel: 0342-911 022   Fax: 0342-904 696
Snowboard shops
•The Zeta Shop by Celso Sport
Tel: 0342-901 376   Fax: 0342-901 459
Board/boot hire: L30,000/day
•Pano Snowboard Club
Tel: 0342-90 376
These are the people in the know - they organise monthly shows and races, inevitably followed by huge quantities of spaghetti and alcohol. Italian halfpipe rippers Mac Perrotti and Michelle Tognazzi are members.
Snowboard schools
•The Zeta Shop by Celso Sport
Tel: 0342-901 376   Fax: 0342-901 459
Private lessons: L35,000 - L50,000 (dependent on the season).
•Bormio 2000
Tel/Fax: 0342-903 135
Two hour group lessons for three days: L110,000

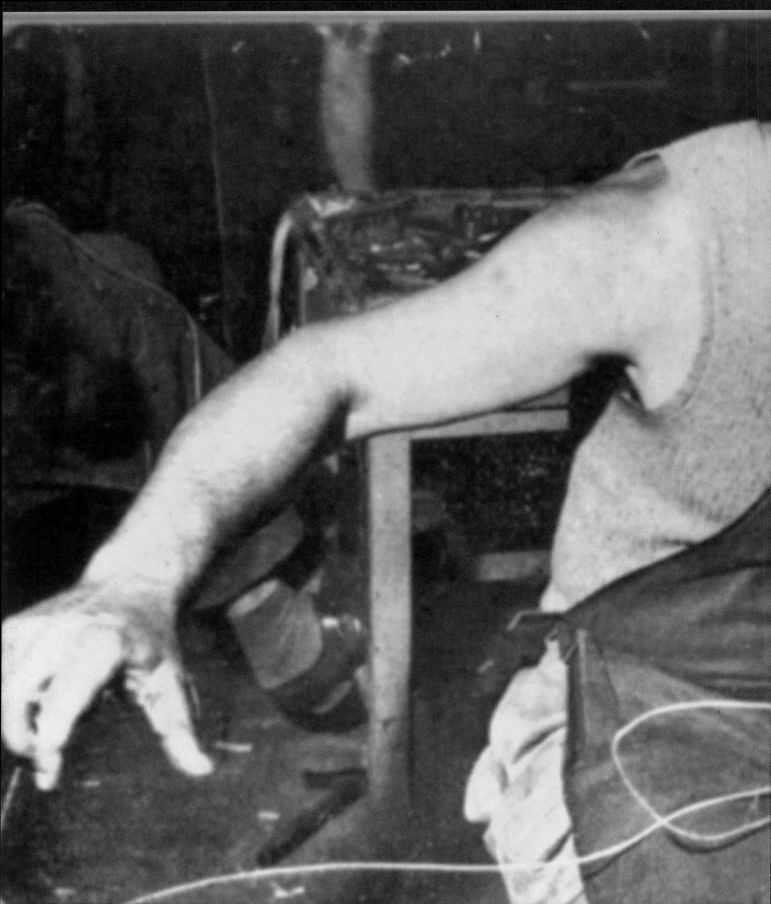

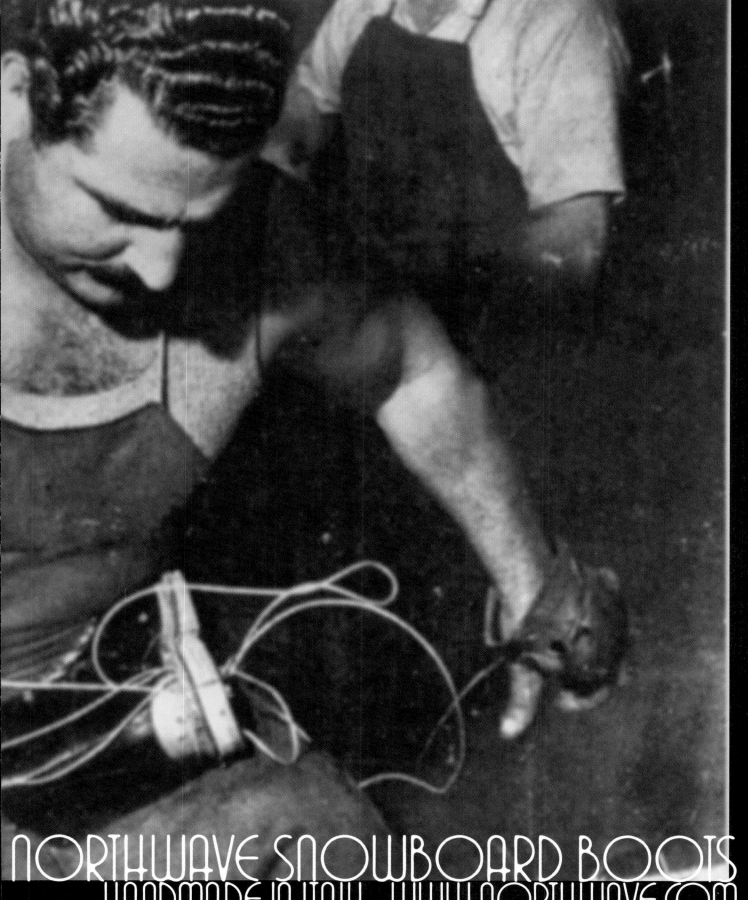

NORTHWAVE SNOWBOARD BOOTS
HANDMADE IN ITALY WWW.NORTHWAVE.COM

Mountain Information

Mountain chain:

Brenta Dollomites

Vertical metre range:

1500m - 2600m

Length of season:

December - April

Number of lifts:

1 cable car, 4 gondolas,

15 chairlifts, 10 draglifts

Snow-making facilities:

There are 357 snow cannons

covering 27kms of piste,

when needed.

Lift pass prices:

1 day: L50,000

6 days: L250,000

 ON THE MOUNTAIN

Go to Madonna - it's a very progressive, snowboard-orientated resort that really welcomes snowboarders and has hosted a number of competitions. In Febuary 1996, the eighth ISF European Snowboard Championship took place here and the ISF will organise the World Championships at the resort in 1999.

Snow Conditions

Generally, the conditions are good on the Groste side and on Spinale. Thanks to all the snow cannons, snowboarding is possible even when there has not been a great snowfall.

Freeriders

There are four main areas to Madonna Di Campiglio:

Cinque Laghi: To the west of the village, take the cable car to the Palon restaurant. There are intermediate and advanced runs, including some great detours back to the village through the trees. Access east-facing intermediate runs by taking the Patascoss chair to Panculoga. Alternatively, take the Tre chair for some intermediate runs that end up on the Panculogo pistes and the more advanced Three Tre World Cup run, which is a tortuous north-east facing run that ends in a narrow tree-lined piste.

Are Pragadalago: The Fiscco di Neve chair accesses the Genzianna piste, which provides intermediate north-east facing runs to Genziana. Monte Vigo provides descents to Marivella or Fogarida.

Groste Are: Take the Groste gondola to the mid-station in order to reach the Passo Del Groste, a wide open plateau from which two chairlifts rise to 2,440m. From the top, there are two red runs and two blue runs to Rif Graffer, and a subsequent red and blue run which leads back to the base of the Rododendro chair. This area has great opportunities for off-piste riding.

The Monte Spinale: This area is accessible from either the new gondola next to the skating rink or the chairlift at the Campo Carlo Magno. From the top restaurant, turn let and to the west side of the top station for a hard run back to Madonna. There are three chairlifts accessing north and north-west facing slopes with good snow retention.The best is La Direttissima dello Spinale, which should not be missed when there is powder.

Freestylers

The best area is the Groste, where natural pipes and moguls dominate. The resort has an impressive halfpipe and funpark at Belvedere.

Carvers

Carvers should head for the Cinque Laghi area for the Three Tre piste, where the European Cup giant slalom and slalom were held last season. Predalago is very good, too, particularly now that the Amazzonia, which is very technical and demanding, has been recently created.

 Mountain fare

The best restaurant on the mountain is the Riff Boc, which is accessed by the gondola Groste. Alternatively, make a packed lunch with ciabatta bread and lots of fresh goodies from the local delis.

pic: Roby Tarbucchi

IT'S A VERY PROGRESSI SNOWBOAR ORIENTATE RESORT

pic: Roby Trabucchi

Essential Information

Tourist office

Tel: 0465-442 000   Fax: 0465-440 404

Snowboard shops

Sport 3-Tre   Tel: 0465-443 53

Board/boot hire: L35,000/day

Snowboard clubs

Sporting Club Madonna di Campiglio

Tel: 0465-415 61

Contact: Antonio dalia Giacomo

Snowboard schools

Professional Snowboarding by Paolo Fazi

Tel: 0465-443 251

10 hours in 5 days: L230,000

 ABOUT TOWN

Madonna is a lovely village set among the stunning scenery of the Dolomites. A high percentage of its visitors are affluent Italians, who come out in the evenings promenading the latest fashions from Milan - a rather amusing spectator sport. Don't let that put you off though. It's a friendly town, cheaper and more welcoming than the more upmarket Cortina, which has a humming snowboarding scene.

 Getting there

By air: The closest airport is Verona, a two hour transfer away, while Milan is a 3.5 hour transfer away.

By train: Trento is the closest station, from where there are bus transfers.

By car: Follow the Milano-Brescia motorway, take the Brescia east exit and then join the A-road for Vestone, Tione, Pinzolo and Madonna di Campiglio.

 Accommodation

There are a number of three and four star hotels, but if you're really hard up camping is available at S. Antonio di Mavignola (6kms from Campiglio) - Tel: 0456-511 78 and Parco Adamello a Carisolo (11kms from Campiglio) - Tel: 0456-443 355. For more details, contact the local tourist office.

 Food

Aside from the hotel restaurants, there are 18 eateries in town, varying from inexpensive pizzerias like the Belvedere to more exclusive cafés - take your pick. The American Bar serves up cold draughts and pizzas till late. For a swanky feed, try Montagnoli on the piste of Monte Spinale - Tel: 0456-443 355.

Nightlife

The Stork Disco is the largest and most popular night-club, but if you're up for a snog try the intimate Des Alpes.

Other facilities

Check out the natural skating, sports centre, paragliding, five public and hotel pools, sauna and cinema.

 Thanks to

Paolo Fazi.

Val Gardena Selva
Arabba Cortina d'Ampezzo

Mountain Information

Mounatin chain:
Dolomites

Vertical metre range:
Cortina 1,224 - 3,243m
Arabba 1,602 - 2,550m
Selva 1225 - 2930m

Length of season:
December - April

Number of lifts:
4 cableways, 23 chairlifts,
47 draglifts.

Snow-making facilities:
Portable and fixed snow cannons
can cover 90kms of piste.

Safety: Avalanche indicator boards
at the bottom and top of the lifts.

Guides: In Arabba, the Marmolada
itineraries are hair-raising and
require a guide. One of the best in
the area is Luciano Pioli, a pro-rider
contactable through the tourist
office. In Cortina, the most radical
tour is with Creste Bianche, which
organises heliboarding trips to the
Antelao glacier -
Tel: 0436-868 505.

Lift pass prices:
1 day: L51,000
(Superski L56,000)
6 days: L255,000
(Superski L279,000)
Season: L570,000
(Superski L890,000)
The cheaper prices quoted above
are for Cortina d'Ampezzo and
cover all the lifts in Cortina and
San Vito di Misurina, plus the ski
buses. The Dolomite Superski pass
covers Cortina, Plan de Corones,
Alta Badia, Val Gardena, Val di
Fassa Carezza, Araba, Alta
Puteria, Fiemme Obereggan and S.
Martion di Castrozza - a total of
464 lifts and 1,180kms of piste.

ON THE MOUNTAIN
One of the most startling things about this area
is the scenery; don't forget to look up at the
crumbling spires and craggy cliff tops - it's
almost enough just being amongst these
spectacular mountains. Take a map wherever
you go as the area is vast, and it's possible to
end up many miles from where you started.
Heliboarding is also available and it is an
unforgettable experience; price L90,000 for a
minimum of three people - Tel: 337-354 862.

Snow Conditions
The snow levels can fluctuate, and often, as in
the '95/'96 season, the Dolomites end up with
great snow when the snowfall is poor on the
north side of the Alps. Generally the best
periods are February through March.

Freeriders
With so much terrain, the possibilities are
endless. To orientate yourself, take the Sella
Ronda tour, a 25km ride from Cortina to Selva.
There are seven villages to visit en route, just
don't stop and drink at every one of them! The
trip takes about four hours and is suitable for
intermediate to advanced riders.
After the tour, head for Val de Tita, which has
wider steeps with lots of rocks to jump off and
a large windlip further down the run. For
awesome chutes, head to the Piz Boe. Powder
junkies should head for Marmolada, which has
long, open runs accessible by gondola. In
Arabba, all the pistes from Porto Vescovo offer
different types of terrain which provide an
unforgettable experience. In Cortina, the most
popular area is the Cristallo-Faloria.

Freestylers
The halfpipe and funpark are situated on the
Seleda Plateau, accessible from both St Christina
and St Ulrich. The halfpipe, made by hand and
snowcats, is 80m long and best for intermediate
riders. There are various parties throughout the
season, such as in mid-March when the Snow
Count Down hosts a week long party with live
music, bands and DJs.

Carvers
There are many long wide pistes for carving and any
gondola accessed area is sure to be a leg-burning
experience for speed freaks. Try Ciaminoi, Sas Lonch
or Dantercepies for a screaming good time.

Lifts to avoid
None. They all offer good terrain and great views.

Mountain fare
All the restaurants are of a fairly high standard. The
stand-up snack bars are the cheapest option. A hot,
sit-down meal of meat and pasta, plus a drink, costs
around L12,000 to L18,000. Most places offer pizza
by the slice from L3,500 and hamburgers from L4-
5,500. Put your feet up in the sun at either
Gamsbuthütte or Lupo Bianco. And don't forget to
grab a guick grappa at one of the many snow bars.

HELIBOARDING IS AVAILABLE
AND IT IS AN UNFORGETTABLE
EXPERIENCE

Rider. Dave Hatchett pic: Richard Walch

Essential Information

Tourist offices

Arabba Tel: 0436 791 430

Cortina Tel: 0436 3231 Fax: 0436 3235

Selva Tel: 0471-792 277 Fax: 0471-792 235

Snowboard shops

•Cortina Olimpia Sport - Tel: 0436-2200

Board/boot hire: L40,000/day

Board/boot hire: L180,000/6 days

•Best Sport   Tel: 0436-868 349

•Arabba Mode Sport   Tel: 0436-791 42

Board hire only: L25,000/day

Board hire only: L90,000/day

•Ski Service Nico - Tel: 0436-794 45

Snowboard clubs

•Arabba Snowboard Team Happy Bears

Tel: 0436-791 39

Contact: Stefano and Sebastian Cattaneo.

•Cortina Dolphin Club Cortina Tel: 0436-4478

Contact: Bruno D' Andrea.

•The Wave Tel: 0436-866 156

Contact: Nicola Bizzari.

Snowboard schools

•Arabba Tel: 0436-791 60

1 hour individual lesson: L45,000

18 hours of lessons in 6 days: L160,000

•Cortina Tel: 0436-2911 Fax 0436-3495

1 hour individual lesson: L62,000

12 hours of lessons in 6 days: L270,000

(afternoons) L400,000 (mornings).

•Noleggio Snowboard Centre

Tel: 0436-866 635

 ABOUT TOWN

The town of Selva, in the heart of the area, is an appealing mix of charm and convenience; thanks to its cobblestone streets, the town has an old world feel and the lifts are centrally located. If it's a grim day, poke around the shops and admire the many local crafts, including hand-carved, life-size wood replicas of great mammoths. In Val Gardena, the local dialect is Ladino, a cross between Rhaetaina and Latin dating back to 15 BC. Buses connect all the surrounding villages.

 Getting there

By air: The closest airports are Venice, Munich Innsbruck, Milan and Verona, from where transfers take about three hours.

By train: The closest station is Bolzona, from where it's a 30 minute bus transfer.

By car: Head towards Bolzona and then to Selva. This route was once used by Marco Polo and the scenery en route is stunning - look out for the castles camouflaged among the rocky outcrops.

 Accommodation

There are a number of options. For those on a tight budget, there is camping in Cernado - Tel: 0436-867 575. There are also grounds at the Dolomite Camping Centre - Tel: 0436-2485 and Camping Olympia - Tel: 0436-5057. Arabba has 10 hotels priced from L70,000 to L130,000; Pensione Evaldo and Hotel Porto Vescovo are among the cheapest. Cortina, there are about 60 hotels, is not as cheap - prices range from L80,000 to L230,000. For a whole plethora of options, contact the local tourist offices.

 Food

The supermarket sells all that you might need for a picnic lunch, including meats, cheeses, bread, fruit and nuts; prices start from L5,500. For a hot sit-down meal, look out for the 'turistico menu' sign, where special deals on a salad, meats, bread and a drink are to be had. Pizza slices start from L3,500 - most of the pizzerias are of a high standard.

 Nightlife

One of the best bars is the Igloo Bar, a glass dome at the Selva Mina lift base station, where the après-ski is brilliant and you can kick off your evening in style. The only other place for a good drink is Yeti's Umbrella Bar in Santa Christina, which has two-for-one shots at happy hour and is open till 1.00am, as is the lively Hotel Wolkenstein. In Selva, the best place to move and shake is in front of the mirrors at the Dali Disco. In Cortina, hit the Area Disco once you've been to the cool Pub Clipper and absorbed the snowboard vibe. In Arraba, the recommended watering-hole is the Pub La Stube, near the Hotel Vescovo.

Other Activities

There are pools (entry fee L5,000) at the Community Centre and most of the big hotels. There is also an ice rink, bowling alley and rifle range at the Sport Pavillion.

 Thanks to

Christina Demetz from the tourist office, Hotel Antares, Kari and Fame at the Yeti's Umbrella Bar, Air Service Centre, the Alpin School Catores for our guide Othmar Pinoth, Walter (the Dutch bartender) at Hotel Wolkstein, Bruno D'Andrea and Sebastian Cattaneo.

French Alps

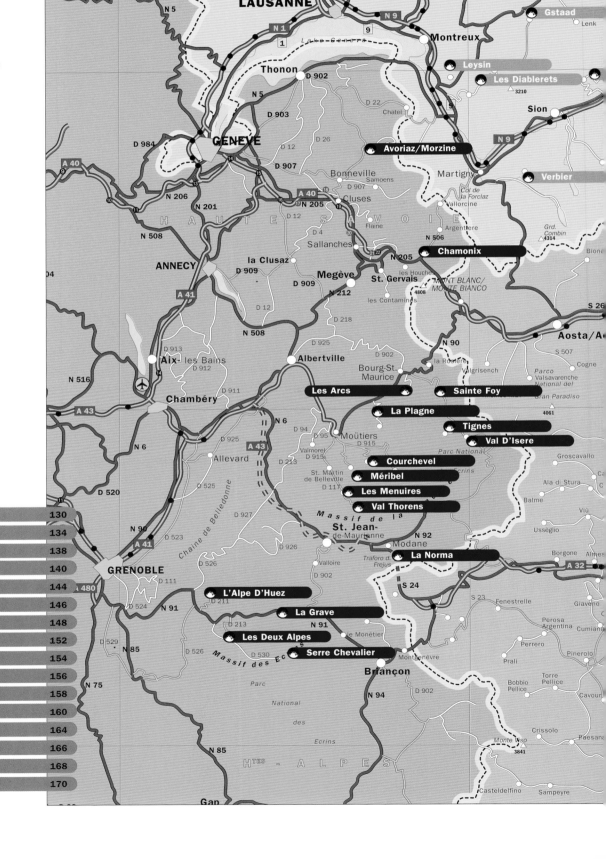

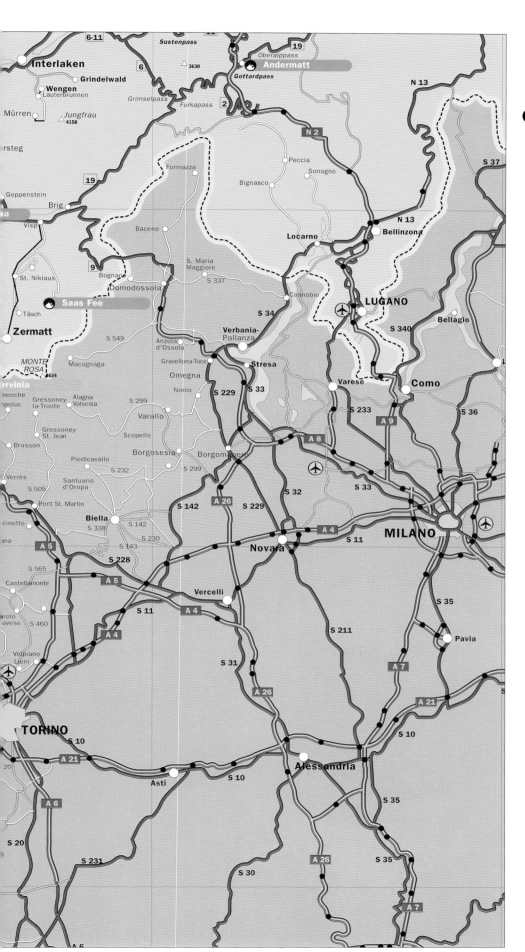

Further Informaiton

Number for main railways

Tel: SNCF 36 35 3535

English speaking travel advice:

Tel: 42 82 50 50

Number for main airlines:

Air France - Tel: 0144 08 2222

Air France: Welcome service:

Tel: 0146 75 78 00

Air Inter - Tel: 014546 9000

Airports

Airport informaiton

Tel: 014408 2222

Main bus company

Paris Eurolines - Tel: 0149 725151

Mountain weather services:

Meteromontagne - Tel: 3668 1234

or 36 68 0404

Number for recorded snow forecasts:

Tel: 36 68 0101

Sk France: 0142 66 64 28

Road traffic:

0148 94 3333

Weather reports:

Seen in all newspapers and after the news,
early in the morning (6 -7am at midday
and 8 9pm).

Snowboard on television:

Watch TV cable channel 'Eurosport'
(broadcasted snow shows occasionally)

National snowboard magazines:

Snow Session, Snow Surf, Freestyler,
Snowbeat, Snowboard Mag, White Spirit

National Snowboard Assocation:

•Snowboard Montbonnot

Tel: 0476 52 37 74

Main tourist board details

•Ski France

61 Boulevard Haussmann, 75008 Paris -

Tel: 01-47 42 2333   Fax: 01 426615 64

•France Ski International

Maison de la Savoie, 31 Avenue de L'Opera

75001 Paris - Tel: 0142 61 3321

Ask for cheapest prices and discounts on:

Minitel 3615 Degrifneige or 3615 Reucneige

WARNING:
Do Not Be Fooled. Many snowboard boots will claim to be "NICE"... Protect yourself. Check the label. If it does not say "NICE", it probably isn't.

pic: Nick Hamilton rider: Kenlie

pic: Nick Hamilton - Avoriaz

Avoriaz

Mountain chain:

Portes du Soleil

Vertical metre range:

1,165m - 2,275m

Length of season:

mid-December - beginning of May

Number of lifts:

1 cable car, 2 gondolas,

20 chairlifts, 14 draglifts

Snow-making facilities:

10 snow guns.

Safety:

An avalanche indicator board,

which is regularly updated, is

located at the top of the Les

Prodains cable car.

Guides:

Contact either the tourist office

or Chalet Snowboard.

Lift pass prices:

1 day: 195F *

6 days: 885F

Season: 3,000F

(* This is a Portes du Soleil

pass - a pass for Avoriaz only

costs 147F.)

Lift pass alternatives:

Avoriaz is part of Portes du Soleil

and is, therefore, linked to

Morzine, Les Gets, Châtel,

Champéry, Les Crosets, Morgins,

Champoussin and a number of

smaller resorts.

 ON THE MOUNTAIN

Of all the Portes du Soleil resorts, Avoriaz is best suited to freestyle/freeriding. The terrain is 'small', but packs in great variety - it has trees and gullies, track jumps and the like. Avoriaz is split into five areas: Hauts Forts, Arare, Chavanette, Lindarets and Super-Morzine.

 Snow conditions

As the resort is mostly north-facing, the snow holds well throughout the season.

Freeriders

Hauts Forts is the steep, black area with the longest runs. It's best known for its powder runs and the excellent 'Jumps/Home Run' down to Les Prodains - check on conditions before you go, as the area is avalanche prone at the top. Chavanette has the best snow early and late in the season, and is the prime area for alpine riders. Lindarets is the tree and restaurant playground - after a fresh fall, there are plenty of routes through the trees on both sides of the valley.

 Freestylers

The competition halfpipe is at the bottom of Arare, but is rarely serviced and quickly becomes a shallow snow-filled bowl. The funpark is located to the right of Arare, by the Lac du Bleu run. It's a good sized park, running from the top to the bottom of the Lac du Bleu draglift. A big, obligatory kicker starts the run, followed by rails, a picnic table and little table tops. There is also a spine, longer rails, a shallow 'pipe' with table tops and a couple of 'big-as-you-like' kickers.

 Carvers

The best runs on the Chavanette bowl, the main Arare piste and over the Swiss border in Les Crosets.

 Lifts to avoid

If you're staying in Morzine and are uncomfortable with draglifts, avoid using Super-Morzine lifts to reach Avoriaz. The chairlifts in Chavanette are slow and can be cold.

Mountain fare

For lunchtime breaks, go down to the multitude of restaurants in Lindarets, in particular the Pomme de Pin.

⌂ ABOUT TOWN

Avoriaz is purpose-built on a grand design, making it perfectly functional. It's also car-free, which is great for ride-to-the-door convenience. Its location, perched on a dramatic, sheer cliff, is a huge advantage, giving it a spectacular back-drop.

→ Getting there

By plane: Geneva is two hours away by bus or train.

By train: The nearest train station is Cluses, from where there is a bus 2-4 times a day.

By car: Go by car to junction 18 on the A40 Autoroute Blanche to Chamonix, then follow the signs to Morzine.

⌂ Accommodation

The only snowboard operator is Chalet Snowboard which doubles up as a Burton test centre. The Chalet does packages that include full board and flights from Britain; prices start from £550.00 - Tel: 01235-767 182 (in the UK). For a wide choice of apartments, try Pierres and Cacances - Tel: 5074 1022 or Avoriaz-Location - Tel: 5074 0453. For hotels, try Dromonts - Tel: 5074 0811 or Hauts Forts - Tel: 5074 0911. Contact the tourist board for other options.

⦿ Food

For a cheap burger and fries, try the joint down from Codec. For lunch, the local patisserie does great pastries and pies. There is a good Tex Mex and Pizzeria Barbara serves the best pizza.

⊗ Nightlife

The best bar in Avoriaz, which is the pick of the bunch in the early hours of the evening, is Taraillon. Both Chouca and The Place often stage live music and always have a good atmosphere. Les Ruches is the place to play pool. Later in the evening, try the nightclub Midnight Express, where entry is free but the drinks are expensive.

Other activities

There is a bowling alley, and an ice rink.

✓ Thanks to

Ian Trotter from Chalet Snowboard.

pic: Jeff Webb rider: Terje

pic: Nick Hamilton rider: Becci Malthouse

Essential Contacts

Tourist office

Tel: 5074 0211   Fax: 5074 1825

Snowboard shops

•Street Trash   Tel: 5074 1019

•Emery Pro Shop Tel: 5074 1264

Snowboard schools

•ESF   Tel: 5074 0565

•The Snow Sports School   Tel: 5074 0218

G-SHOCK, SURVIVES THE IMPACT OF HARD-CORE BOARDING

SHOCK RESISTANT.
ELECTRO-LUMINESCENT
BACKLIGHT.
1/100 SEC. STOPWATCH.
COUNTDOWN ALARM.
DAILY ALARM.
WATERPROOF 200M/100M.

CASIO
G-SHOCK

  **gravityshock**

pic: J.M. Favre rider: Hans Roesch

Chamonix

Mountain Information

Mountain chain:

Alps

Vertical metre range:

1,035m - 3,840m

Length of season:

beginning of December - May

Number of lifts:

Le Brévent: 1 gondola,

1 cable car, 3 draglifts,

4 chairlifts

La Flégère: 1 gondola,

4 chairlifts

Les Grand Montets:

2 cable cars, 1 gondola,

6 chairlifts

Le Tour: 1 cable car,

4 draglifts, 2 chairlifts

Snow-making facilities:

Not generally used.

Safety:

A daily report is posted at the main
lift station and the tourist office.
Chamonix has many areas prone to
avalanche, so ask the piste patrol
for advice. For more information,
contact the Mountain Police -
Tel: 5053 1689.

Guides:

Compagnie des Guides de
Chamonix Mont-Blanc
Tel: 5053 0088

Lift pass prices:

1 day: 150F

6 days: 920F

(full valley pass)

Season: 4,100F

(full valley pass)

 ON THE MOUNTAIN

**Something of a snowboard Mecca. The area
comprises a series of resorts strung together
along the Chamonix Valley. Le Brévent is the
area above the town of Chamonix, La Flégère is
further down the valley towards Argentière
(where the famous Les Grands Montets rise
above the village) and the Col de Balme rises
up from the satellite town of Montroc.
Between them, they offer some of the finest,
purest and most heart thumping off-piste
terrain to be found in the Alps. The longest run
is 4kms down the glacier from the famous
Vallée Blanche and is a 'once in a lifetime'
experience.**

 Snow conditions

The most reliable snow areas are the north-
facing runs above Argentière and the Col de
Balme area above Le Tour. Le Brévent, Les
Houches and La Flégère are south-facing and
at a lower altitude, so they lose snow quickly
when the weather warms up.

 Freeriders

The off-piste in the Chamonix Valley is
unsurpassable, but before you get too excited,
a word of caution: this mountain is dangerous
and we strongly recommend you take a guide
if you want to avoid going home in a box.
There are four main freeriding areas listed
below. We recommend the areas and runs we
think you'll enjoy most...

Brévent: Below the Col Cornu, there are
steeps, chutes and cliff drops. Another run with
the same fare is to the left (facing down the
mountain) of the Brévent top station. To the left
of the Plan Praz are tight fast runs through trees.

Le Tour: Off the Charamillon Chairlift (C), there
is an awesome bowl (red dotted line No.3 on
the Le Tour Trail map) with endless variants.
Underneath the adjacent Chairlift D, there is a
popular boarding run with hits, spines and
quarterpipes. The area to the left of Lift E also has
big quarterpipes, natural gullies and gap jumps.

Argentière: Les Grand Montets is famed
worldwide for its stunning views and exhilarating
riding. However, a supplement of 32F is charged
every time you ride up in the top cable car. There
are lots of off-piste variations. The most scenic piste
(Marked No.1 on the map) is the Point de Vue, from

where the crevasses of the glacier are awe-inspiring.
Run No.2 goes down to a natural bowl with windlips,
small gullies and jumps. At G G (Marked No.9 on the
map), there are fast tree runs with drops, gaps and
piste jumps. This area is a great escape in flat light or
poor weather. The various runs down the Combe de
la Pendant are as amazing as they are dangerous.
There are loads of cliffs, chutes, hits and jumps, but
the area is avalanche prone, so seek advice before
you set off. Under cable car A, there is a plethora of
wild tree runs, which are at their best just after a
snowfall.

Flégère: To the right of L'Index (marked with orange
dots), there is a long traverse which leads to a wide
bowl, the Combe Lachenal. Another area, with more
hits, jumps and windlips, is directly below L'Index. In
times of flat light and poor weather, there are some
tight tree runs by Lift D.

 Freestylers

There is a funpark at Charamillon (Le Tour/Col de
Balme), which has table tops, gap jumps, rail slides
and quarterpipe jumps. The halfpipe proposed for the
'96/'97 season will be 150m long and maintained by
a pipe dragon.

 Carvers

There are over 140kms of piste from which to choose,
but for scenery and steepness the best runs are off the
Grands Montets, the Point de Vue and Pylones. Le
Brévent and La Flégère have easier gradients to cruise.

(X) Lifts to avoid

The lifts at the top are exposed and get fairly cold.

Mountain fare

Most of the places on the mountain are pricey, so it's
advisable to take a packed lunch.

pic Peter Mathis - Chamonix

ABOUT TOWN

Chamonix is a French village, not just a purpose-built resort, which makes the atmosphere somewhat less transient and the locals more welcoming. In fact, it's a great place to watch rural French Alpine life go by. The village has everything from pubs to clubs to restaurants serving all sorts of international cuisines and gift shops to a busy Saturday market. Most people choose to stay in Chamonix, as that's where most of the amenities and nightlife are based, plus it's central. The nearby towns of Montroc, Les Houches and Le Tour are slightly less expensive, but riding in areas other than where you stay becomes a hassle. Argentière is where most of the seasoners hang out.

Getting there

By plane: The closest airport is Geneva, from where the transfer by bus or train takes about an hour.
By train: The station in the resort is on the St. Gervais-Le Fayet/Valorcine line.
By car: Chamonix is 80kms from Geneva, along a fast easy road on which there is a toll of about 60F(valid on all Swiss freeways for one year).

Accommodation

The cheapest option is the youth hostel or the UCPA, where prices start at 60F per night - Tel: 5053 1496. Another cheap option is to hire an apartment, prices start from 1,800F per week (for 2 people). For more information about hostel and hotels, phone the Centrale de Reservation - Tel: 5053 2333. For more information about apartments, contact the Agence Immobiliere Geralp - Tel: 5053 4096.

Food

There are supermarkets and speciality food stores all through the valley, as well as a market on Saturdays. The Et Café serves delicious, cheap sandwiches and beers. The Tex Mex-style restaurant, La Cantina, has great food, such as T-bone steaks and nachos, at reasonable prices, plus a very friendly atmosphere. Another place for solid, satisfying food is the Wild Wallaby, which doubles as a great bar.

Nightlife

The best bars for a pint and a chin-wag are La Cantina and the Wild Wallaby. The DJs at La Cantina play an eclectic mix of jazz, funk, hip hop, house and jungle throughout the season. The Wild Wallaby offers drinking games, pool tables, live Sky TV and is renowned for its rowdy, late night drinking sessions, when the Scandies and the Brits get well into the action. For more late night drinking, La Refuge, Le Bumble Bee and Moonlight can rock, but given their choice of music, it pays to be well inebriated.

Other activities

For rainy days, there is a mini ramp in Passey, 10 minutes down the valley.

Thanks to

Johnny Barr Super Star.

Johnny Barr about to initiate a Wu Tang Death Lunge pic: Marc Hare

Essential Contacts

Tourist office
Tel: 5053 2333   Fax: 5053 3615
Snowboard shops
Chamonix Mountain Bike Tel: 5053 5476

pic:Jeff Webb rider: Babbs

More Mountain Information

Lift pass alternatives:
There are cheaper day passes covering the individual areas of Le Brévent, La Flégère, Balme, Les Houches, Les Grand Montets, Argentière and Le Tour. The Grands Montets cable car costs an extra 32F per ascent. All passes valid for more than two days can be used on the Val Veny/Courmayeur lift system in Italy for two days less than the amount of time on the pass (e.g. a six day pass will allow you to ski for up to four days in Italy).

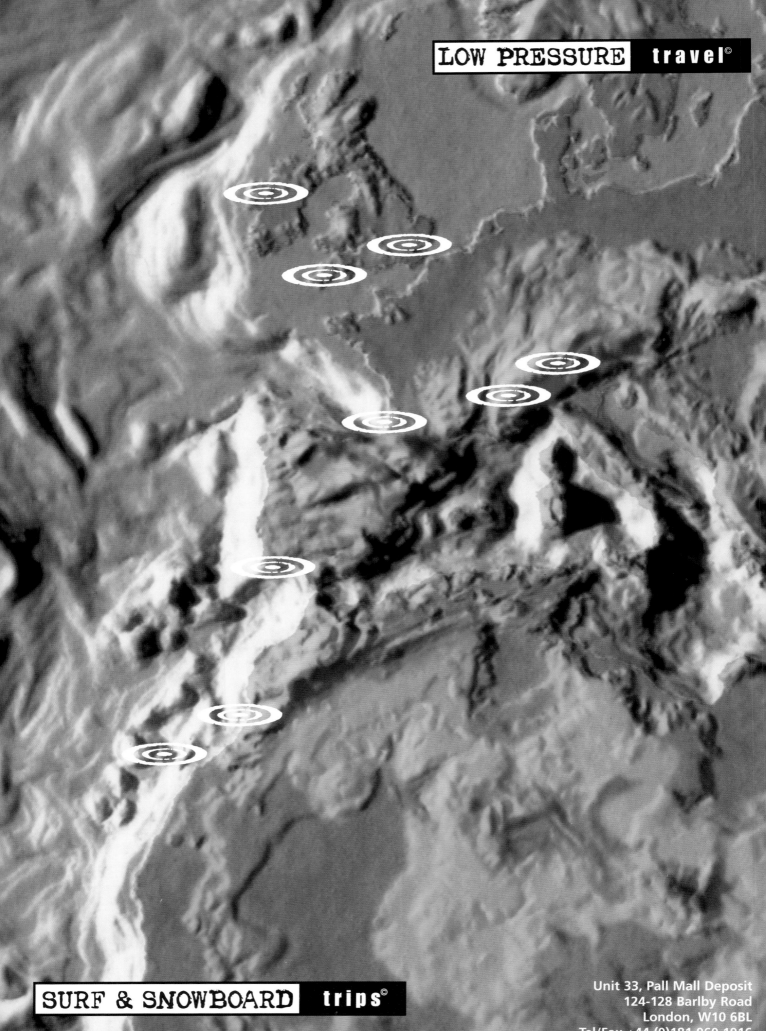

Val D'Isere pic: Peter Mathis

l'espace killy

Val d'Isère

pic Helmut Wahl

Mountain Information

Mountain chain:

Alps

Vertical metre range:

1,550m - 3,500m

Length of season:

beginning of December -

last week in April

Number of lifts:

2 mountain railways,

4 cable cars, 6 gondolas,

49 chairlifts, 41 draglifts

Snow-making facilities:

200 snow cannons cover 24km of

pistes, when needed.

Safety:

Listen to the latest weather

conditions and avalanche

information from the piste patrol on

Radio Val Frequency 96.1FM.

Strictly adhere to all signposts.

Guides:

Contact the Mountain Guides Office

for more details - Tel: 7906 0234

Lift pass prices:

1 day: 209F

6 days: 960F

Season: 4,810F

NB: If a pass valid for between 3

and 15 days is purchased, and all

the lifts are shut due to bad

weather, you will be reimbursed for

the days when it could not be used.

Lift pass alternatives:

If you purchase a pass valid for one

day or more, it can be used for one

day in either La Plagne or Les Arcs.

If it is valid for six days or more,

the pass can be used for one day

in each of Les Trois Vallées,

Pralognan-la-Vanoise, Les Saisies

and Valmorel.

 ON THE MOUNTAIN

Val d'Isère, one of Europe's best known resorts, is part of the vast Espace Killy, which is renowned for its extensive and varied terrain, and is linked by lifts to Tignes. All boarders will find something to relish: huge piste and off-piste areas, a well-kept halfpipe and some the liveliest nightlife in the Alps.

 Snow conditions

Val d'Isère can usually be assured of having snow, as most of the slopes are north-facing and at high altitude.

 Freeriders

The connection from Val d'Isère to Tignes is worth a ride. Go up the Fornet, the only car available on stormy days that has a sheltered run - there are some radical gullies to the left of the car and the wooded areas below provide great entertainment. Continue ascending to the beautiful Pissaillas glacier, which is open all year round and try out the Col Pers, which starts with a traverse from the top chairlift on the glacier. The area then opens up into a wide bowl with endless variations. At the bottom, at the source of the Isère river, cut into the narrow Gorges de Malpasset and eventually the runs arrive back at the cable car. Go left off the Solaise Express and head down Les Danaides, another sheltered valley which often harbours great snow.

La Daille has the longest, and one of the best, runs, if there has been no fresh snow. The gradient is perfect, with a great variety of jaunts into trees and banks, plus hits and rollers.

Under the Rocher de Bellevarde, there are some cliffs and steep, hair-raising chutes. Be wary of the cliffs directly at the top - the further you go to the right, the better.

At the top of the Mont Blanc chair, there is a double bowl with a wicked jump. Other notables are the Col de la Madeline, the Banane, Spatule, Cairn Col Pers, Marmottons and Cugnai.

 Freestylers

The halfpipe is located at the bottom of the Santel Express chairlift, and is generally in good condition during January and February (due to the cold and snowfall). After that, it seems to lose shape, mainly due to lack of maintenance. The 3,500m² funpark is located at La Daille, near the bottom of the Funival train. It consists of fun boxes, hits, quarterpipes, small gaps and a radical table top. The locals are excellent boarders and service the park constantly.

 Carvers

The OK piste at La Daille has high speed carving from top to bottom. Also, try out the higher glacial areas for long prepared pistes. The run over to Tignes has a great gradient with a multitude of pistes and treacherous moguls.

 Lifts to avoid

On windy days, riding the chairlifts can give you frostbite as Val d'Isère is an open ended valley, which acts as a wind tunnel and is extremely exposed.

 Mountain fare

There are a number of mountain restaurants, but none is outstanding - and most are expensive.

French Boys Bong Hard

 Thanks to

Gregs, Matthieu and Lloyd Rogers.

 ABOUT TOWN

This is the place which has everything: good riding and big-time party action. The drive into Val d'Isère is stunning - so stunning you may crash your car. La Daille is the first part of 'Val' (as it's nicknamed), but it's the cheaper alternative, the ugly sister to the main town, which is a further five minute drive away. Val main town is the Alps answer to Aspen: expensive, luxurious and a good laugh.

 Getting there

By plane: From Geneva and Lyon, it's a 4.5 hour trasfer; from Chambéry, it's a 3.5 hour transfer.
By train: The closest station is Bourg St Maurice, from where there are regular connections.
By car: Go to Bourg St Maurice on the N90 and Val d'Isère is a further 30kms away. Avoid driving in on a Saturday, as the rest of Europe will be doing the same and the traffic can back up as far as Bourg St Maurice.

 Accommodation

For information about self-catering studios, call Val Location (Central Reservations Office) - Tel: 7906 1890. For low budget hotels, call Val Hotel - Tel: 7906 1890. It's definitely a good idea to make a booking, as Val d'Isère is extremely popular and is often full.

 Food

There are over 70 restaurants in Val d'Isère - a whole brochure has been published with what's on offer - and the menus and prices are incredibly varied. However, standards are generally high, on account of the demanding French clientele. The recommended cheap options are the satisfying fare at G-Jays and Bananas, and the ample portions of pasta served at the Pacific. Avoid the Billabong Café - the portions would leave an anorexic with the munchies.

 Nightlife

For a great night out, try this menu: warm up at the English-run Morris Pub, where satisfying bar snacks and live music (best from about 10.30pm to 1.00am) are the order of the day, or G-Jays. Next, head to Café Face, a dance venue, and intoxicate yourself with sublime drinks, such as chocolate jelly vodkas. Directly across the road is Dick's T-bar, a late night disco which has a heel-kicking clientele ready to party till late. Then there's Club 21 nearby, geared more to the classy, cosmo-type French socialite, but it's open till 6.00am, which is when the local patisserie opens. Party on!

Other activities

Ask at the tourist office for more information about the following activities: the climbing wall, ice-skating rink, swimming pool, sauna and cinema.

Pic Al Green : The Half pipe

Tignes

 ON THE MOUNTAIN

Besides having a link to Val d'Isère, Tignes has a huge amount of its own varied terrain: between Tignes Les Brevieres at 1,550m and the glacier Ski d'Eté at 3,500m lie absolutely every terrain imaginable. The main resort area, at 2,100m, has an excellent halfpipe and funpark. Below the village are the wooded areas, which are superb when there is snow. A number of boarders come for the season, and stay, as Tignes has a long tradition of summer camps and early season competitions, such as the Kebra Classic Cup. For more information, contact the Kebra shop.

TIGNES HAS ABSOLUTELY EVERY TERRAIN INCLUDING AN EXCELLENT HALFPIPE AND FUNPARK

 Snow Conditions

Tignes is one of most snowsure resorts in the Alps, because of its height and the snow-making facilities on the lower slopes.

 Freeriders

One of the best runs is long, radical and has many variations - start at one of the great chutes on the Aiguille Percée, ride all the way down to Les Brevières via a long black run, and enjoy the many dippers and hits on either side of Des Sache. To the left of the Col des Ves, there are some great couloirs with steep run outs, most of which you'll spot from the chair. The tree run down to Les Brevières is also worth riding, but be careful because the area is avalanche prone.

 Freestylers

The halfpipe, located near the town, is manned by a free 'Millonex' draglift. Made for French Cup Competitions, it is maintained in Jane Fonda shape by the locals. The well-kept funpark, roughly 800 metres long, is located above the halfpipe at the top of the Palafour chair. It's built into a natural gully and there are quarterpipes, fun-boxes, and objects to jib and slide all the way down. One of the big bonuses for 'stylers is the year-round halfpipe on the Grande Motte glacier, which is used in summer and autumn, but is not usually maintained in winter.

 Carvers

The motorway down to Val Claret from the Grande Motte is sublime in both smoothness and speed.

 Lifts to avoid

If the weather is bad, avoid the chairlifts.

 Mountain fare

L'Escale Blanche, the restaurant underneath the Refuge Hotel, is a great place to get a 40F meal; eight francs more will buy you steak and chips. On the walls there are pictures of the Tignes valley - as it was before someone vomited the resort all over it.

Mountain Information

Mountain chain:

Alps

Vertical metre range:

1,550m - 3,500m

Length of season:

beginning of December - first week in May, although the glacier is open all year.

Number of lifts:

1 funicular, 1 cable car, 2 gondolas, 26 chairlifts, 19 draglifts.

Snow-making facilities:

115 snow cannons cover 24 kms of piste, when needed.

Safety:

For up-to-date information - Tel: 7906 5644.

Guides:

Available through the snowboard shops (see opposite page).

Lift pass prices:

1 day: 209F

6 days: 1,044F

Lift pass alternatives:

A one day pass is valid in either La Plagne or Les Arcs. If you buy a pass valid for six days or more, you can use it for one day in Les Trois Vallées.

pic: Peter Mathis rider: Sean Nerva

pic: J.M. Favre

ABOUT TOWN

Tignes is a purpose-built resort comprising three villages: Val Claret (the largest), Le Lac and Le Lavachet. The resort's boarding scene is alive and healthy, but the nightlife isn't quite up to speed and the village could do with a serious face lift.

Getting there

By plane: Geneva and Lyon are 4-5 hours away, while Chambéry is only a 3.5 hour transfer.
By train: The nearest stop is Bourg St Maurice, from where it's a 25km bus ride.
By car: Travel on the N90 to Bourg St Maurice, from where Val d'Isère is a further 30kms, then follow the signs to Tignes.

Accommodation

With over 28,000 tourist beds in Tignes, there is plenty of choice and it's hard to make particular recommendations. A number of tour operators offer cheap, all-inclusive package deals. Otherwise, check out the huge number of chalets and hotels on offer. For more help, call the tourist office.

Food

Tignes has a number of restaurants specialising in traditional French food and local Savoyard specialities - take a look at the tourist office's restaurant guide for menu and price details. The Wobbly Rabbit (see below) is worth a visit and has a large varied menu, including Thai and English favourites. The Tex-Mex at the Cavern is also said to serve filling portions of tasty food.

Nightlife

At Val Claret, both the Caveau and the Pouteriee offer a relaxed atmosphere with live jazz and blues. The nearby Wobbly Rabbit has lethal tequila jugs at happy hour. If you want some late night action, try Playboy and Chandelles, which both have Euro disco-type DJs. In Le Lac, have a pint at the locals' bar, the Café de Post, and for a late night strut, try the Caves. In Le Lavachet, a favourite drinking haunt is Harri's, which has pool tables.

Other activities

There's a natural skating rink, hang-gliding, para-gliding helicopter rides, snow-mobiles, husky dog-sleigh riders and diving beneath the ice on the lake.

Thanks to

Marc and Scotty 'Bwoy' Nixon.

pic: Marc Hare

Essential Contacts

Tourist offices
Le Lac Tel: 7906 1555
Val Claret Tel: 7906 5009
Le Lavachet Tel: 7906 3973

Snowboard shops
•Kebra Surfing Tel: 7906 4337 Fax: 7906 4490
Kebra is the pick of the snowboard shops and hosts the Kebra Classic Cup, which has been going almost 10 years.
•Le Lac: Sweet Snow Surf Shop Tel: 7906 3992
•Snowboard Centre Tel: 7906 4650
•Surf Feeling Tel: 7906 5363

**JULIEN
JACQUIER**

pic: J.M. Favre - Les Arcs rider: Matthieu Petral

Les Arcs

pic: SCALP rider: Axel

 ## ON THE MOUNTAIN

This is the home of the legendary Regis Roland, who founded A snowboards and who can sometimes be seen out on the mountain. It's no real surprise that he and his team hang out in Les Arcs, because the terrain is incredible. Most of the runs have plenty of hits and rollers, and most of the clean, steep chutes can be walked to from the lifts. As one of the locals so succinctly put it "Eet ees magic 'ere"!

✳ Snow conditions

Many of the slopes are north-facing and located at high altitude, so the snow is reliable throughout the season.

THIS IS THE HOME OF THE LEGENDARY REGIS ROLAND. IT'S NO REAL SURPRISE THAT HE AND HIS TEAM HANG OUT IN LES ARCS, BECAUSE THE TERRAIN IS INCREDIBLE

◖ Freeriders

Situated off Gollet 12, there are adrenaline pumping tree runs rife with jumps and rollers. The run located under Plan Bois 69 has great right and left quarterpipes, and rocks after a powder fall.

Take either the 'Transarc' cable car or one of the other lifts to the 'Col d'Entreporte' area, where there is superb off-piste terrain - some of the best spots are a ten minute hike along the ridge.

Over in Les Arcs 2000 area, there is a good fun jibby run under the Clocheret chair. The north couloir of the Aiguille Grive at 1800 offers a radical run.

◖ Freestylers

The halfpipe is located at the bottom of the Carreley blue run - it's only open till the end of March, but it is well-looked after. The funpark, open all season, is located between the Arpette chairlift and the Frettes draglift. Six hundred metres long, it is full of gap jumps, fun boxes, hits and quarterpipes.

Les Arcs Funpark pic: Mark Hare

 ### Carvers

The lower slopes at 1800 are the main carving areas, because the gradient is neither too steep, nor too shallow. Alternatively, try the Froid Fontaine piste, purportedly one of the best in Les Arcs, or the Grand Renard at 1800 - it's a natural downhill course for speedsters.

 ### Lifts to avoid

Queues can bottle-neck at 1800 early in the morning and late in the afternoon.

 ### Mountain fare

The restaurant near the Col de la Chal has an incredible panorama, but the food is mediocre and the service is marginal. Take a packed lunch!

Mountain Information

Mountain chain:

Les Arcs

Vertical metre range:

1,100m - 3,226m

Length of season:

first week of December -
last week of April

Number of lifts:

1 cable car, 1 gondola,
34 draglifts, 30 chairlifts

Snow-making facilities:

There are a handful of snow
cannons covering essential areas.

Safety:

The tourist office has daily details.

Guides:

For more information -
Tel: 7907 7119

Lift pass prices:

1 day: 208F

6 days: 960F

Season: 3,160F

Lift pass alternatives:

La Plagne, La Rosière and La Thuile are also covered by this pass. A pass valid for six days (or more) gives you a free day of riding in Tignes-Val d'Isère, Les Trois Vallées and a 20 percent reduction on tickets for Sainte Foy.

Tourist office

1600 - Tel: 7907 7070

1800 - Tel: 7907 1257 (main office)

2000 - Tel: 7907 1378

Snowboard schools

•Tip Top Tel: 7907 2800   Fax: 7907 4083

Lessons: 250F/day

•In Extremis

Tel: 7907 2172   Fax: 7907 2176

Snowboard shops

•New School   Arc 1800   Tel: 7907 4334

Make this your first stop, as it's the hard-core spot, where the staff will answer all your queries about the nightlife, prime boarding areas etc. Stephane is the main man.

•In Extremis Surf Shop

Arc 1800 Tel: 7907 2172

 ABOUT TOWN

The happening part of town is in the Charvet block at 1800, which has all the essential facilities such as nightclubs, shops and the main tourist office. Arc 1600, about 2kms down the road and connected by lifts to 1800, is packed with accommodation. Arc 2000 is 12kms away, on the other side of the mountain, and like 1600 has cheaper accommodation than 1800, but absolutely no atmosphere. There are free shuttle buses between all three stations at regular intervals. Once again, contact the UCPA for deals and cheap alternatives when planning your trip.

 Getting there

By plane: Geneva, Lyon and Chambéry are between a two to four hour transfer away.

By train: The closest station is Bourg St Maurice, from where there are frequent buses and a funicular direct to the resort.

By car: From Moutiers, head for Bourg St Maurice, then follow the signs to Les Arcs.

 Accommodation

The best option at Les Arcs is self-catering as many of the restaurants are expensive, however there is a wide choice of cheap and mid-range hotels. One of the more popular with snowboarders is the Freeride Hotel in Peisey-Nancroix (Rad Air affiliated) - Tel: 7907 9937 or 0181-960 0555. For the UCPA - Tel: 7907 0750. Check with the tourist office for more details.

 Food

At the Tex Mex and Savoyarde, there are tempting morsels such as roast chicken and pizzas to be sampled. The locals tend to eat (and party) at Chez Matthieu in Villards and the Mountain Café in Charvet. If travelling to Les Arcs by car, the best place for bulk shopping is en route, at Bourg St Maurice or Moutiers.

 Nightlife

Try the late night Blue Bar, which often has live music, or the Hotel du Golf in 1800, which has a jazz bar and disco. The snowboard crowd tends to congregate in Carré Blanc in Les Villards.

Other activities

Parapenting, horse-riding, ice-skating, a swimming-pool and cinema are on offer.

✅ **Thanks to**

Lloyd Rogers, Stephan at the New School shop and all the nutters who made our visit so enjoyable.

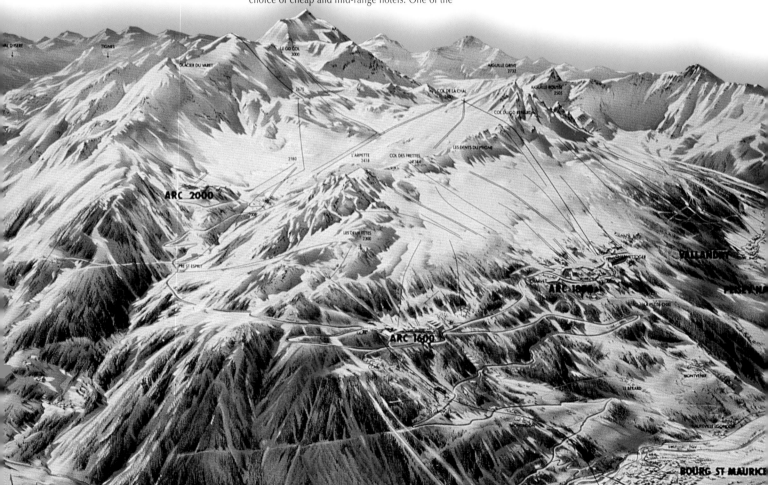

Sainte Foy

Mountain Information

Mountain chain:

Tarentaise

Vertical metre range:

1,550m - 2,620m

Length of season:

mid-November - mid-April

Number of lifts:

3 chairlifts

Snow-making facilities:

The Gods.

Safety:

The tourist office has daily updates.

Guides:

Ask at the tourist office - a guide is essential above the second lift.

Lift pass prices:

1 day:	94F
3 days:	270F
Season:	925F

More Essential Information

Tourist office

Tel: 7906 9170

Fax: 7906 9509

Snowboard shops

•Zig Zag   Tel: 7906 9420

Snowboard schools

•ESF   Tel: 7906 9519

 ON THE MOUNTAIN

Sainte Foy is a still undiscovered gem in the Alps, as it has only existed since 1990. An un-pisted heaven, it has vast, wide open bowls, a grand forest fairyland, and almost never gets crowded, - there are only 250 tourist beds in the local village. What's more, it is usually open when resorts such as Val d'Isère and Tignes are shut, due to bad weather and visibility. The Vincent Bros have their winter camp here called La Limace (The Slug) - the place is always filled with travelling boarders from all over the world. If you don't love snowboarding at Sainte Foy then you may be missing the point.

 Snow conditions

Sainte Foy is south-facing and mostly in the sun, which means that the resort tends to lose snow quickly at the end of the season, resulting in icy mornings and slushy afternoons.

 Freeriders

Try the Crystal Dark, an official route from the highest point on the mountain (2,620m). Traverse along the ridge and you'll find fresh snow all day. Continue down, through the trees, and you will make your way back to the resort. Another official route is the Cret-Ceru, from the top down a gentle, open slope, through trees, to the bottom of the second lift.

You must be careful, however, as both these routes are avalanche prone. With a guide, take the Foglietta or the route to Les Pigettes and the resort will arrange a free bus back to the town, if you let them know in advance. The L'Arpettaz takes you up to some steeper tree runs and an un-pisted cat track. For powder runs and long chutes, go to the top of the L'Aiguille and hike out along the ridge for 40 minutes. Once again, check for safety.

 Freestylers

There's no funpark or halfpipe, because they don't need one! Val d'Isère is close by if you're desperate.

Carvers

There are only nine pistes, but they are generally better prepared than those in Val d'Isère.

Mountain fare

La Maison Colonnes, at the bottom of the main lift, is a relaxing place for lunch - a feast of provincial French food (three courses from 105F) and carafés of red wine (from 35F). Snacks cost between 20F and 35F. At Plan Bois, there is a ghost-like restaurant. At first glance it looks uninhabited, because there are haphazard benches scattered around, but if you look again, there is a menu offering basic, rustic French food. It only serves snacks before 12.30pm.

IF YOU DON'T LOVE SNOWBOARDING AT SAINTE FOY THEN YOU MAY BE MISSING THE WHOLE POINT

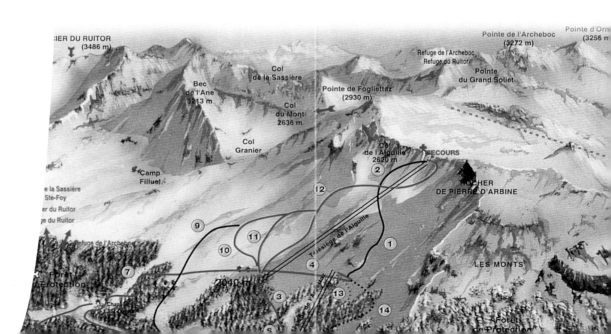

pic: Mark Junak rider: Lloyd Rogers

Back of Fogliettaz pic: Mark Junak

SAINTE FOY

TARENTAISE

Nant Cruet 3805 m
s Plates des Chamois
s Mines 3420 m
e la Gde Sassière 3747 m

Pointe d'Ormelune

Pointe de l'Archeboc

Col du Lac Noir

Col du Rocher Blanc

raire du Monal

Les
Pigottes

étude du Monal

◉ ABOUT TOWN

Nothing much happens in Sainte Foy, because it's little more than a tiny clutch of old farmyard buildings. If you want nightlife, go up the road to Val d'Isère. If R & R (riding and relaxing) is a priority, then kick-back, enjoy the sumptuous food and savour the real spirit of the mountains.

➔ Getting there

By plane: Geneva, Chambéry and Lyon are all a three to four hour transfer away.

By train: The closest station is Bourg St. Maurice, from where Sainte Foy is a bus journey away.

By car: Go to Bourg St Maurice on the N90, and Sainte Foy is a further 20kms up the valley in the direction of Tignes and Val d'Isère. Take care, because the road from La Thuile is one of the least maintained roads in the Alps and has some treacherous hairpins and huge potholes. It's a sick ride in itself.

◉ Accommodation

Chalet Number One is run by Sarah and Lloyd Rogers, who arranges packages from Europe - Tel: 7906 9533. Chalet Yellow Stone is another tour operator specialising in the area. The tourist office in Sainte Foy runs a reservation service that will book everything from campsites to apartments - Tel: 7906 9516.

▦ Food

The English-run Il Capriccio has a wide variety of food, from Italian and Chinese (the chow mein is wicked) to French. Chez Lea in Villaroger is run by a 90 year-old woman and her daughter - 110F will buy you a multi-course traditional French dish, and servings are replenished as needed. La Becqua is another, typically French restaurant serving food at moderate prices. For a culinary experience, try Le Miroir, which is incredibly expensive (300F for the set menu), but the food is exquisite and the portions are said to be unfinishable.

(××) Nightlife

The stars are beautiful, the air is crisp and, on a clear night, the whole valley is visible. That's it folks!

✓ Thanks to

Lloyd Rogers, Gregs, Monsieur Gacon and Joanna Neall.

View from our kitchen pic: Marc Hare

La Plagne

ON THE MOUNTAIN

La Plagne has an amazing variety of radical and unusual terrain; Luke Skywalker would feel at home in the lunaresque, crater-like landscape - riders will also enjoy the resort's anti-gravitational nature. The area is comprised of seven linking areas, totalling over 215km of pistes. The off-piste areas are also limitless. Some areas of the resort are prone to lengthy flat spots, so if you don't know where you're riding, go fast.

✳ Snow conditions

La Plagne has mostly north-facing slopes lying at high altitude which means the resort is snowsure. Later in the season many of the lower areas lose their snow quickly making access difficult from the higher areas.

Freeriders

A good run for intermediate to advanced riders starts at the top of the Bellecote glacier, and sweeps down a steep, accelerating gradient, ending at Les Bauches restaurant. Another exhausting run, the Mont de la Guerre has a vertical drop of over 1,250m from the Grande Rochette to Champagny.
Around the Belle Plagne fast chair there are great natural quarterpipes in the gullies. Head to the left of the 34 Blanchets and you will find steeps, chutes and cliff lines running out to the

piste. At the top of the Grande Rochette gondola there are a number of steep chutes which also have pisted run outs. Around Le Becoin there are several areas of open off-piste; look out for a long natural windlip running across the top (in all conditions). For long, fast, tree runs head towards TK 10 Bouclet 1 Lift.
On the other side towards Vers Champagny, there are plenty of hits and radical cliff jumps.
Continuing down the ridge, there are more wooded areas, appealing in poorer weather.

Freestylers

Plans are underway for a funpark at present, however, in the interim, there are a number of natural quarterpipes located in the area above the Plagne Centre. The whole area is a freestyle playground, so you won't be disappointed.

Carvers

La Plagne has 215km of well-kept pistes for hours of carving entertainment!

✗ Lifts to avoid

All the lifts are fine, but note in high season, there can be large queues at the high-altitude areas.

Mountain fare

There are a number of mountain restaurants which all serve reasonable food at resort prices. One recommended restaurant is located at the top of the Champagny gondola with friendly, efficient staff, hearty fare, and stunning views.

Mountain Information

Mountain chain:

Vanoise

Vertical metre range:

1,250m - 3,250m

Length of season:

first week of December - beginning of May

Number of lifts:

1 cable car, 8 gondolas, 30 chairlifts, 74 draglifts

Snow-making facilities:

62 snow cannons

Safety:

Weekly avalanche predictions are posted around the town.

Guides:

Ask at the tourist office for more details.

Lift pass prices:

1 day: 209F

6 days: 960F

Season: 4800F

Lift pass alternatives:

A six day pass covers Les Arcs, plus a day in Les Trois Vallées, Val d'Isère-Tignes, Pralognan-la Vanoise and Les Saises.

⌂ ABOUT TOWN

La Plagne is made up of 11 linked resorts, and for this reason seems fragmented with no particular focal point. Seven of the resort towns are purpose-built and make slope access convenient, but the other four, at a lower altitude are the first to lose snow, and access can be difficult. The nightlife is rather tame, and often the resort is besieged with French families, but, the boarding is phenomenal.

⌂ Accommodation

Bed and breakfasts located at 1,400m are the best value for money, but they are a hassle for lift access if there is lean snowcover. Plagne Bellecôte is a students town; accommodation is cheap and cheerful in this area. Bob's Café is recommended for budget accommodation, (also has great food too!). The UCPA has an office here at 1800 - ask the tourist office for more details and bookings.

☺ Nigtlife

Not much to write about, save for a couple of ordinary bars for a quiet drink (Tom's bar at Plagne 1800, and the Showtime Café in Bellecote). The King Café in Plagne Centre is a relaxing place for a drink and a pizza. Locals say the nightclub Le Must is fun; entry costs 70F, and jeans and trainers aren't allowed - all three factors were deterrents for our crew.

La Plagne Panorama pics: Marc Hare

➔ Getting there

By plane: Geneva, Lyon and Chambéry are all a 3.5 hour transfer.
By rail: The closest station is Aime, an 18km transfer.
By car: Follow the N90 to Aime and then via Macot La Plagne.

¶ Food

There is a supermarket at every resort station, and a large shop is based in the commercial centre of La Plagne. Local dishes such as raclette and Savoyard fondues are popular (The Cheyenne Café in Belle Plagne, or La Ferme in Plagne Bellecôte) - there are also plenty of pizzerias and creperies around. Bob's Café (mentioned above) does various menus at reasonable prices.

✓ Thanks to

Florence Valette from the Tourist office.

THE NIGHTLIFE IS RATHER TAME BUT THE **BOARDING**, IF THAT'S YOUR FOCUS, IS **PHENOMENAL**

Essential Contacts

Tourist office

Tel: 7909 7979   Fax: 7909 7010

Snowboard shops

There's no dedicated snowboard shop, but the big local sports shops, such as Armand Berard Sport and Belle Plagne Sports, hire out quality equipment.

Snowboard shops

There's no dedicated snowboard shop, but the big local sports shops, such as Armand Berard Sport and Belle Plagne Sports, hire out quality equipment.

Snowboard schools

•ESF Tel: 7909 0058   Fax: 7909 2933

3 half days: 480F

•Oxygen Ski/Surf

Tel: 7909 0399   Fax: 7909 2055

Offers a free introduction to snowboarding.

chez nous en Bretagne, le snow, on connaît.
c'est juste qu'on a pas eu de neige depuis longtemps...

kana beach™

rien a foutre

Les Trois Vallées

Courchevel
Méribel
Les Menuires
Val Thorens
La Norma

pic: Nagel Photo - Méribel rider: Mark Rothwell

Courchevel

Mountain Information

Mountain Chain:

Vertical metre range:
1,300m - 2,740m

Length of season:
first week of December
- first week of May

Number of lifts:
1 cable car, 9 gondola lifts,
16 chairlifts, 41 draglifts,
1 basket lift.

Snow-making facilities:
A large of area of the piste
(60kms) is covered by snow
cannons when necessary.

Safety:
Ask the pisteurs for advice.

Guides:
Contact the tourist office.

Lift pass prices:
1 day: 176F
2 days: 313F
6 days: 776F
Season: 3,850F

Lift pass alternatives:
The prices listed are for
Courchevel, which is part of Les
Trois Vallées.

 ON THE MOUNTAIN

Courchevel (or GroovyGirl town, as I prefer to call it) has a happening snowboard scene. The Tourist Office realises that your money is as good as anyone's and it is doing everything it can to encourage you to hand it over. The three main stations are 1550, 1650 and 1850, between them you'll find everything you desire. 1850 is the crossroads that links all the stations. From the top of Saulire at 2740m you can reach all five stations including Le Praz and La Tania or you can drop over the other side to Meribel. The lower stations provide sick tree runs, when the weather sucks.

 Snow conditions

As many of the slopes are north-facing, at medium to high altitudes, Courchevel is snowsure for most of the season.

 Freeriders

With a wide variety of pleasures from which to choose, freeriders will be in their element. Most of the pistes in 1850 have hits and rollers. For example, to the right of the Saulire lift riders will discover a number of chutes and cliff drops with steep run outs. One of the more radical couloirs is known as Butcher's, after a local butcher who used the run as a wake-up hit - probably cheaper than an expresso and it certainly gets the adrenaline going faster. There are cliffs and more steep chutes just off the Chanrossa lift. To the right of the Roc Mugnier, there are more long, well-pitched chutes running out to the lift stations. For tree runs, ride down to 1300, where the variations are numerous. Even further down, at La Tania (alias Kiwi Town), the snow cannons create some great hits and rollers.

 Freestylers

There is a long halfpipe, kept in top-notch condition, over at Marmottes. It's used by the Courchevel locals, but often attracts a regular contingent of boarders from surrounding resorts. There is no funpark as yet, but don't you worry about that, plans are afoot.

 Carvers

The pistes, which vary in steepness, are kept in good condition. From the top of Chanrossa there are heaps of wide open spaces down to 1650

 Lifts to avoid

Generally, all the lifts are snowboard friendly and there are few queues.

Mountain fare

Most of the restaurants we saw served standard mountain fare and were expensive. Our advice - take a packed lunch!

 pic: J.M. Favre

rider: Becker   pic: J.M. Favre

 ABOUT TOWN

Courchevel is actually a collective of villages, unimaginatively named after the varying altitudes at which they are located. The main centre, where most of the shopping and eateries are found, is 1850. The most attractive area, and the least expensive, is 1300, which has managed to maintain its village charm. 1550 has cheaper accommodation, but is not well serviced. 1650 has a good mix of affordable options and some good nightlife.

Getting there

By plane: The nearest airports are at Chambéry (a 2.5 hour transfer away), Geneva and Lyon (which are both a 3.5 hour transfer away). At weekends, there are direct flights from London to the Courchevel altiport.

By train: The closest station is Moutiers, from where buses run regularly.

By car: Head along the A43 to Moutiers and take the Courchevel exit, from where the resort is a further 25kms away.

Accommodation

A number of tour operators organise packages to Courchevel. For more information about chalets, hotels or apartments, contact the main reservations line - Tel: 7908 0029 or Fax: 7908 3354.

Food

Courchevel has loads of restaurants. For good value eats, the Kalico (on the piste at 1850) serves grills, pizzas and Savoyard specialities - good music and pool tables add to the restaurant's appeal. Other recommended cheap eats are the Cortona pizza place and the Hotel L'Adret (for French food) in 1550. There's a Thai restaurant offering a 250F menu for two people. Those with epicurean palettes (and a wadge of cash) should try the two-star Michelin rated Chabichou and Le Bateau Ivre in 1850. Self-caterers and budget eaters will find a reasonably priced supermarket in the centre of 1850.

Nightlife

The nightclub Kalico is the main hive for boarders. It boasts a loud sound system run by British DJs, a raging pit dance floor and reasonable (for a nightclub) bar

Ice climbing wall   pic: M. Hare

prices. Tee-Jays, another boarders' venue, is a great place to fuel up first, and offers live bands, beach parties, funk and acid jazz. If you're on 'the crawl', try L'Euippe, which has decent music, a video screen and live bands, or the Dakota, a rock bar playing blues and jazz. If you're out on the pull, bear in mind that the chalet girls night off is on Tuesday!

Other activities

Courchevel has an Olympic ice-rink, a bowling alley, an indoor climbing wall, ice-climbing and cinemas.

WITH A WIDE VARIETY OF PLEASURES FROM WHICH TO CHOOSE, FREERIDERS WILL BE IN THEIR ELEMENT HERE

 Thanks

Ilse Le Grand, Adi Kipping Sue Tubb and Andrew

Essential Contacts

Tourist office

Tel: 7908 0029 Fax: 7908 1563

Snowboard shops

• Snow Coco Tel: 7908 3761.

• Hookipa -Tel: 7908 3719 Fax: 7908 7261

Snowboard schools

• ESF -Tel: 7908 0772 Fax: 7908 1459

• Ski Academy Tel: 7908 2608 Fax: 7908 0327

• Ski Masterclass Tel: 7908 2200 Fax: 7908 3991

Méribel

 ON THE MOUNTAIN

Méribel is an excellent resort, which looks after boarders well and, in the '95/'96 season, hosted the British championships. It is in the centre of, and thus well-connected to, Les Trois Vallées. It has an extremely efficient system of 200 lifts, which means that queues are never a problem, and it has 600km of pistes, so the boarding possibilities are seemingly limitless. As with every resort, check with local riders or pisteurs before going off-piste as areas of this resort are avalanche prone.

 Snow conditions

As Méribel lies at a lower altitude than the surrounding areas, the snow reliability isn't as good. To compensate, the lower runs have a substantial number of cannons - 1,200 of them in fact!

Freeriders

Here are some suggestions:

Col du Fruit: A 20 minute flat walk in from the Grande Rosière lift, through the Reserve Naturelle de Tueda, which is insanely beautiful. However, there is another 20 minute flat walk out back to the Mottaret lifts.

K2 Couloir: Heading down from the top of the Mont Vallon lift, turn right after the first corner on the piste and before you is a radical couloir.

Back of Mt Vallon: Pick out the steep cliff-jumps and ride the powder.

The Spot: Traverse right off the piste at the top of the drag and you will find an inviting field.

The Glacier du Gebrouloz: Take an upward 45 minute hike from the Col chairlift and embark on a 15km run, starting on a spectacular glacier. Exit at the bottom of the Col du Fruit.

To Raffort: Traverse to the right of the Olympic express and go for a ride...

Christmas trees: Dismount halfway up the Burgin Saulire cable car, then head straight for the pisteur's hut and descend down through the trees for a grand powder run. **Col de la Loze:** Traverse right from the top of the Rocher de la Loze and ride down wherever you like.

Freestylers

A halfpipe and funpark are located at the top of the Altiport Lift. The pipe was built by hand, and maintained, by the staff of Sport 1600 and the Méribel Massive. However, due to the low altitude of the area, it suffers when there is little snow.

Carvers

The Saulire mountain is a massive wide descent, which you can charge down at great speed. Everywhere above the tree line in Méribel is a carver's paradise.

Mountain fare

The Rond Point bar has a large sun terrace and delicious food - they serve huge baps and you can bludge the odd glass of water. This is where the local crew congregate at sundown.

QUEUES ARE NEVER A PROBLEM AND WITH 600KM OF PISTES, THE **BOARDING** POSSIBILITIES ARE SEEMINGLY **LIMITLESS**

pic: Nagel Photo rider: Mark Rothwell

pic: J.M. Favre

By train: Take the train to Moutiers and catch one of the many connections for the final 18kms.

By car: Take the A43 motorway to Albertville, then the N90 trunk road to Moutiers and follow the signs for Méribel along the D90.

Accommodation

There are a number of places from which to choose, as well as a wide variety of British tour operators. For information and reservations - Tel: 7900 5000 or Fax: 7900 3119.

Food

The town is littered with the usual, cheap mountain restaurants offering pizzas and fondues - prices start from 50F for a meal. We recommend the English-staffed French Connection, which is a relaxing place to eat and drink.

Nightlife

Try this for starters, but improvise at will. Start off at Le Taverne, a relaxing place for a 35F Guinness, then head to Le Capricorn where you should try Muttzig, the local beer (7.5 percent alcohol), and watch Eurosport. Later, head to Jacks, a popular drinking-hole with the resort staff, and, even later, slide on your late night beer goggles at the Artichaub, open till 5.00am. On Sundays, French Connection has happy hour drinks, priced from 10F to 20F, all day long. Just don't blame us for the morning after!

Other activities

Méribel has an Olympic ice rink, bowling, a swimming-pool, hang-gliding, parapenting and cinemas.

Thanks to

Scotty 'Bwoy' Nixon and the entire Méribel Massive, Christophe and the Sport 1600 store, Nick and Shane's Hotel.

Méribel pic: J.M. Favre

ABOUT TOWN

Unlike its neighbours, Méribel has managed to retain much of its village charm, thanks to strict building rules. All the chalets are wooden and low-rise, making the town look quite picturesque. It actually consists of two main villages: Méribel Centre (the original resort) and Mottaret, which is a cheaper place to stay. Les Autres Quartiers is home to Sport 1600, which is the happening place to hang-out - many of the locals live close by and it's just a piste slide from the centre of town, which is handy at 5.00 in the morning.

Getting there

By air: The nearest airports are Lyon and Geneva (both a 3.5 hour transfer away) and Chambéry.

Les Menuires

Mountain Information

Mountain chain:

Alps

Vertical metre range:

1,400m - 2,850m

Length of season:

end of November - late April

Number of lifts:

20 draglifts, 18 chairlifts,

6 gondolas, 4 cable cars

Snow-making facilities:

280 snow cannons cover

60kms, when needed.

Safety:

For up to date information on

conditions - Tel: 7900 6447.

Guides:

Available through the

ski/snowboard schools.

Lift pass prices:

1 day: 175F

6 days: 850F

Lift pass alternatives:

The Les Menuires pass includes

St Martin de Belleville, a little

further down the valley. The Vallée

des Belleville pass includes Les

Menuires, St Martin and Val

Thorens. If you buy an Espace

Olympique Savoie pass lasting for

six days or more, you can ride in

Espace Killy, Val d'Isère, Tignes,

Espace La Plagne, Peisey

Vallandry, Les Arcs Pralognan,

La Vanoise and Les Saisies.

 ON THE MOUNTAIN

Les Menuires has something for all kinds of riders - freeriders will find themselves in off-piste paradise at La Masse, 'stylers will love the halfpipe and funpark with its local flavour, and carvers will appreciate the wide open pistes. The mountain is well marked out, making routes easy to follow. Besides its own bountiful playgrounds, Les Menuires has easy access to the rest of Les Trois Vallées.

 Snow conditions

On the side of La Masse, riders can be assured of snow cover for most of the season because of the slope's altitude and north-easterly orientation. On the opposite, west-facing side of the resort, a battalion of 280 snow cannons ensures adequate cover.

 Freeriders

The hard-core, off-piste areas are found on the Pointe de la Masse, which rips. Head left down the Du Lac Noir to find cliff jumps and steeps. The Lac du Lou has wide open fields, undulating towards Val Thorens. The hits won't take long to find, because they're plentiful and usually perfectly pitched. Under the Chambre 2, small drops and hits can be charged.

 Freestylers

A halfpipe is maintained by the locals, including staff from Absolu. The small funpark, a popular hang-out for locals, has many enticing features, such as quarterpipes, a small rail and a good sized fun-box. The location of these facilities may change from season to season - ask at the Absolu shop if in doubt.

Carvers

This place is nirvana for carvers. In between Petits Creux and Les Boyes, there are exhaustive amounts of huge, wide open pistes to charge down.

Lifts to avoid

All the lifts are snowboarder friendly, but the queues can be long, particularly late in the day at La Masse.

FREERIDERS WILL FIND OFF-PISTE PARADISE AT LA MASSE, FREESTYLERS WILL LOVE THE HALFPIPE AND FUNPARK WITH ITS LOCAL FLAVOUR, AND CARVERS WILL APPRECIATE THE WIDE OPEN PISTES

 Mountain fare

There are restaurants a-plenty, but crepes and pizzas are the best deals. Check La Chouette next to the Absolu shop if you're after a cheap meal.

Les Menuires - Little Marbella pic: Marc Hare

Nightlife

There are two main hang-outs - the Yeti Bar and The Moose. Seasoners and locals relax at The Moose, which has decent music, food, moderately-priced drinks and pool tables. The nightlife after 1.00am is pretty tame - Liberty is where the natives go, it's expensive but you might like it. If you need to party, go to Val Thorens - just around the mountain.

Other activities

There is an ice-skating rink and an outdoor heated pool located in the centre of town, or you can try a paragliding flight.

Thanks to

Nico Sanchez from Absolu Le Proshop and Abi Dean.

Nico pic: Marc Hare

More Essential Information

Tourist office

Tel: 7900 7300 Fax: 7900 7506

ABOUT TOWN

This place needs serious cosmetic surgery, because it resembles an upmarket council estate. However, it is functional and the atmosphere is a redeeming feature. Val Thorens, however, has a much better nightlife.

Getting there

By plane: The nearest airports are Chambéry and Geneva (both a 3.5 hour transfer away), and Lyon (a 2 hour transfer away).
By train: The TGV pulls right up to the Moutiers railway station, from where there are frequent connections to Les Menuires.
By car: There is a motorway all the way to Albertville, where there is a turn-off to Moutiers and Les Menuires.

Accommodation

Les Menuires is full of apartments, which can be booked either through the tourist office or a tour operator package. For something cheaper, with more character, the traditional Savoyard village of St Martin de Belleville is a 15 minute drive down the valley. The only problem is access, as it takes 25 minutes to ride up the mountain-side by lift and the route down can be a problem if there is no snow. Central booking office for accommodation - Tel: 7900 7979 or Fax: 7900 6092.

Food

Cheap, hearty fare at the Yeti Bar costs from 40F, while the Hacienda serves tasty Mexican food and hard-core margaritas.

LA MASSE Looking Sick pic: Marc Hare

Val Thorens

Mountain Information

Mountain chain:

Péclet - Caron

Vertical metre range:

2,100m - 3,200m

Length of season:

late November -

first week of May

Number of lifts:

1 cable car, 4 gondolas,

10 draglifts, 12 chairlifts

Snow-making facilities:

72 snow cannons cover

60kms of piste.

Safety:

An avalanche indicator board is

located beside the Setam office.

Guides:

Go to the tourist office between

6pm and 7pm on the eve of the

day that you require a guide, who

will cost 1,300F for the day and

will take up to five people.

Lift pass prices:

1 day: 175F

6 days: 770F

Season: 3,300F

Lift pass alternatives:

The Vallée de Belleville pass

includes Les Menuires, St Martin

de Belleville and Val Thorens - for

an extra 40F per day. If you buy

the Espace Olympique Savoie pass

for 6 days or more, you can ride in

Espace Killy, Val d'Isère, Tignes,

Espace La Plagne, Peisey

Vallandry, Les Arcs Pralognan, La

Vanoise and Les Saisies.

 ON THE MOUNTAIN

The boarding area is vast and easily accessible through a highly efficient lift system, which connects Val Thorens to the wider Les Trois Vallées. One of the highest resorts in Europe, at 3,200m, it has an enormous number of off-piste routes from the mountain top to the village, providing board-to-door convenience. When Val Thorens has fresh snow, there are windlips, cliff drops, couloirs, banks, hits and good clear powder runs, and, even in leaner times, there is plenty to be enjoyed. Bad weather is bad news, however, as sheltered runs are few and far between, and there are no trees.

 Snow conditions

Val Thorens is almost unbeatable for reliable, quality snow cover, due to its great altitude and the north-facing orientation of the slopes.

 Freeriders

The Lac du Lou run leaves from the summit of the Cime de Caron and joins runs from the La Masse area of Les Menuires.

From the top of the Plein Sud, there are several cliff drops, with couloirs in-between. Down the face of the Cime de Caron, there is a fast, black run for speedsters. Another run with various hits is located to the right of the Cascades - look out for two good spinning hits located on the left, towards the lift.

Another run from the Moutière lift is a small valley, with jumps and piste drops.

Take a guide or listen to the advice of the locals, particularly if it's your first visit to the resort, as the area is avalanche prone.

 Freestylers

There is a funpark, located at the Funitel Lift, which is well-maintained, but without good snowfall it's not usable. Marielle Goitschel, ex-Olympic ski gold medallist, who rules the roost at Val Thorens, believes this area should be policed! Hopefully her son, who prefers to slide sideways, will persuade her that snowboarders are not criminal outlaws - Tel: 7900 0286 or Fax: 7900 0010.

 Carvers

Val Thorens is excellent for carving. Most of the pistes are kept in good condition giving carvers plenty of scope for choice. Highly recommended, for length and gradient, are the runs off the Cime de Caron.

(X) Lifts to avoid

None! Try them all - it'll take at least three days.

Mountain fare

The Plan Bouchet is one of the best restaurants for food and a convivial atmosphere, otherwise there are the usual array of standard places where prices vary between 70F and 120F for a meal, with one beer.

pic: Face Shots

pic: Marc Hare

ONE OF THE HIGHEST RESORTS IN EUROPE, IT HAS AN ENORMOUS NUMBER OF OFF-PISTE ROUTES

pic: Marc Hare

Essential Contacts

Tourist office

Tel: 7900 0808   Fax: 7900 0004

Snowboard shops

•3V sports   Tel: 7900 0172

A hard-core shop coordinating equipment hire, tuition, and a network of local riders and camps.

Snowboard schools

•ESF   Tel: 7900 0286   Fax: 7900 0010

•International Ski Surf/Nature
Tel: 7900 0196

•L'Ecole de Ski   Tel: 7900 0196

 ABOUT TOWN

This is a modern, purpose-built resort, but it is of reasonable taste when compared with its ugly sister, Les Menuires. As Val Thorens is one of the highest resorts in Europe, the vista beyond the village will have you in awe of the grandeur and starkness of the mountains.

 Getting there

By plane: Lyon and Geneva are both a 3-4 hour transfer away.

By train: The nearest main station is Moutiers, from where it's a 35km ride by frequent bus connection.

By car: To access Val Thorens, take the motorway until Albertville, then turn off towards Moutiers. Follow the signs to St Martin de Belleville and head up the valley past Les Menuires to Val Thorens, which is car-free. It is, therefore, compulsory to park in a registered space - book a week early for discounts or park at Les Menuires for free and catch the bus to Val Thorens.

 Accommodation

For all-inclusive package deals, contact the UCPA - Tel: 7900 0139. Self-catering apartments and hotels (i.e. Espace Goitschel from 225F with breakfast) are available through the Centrale de Reservation - Tel: 7900 0106 or Fax: 7900 0649.

 Food

One of the cheapest (35F approximately) and heartiest meals is the local dish, 'tartiflette', a mix of egg, bacon and potatoes. Try El Gringo's Café, which provides a hearty feed that is best consumed with a decapitating margarita or two, and Temples du Soleil, located at the entrance to the sport centre, serving a

wicked pizza for 45-55F. Otherwise, there is a large market on Tuesdays and Thursdays, where bargain wine and food are sold.

 Nightlife

The Frog and Roast Beef is reputedly the highest pub in Europe, some claim to fame! Another pub, O'Connells, pulls a fine Guinness (as it should for 35F) and is the place to make friends with the staff, then you'll soon know everyone in the resort. For pool, try the Viking Bar. The Malaysias nightclub plays hip-hop, while the Underground opts for racy dance music. The Ski Rock Café is good for a laugh, particularly if you're Swedish, ski and like karaoke, otherwise try the Tango Club for a sliding dance.

Other activities

A cinema, paragliding and an awesome sports centre are all on offer.

NB: If you buy Carte Neige Insurance in Val Thorens, you get a week's free pass to the Aquaclub, which has amazing saunas and spas!

Thanks to

Cécile from the tourist office, Fred from 3V sports and Mark & Spencer.

El Gringo Gringo pic: Marc Hare

La Norma

Mountain Chain:

Alps

Vertical metre range:

1,350m - 2,750m

Length of season:

mid-December - mid-April

Number of lifts:

1 gondola, 6 chairlifts,
10 draglifts

Snow-making facilities:

21 snow cannons.

Safety:

Check the avalanche indicator
board in the centre of the town
for daily updates.

Guides:

Contact the ESF Tel: 7920 3310

Lift pass prices:

1 day: 102F

2 days: 200F

2 weeks: 1,160F

Season pass: 1,450F

 ## ON THE MOUNTAIN

La Norma has been purpose-built to cater for
3,500 visitors, but the mountain's lifts can move
up to 7,000 people an hour. A simple arithmetic
reveals that this is one mountain that is unlikely
to be crowded. Moreover, as most visitors are
families, so often the more challenging places
are left untouched. Even after a week of no
fresh snowfall, we found large areas of sick,
untracked powder. Snowboarders have yet to
discover La Norma, so there is no scene at
present, but there are heaps of possibilities.
While it is not linked to Les Trois Valleés, they
are nearby.

 ### Snow conditions

La Norma hums after a dumping of snow and
has a substantial number of shaded areas
where the powder lingers. In bad weather,
there are plenty of forested areas for riding.

Freeriders

There is a plethora of places to play in La
Norma, starting with some great cliff jumps
accessed off the lift at Le Clot. If you go up the
lift La Norma 1 and slide over the back, there
are several cliffs, windlips and steeps. To get
to the main tree areas, go right off La Repose.
In addition, the pistes running through the
trees have plenty of hits down either side.

 ### Freestylers

A local boarder, Gilles from Technicien du Sport, is
the mastermind behind the funpark (marked as 'snow
park' on the map) in La Norma. With a good covering
of snow, the park is excellent, although some of the
jumps are too small and the landings flat.

 ### Carvers

There are a number of well-groomed pistes for
carvers, the steepest of which is off La Norma 1.

 ### Lifts to avoid

No. 16 on the piste map is a rather slow chairlift
- if in doubt, party on it!

 ### Mountain fare

There are two restaurants on the mountain, both
serving good solid food for midday sustenance.
One was built by the owner and there are some rad
pictures to check out.

Other mountain activities

Every Wednesday there is an open derby competition
down the La Norma piste, which is open to all - skiers,
telemarkers, mono-skiers and anything else that slides.
Ask at the tourist office for details.

Gilles at Home pic: Marc Hare

AFTER A WEEK OF NO FRESH SNOWFALLS, WE FOUND LARGE AREAS OF SICK, UNTRACKED POWDER

Essential Contacts

Tourist office

Maison de la Norma

Tel: 7920 3146   Fax: 7920 3655

Snowboard Shops

•Norma Sports - Technicien du Sport

Tel: 7920 3020

Ask for Gilles - he's the best first call!

•Patrick Sports   Tel: 7920 3394

Snowboard schools

•ESF   Tel: 7920 3310

Price for 6 half days: 450F.

 ABOUT TOWN

La Norma, tucked in amongst a beautiful Alpine forest, is a small, purpose-built resort, which harbours a permeating feeling of functionality. Most of the resort's clientele are families visiting from Denmark and Germany, consequently the nightlife is a wee bit strange. Having said that, the resort management has an 'open-arm' approach to boarders and it's a welcoming, inexpensive place to enjoy great, varied riding. Just make no mistake, this area is sublime!

 Getting there

By air: Lyon, Geneva, Chambéry and Turin are less than a two hour drive away.

By train: The closest station to La Norma, a 4.5 hour TGV train journey from Paris, is Modane.
Bus connections run frequently between the station and resort.

By car: There are motorways from Lyon, Geneva and Valence to Albertville, from where the N6 takes you to Modane and the resort is then 6kms in the direction of Haute-Maurienne.

 Accommodation

The Sogenor booking office can sort out apartments priced from 1,016F (low season) to 3232F (high season) - Tel: 7920 3146 or Fax: 79203655.

 Accommodation is also available through Les Portes de la Vanoise, prices start from 1,650F - Tel: 7910 3801 or Fax: 7020 3379. For budget choices, try the UCPA, which offers a variety of all-inclusive packages.

 Food

There are six restaurants in the village - the menus vary from pizzas to local dishes, but the cheapest is the local creperie. The Roi du Soleil is one of the best restaurant/bars for value, with a varied menu starting from 45F for three courses. For a bargain lunch, the supermarket has 'poulet du roti' (roast chicken) - just add a crusty baguette, salad..... and ten beers.

(×ײ) **Nightlife**

Run by Dutch people, the Roi du Soleil (open from 8.30am-1pm) promotes a relaxed Amsterdam vibe, which doesn't mean it's all right to skin up! "This is France!" they said. "What's the point of that then?" we said. But beers are priced from 12F. Later in the evening, try Le Privé or the Piano Bar, both bristle with boisterous boxheads.

 Thanks to

Eric Dournon (director of tourism) and Gilles from Technicien du Sport.

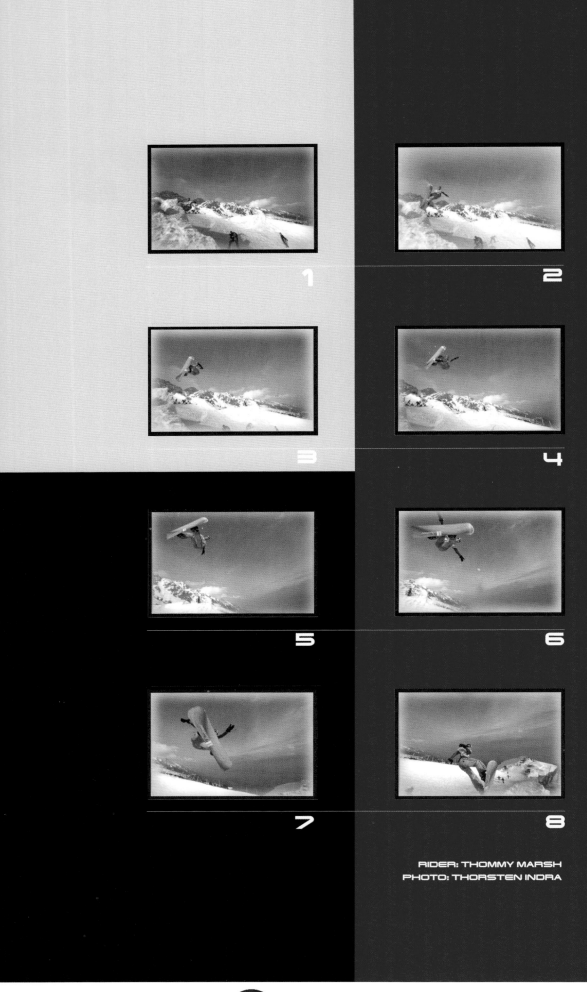

1
2
3
4
5
6
7
8

RIDER: THOMMY MARSH
PHOTO: THORSTEN INDRA

PLUS MINUS COLLECTION

THE PLUS MINUS COLLECTION
CHIEMINGERSTRASSE 19 – 83355 GRABENSTÄTT
TELEFON 08661-9888-0 – FAX 08661-9888-25

Hautes Alpes Intro

Alpes d'Huez

pic: Face Shots rider: Adam Barnes

Mountain Information

Mountain chain:

Massif des Grands Rousses

Vertical metre range:

1,450m - 3,300m

Length of season:

first week of December -
last week in April

Number of lifts:

14 cable cars, 23 chairlifts,
44 draglifts, 1 elevator

Snow-making facilities:

385 snow cannons bolster the
pistes in times of lean snow.

Safety:

Closed runs are signposted at all
major lifts.

Guides:

Can be arranged at the Bureau des
Guides. The best snowboard guide
is Pascal Junique -
Tel: 7680 4255.

Lift pass prices:

1 day: Saturday 165F,
           Sunday 175F,
           weekday 200F
6 days: 960F
7 days: 1,065F
(NB: in the low season, there is a
20% discount)

Linked or nearby resorts:

A pass for 6 days or more includes
1 day's skiing at each of the
Grande Galaxie resorts (Les Deux
Alpes, Serre Chevalier, Puy-Saint-
Vincent and the Milky Way) and
free entrance to the Palais de
Sports, which has indoor football,
gyms and rock walls, plus shuttle
buses.

 ON THE MOUNTAIN

**Alpe d'Huez is a great mountain to visit with
incredible snow conditions and great
freeriding. In addition, the pistes are kept in
immaculate order and provide some great
carving terrain.**

 Snow conditions

Alpe d'Huez has a perfect location in the
centre of the Alps. It is not far enough south to
be ravaged by the sun and warm winds, and is
not far enough north to have the cold
temperatures and avalanches that plague the
likes of Val d'Isère. If, by any chance, an
avalanche does occur, the mountain's plateau
shape means the avalanche peters out on the
lower, flatter slopes. A large portion of Alpe
d'Huez is south-facing and so very deep
snowfalls are usually followed by sunshine,
which results in snow conditions stabilising, but
cooking very quickly after a storm.

 Freeriders

The off-piste is vast, but you must take a guide in
order to find it! The mountain's plateau (mentioned
above) results in enormous cliff bands cutting across

many faces, with only a few routes down. Going
unguided can be, and has been, fatal. If you want an
unguided piece of off-piste bliss, check out the
Glacier de Sarenne, a 16km thigh tester. Go to the top
of the Pic Blanc and head for the back ridge, where
the glacier takes you to the Gorges de Sarenne, then
follow a pretty river valley back to the village. Air
freaks will be in seventh heaven in Vaujany - hit the
DMC cable car and hack right for about 2,200m until
you reach the fun.

 Freestylers

There is no halfpipe as such, but there is a terrain
garden on the signal piste with all the usual stuff -
quarterpipes, gap jumps and table tops. If you really
have to get on to a pipe for the day, Les Deux Alpes
has one that you can ride using your free day pass.

 Carvers

It's heaven for carvers... all the pistes are long and
wide... including the one run that goes for 16km!
We'd advise you to take a packed lunch.

✗ **Lifts to avoid**

Don't ride the DMC lift in the high season.

pic: Face Shots

ABOUT TOWN

It's a large, user friendly resort, with a good mixture of French, Scandinavians, and Brits including the usual hard-core ski and board bums. Avenue de Jeux is where everything happens and it's easy to find. The town is lively the whole week - even on a Tuesday night it's possible to go out till the early hours.

Getting there

By air: Lyon (transfer three hours, Geneva transfer four hours. Grenoble transfer 1.5 hours)
By train: Nearest station is Grenoble with a 1.5 hour transfer by bus.
By car: Motorway to Grenoble then RN91 - follow signs for Alpe d'Huez.

Accommodation

Reservation centre - Tel: 7680 354, Fax: 7680 6954

Food

There are great restaurants in Alpe d'Huez. Cremaillère is one of the best places to eat - it has fantastic pizzas and steaks with Savoyard potatoes, and is open until 4.00am. Cremaillère does free aperitifs, and also has a free taxi service. Pizza Pinnocchio has the best pizza in town, recommended for a huge, hearty feed.

ALPE D'HUEZ HAS A PERFECT LOCATION IN THE CENTRE OF THE ALPS

Nightlife

If you don't go anywhere else go to the Cactus Cafe which plays great music; hip-hop, reggae and blues and rock, but it can munch into your pocket. Le Utop rages until 5.00am, and is the late night place to go. There are plenty of other bars, but the undisputed champion of the resort is the Underground which is the coolest, hippest groove station in the world. It's packed every night and often has live music, the bar staff are ultra cool and it offers freestyle, slalom and off-piste outings.

Other activities

Planetary astrology, billiards, cinema, hang gliding, driving on ice, ice cascades, helicopter rides, swimming, snowshoe walks and hikes - you name it!

Thanks to
Ross Woodhall

Essential Contacts

Tourist office
Tel: 7680 3541   Fax: 7680 6954

Snowboard shops
•Planet Surf Tel: 7680 6228
The best snowboard service on the planet.

Snowboard schools
•Snow surfing (operated by Planet Surf)
Tel: 7680 6228
Instruction at all levels, from beginners to advanced, including pistes for your enjoyment.
Basic tuition: 900F/week
 (1600F with rental equipment),
Advanced tuition: 700F/week
•ESF Tel: 7680 3169
In season there is a snow surfing workshop from 2.30pm - 5.00pm   4 days: 650F

OZ STATION

OZ-EN-OISANS

VILLARD RECULAS

ALPE D'HUEZ

HUEZ

AURIS-EN-OISANS

La Grave

 ## ON THE MOUNTAIN

This is a mountain at it's rawest; it's untouched, unpisted and unrivalled in the Alps, and consequently it's not suitable for beginners or bad attitudes. There are no freeriders, carvers or skiers at La Grave - just people who love to ride mountains. You must be fully competent, and comfortable in most off-piste conditions.

❄ Snow conditions

Usually good, due to it's high altitude, but can get scrappy towards the end of the season, and there are no snow making facilities.

Freestylers

Draglifts moving upwards from the main station take riders to glacier terrain where the snow remains in excellent condition. Head to the left, and you'll find a large open area of powder where you can let rip, and make long, fast arcing turns.Before you get carried away with esctasy, be aware of a sudden change to rocky terrain with large cliffs, steep couloirs and technical boarding. If you don't know the area you can get into serious trouble here - all there is to advise is that you must take a guide. Nearer the bottom, the tree run that rewards you is heaven. Powder covered moguls the size of men litter the forest - head right, towards the town. When you reach the bottom, cross a muddy path leading over a bridge, tread through what seems like someone's back garden, walk up the dark home-made steps and back to the lift station.The other option is heading right from

the dome, where you pass the restaurant, finding yourself in steeper terrain. There are three parallel couloirs here called Les Trifides; the first is a dog-leg couloir which is steep at the top - if you fall, there are rocks below, which can, and have killed.
The second Trifide is fairly straight, but you need to abseil into the third before having a long runout. After you've survived one of these, the run follows a valley back to the village. The top station Dome de la Lauze connects with Les Deux Alps and drops into La Grave, but beware as the lift passes don't crossover, and getting back means spending 105F for a day pass.

Freeriders

The people-sized moguls provide hits right through the tree areas and lower slopes while higher up the moutain you have to ask yourself how rad do you want to ever be. Learn how to freeride, but have lessons first.

Carvers

Ain't no pistes, but the glacial area and powder fields at the top are brilliant. The bottom half of the mountain will be a challenge, but the whole experience may change your attitude.

Lifts to avoid

Well, there are only four...

Mountain fare

Refuge Chancel has a beautiful vista with average fare.

Mountain Information

Mountain range:
Dauphine Region

Vertical metre range:
1450m - 3550m

Season duration:
mid-December - May

Number of lifts:
4 gondolas

Lift pass information
1 day: 170ff
6 days: 750ff

Linked or nearby resorts:
You can board to La Grave from Les Deux Alpes

Snow-making facilities:
Why?

Safety:
1. Take a guide.
2. Take a guide.
3. Take a guide.
Go back to one.

Road Trip - Julien Ettel pic: Richard Walch

⌂ ABOUT TOWN

The town, at first glance doesn't seem up to much; it's a chaotic scramble of old chalets and barns, with an old, timeless feel about the place. It's part mountaineering village, part farm land, and the prices are in line accordingly with rural France. If you want to experience the power and spirit of real mountains, spend some time here, you'll be well rewarded.

→ Getting there

By plane: It's a three to four hour drive from Grenoble, Lyon and Geneva.
By train: The Eurotunnel and TGV to Grenoble run frequently, and from there are transfers by bus.
By car: It is recommended that chains should be carried in this area, as the roads can be treacherous.

⌂ Accommodation

Hotels, furnished lets, B&Bs, camping and caravans are all possible, as well as a number of chalets, one of the best being the package deals at La Chaumine (which include off-piste training). Call the tourist office for prices and further options or the Maison des Hautes Alpes who have information on accommodation throughout the whole region. Tel: 4296 0508 or Fax: 4015 0482.

🍴 Food

A Swedish cook at La Chaumine rustles up a brilliant four course meal; book ahead! Otherwise there are a handful of local restaurants.

A MOUNTAIN AT IT'S RAWEST; UNTOUCHED, UNPISTED AND UNRIVÁLLED IN THE ALPS

Jason Schutz on the Glacier pic: Daniel Strasser

pic: Daniel Strasser

(xx) Nightlife

It's small, quiet and rural. People often chew the fat at La Chaumine, or at the Candy Ass Bar. If for some reason insomnia besieges you, Les Deux Alpes is a half an hour drive down the valley and has nightlife.

Essential Contacts

Tourist office
Tel: 7679 9005   Fax: 7679 9165
Local snowboard shops
• Run by Enzo Colpoi: Kana Surf Shop - opposite the cable car station. Their equipment stock is limited so it's better to be sorted before you arrive.
Snowboard schools:
• Guide's office - Tel: 7679 9021

Les Deux Alpes

 ON THE MOUNTAIN

With a top station at 3570m you're riding at some of the highest altitudes in the Alps. The terrain is hugely varied and the glacier, with ridable snow all year, extends the season till October and makes it possible to ride down to 2,600m till July.

 Snow conditions

The main lift serviced area faces north-west at high altitude, which means Les Deux Alpes is one of the Alps' most snowsure resorts.

Freeriders

Chalance is an off-piste route from the glacier to the bottom of the Combe de Thuit. It is a 1.5km vertical trail, ranging from steep and narrow chutes to wide open powder fields, which eventually joins the lower parts of Les Gours. It is best to go with someone who knows the area. Below the lower section of the Yandri pylons, to the left of the Crêtes on the front face, is a stepped run with 12 or more great hits. It's quite steep, but has undulating ridges, and provides radical air opportunities with safe landings. It is possible to ride through the Dôme de la Loze gateway to La Grave. The vertical drop down to the village of La Grave is 2,000m although Les Deux Alpes passes don't cover La Grave and a day pass to get back will cost 105F. The Tête Moute chairlift from the top of the Diable gondola has a steep black run, which is awesome.

Freestylers

It is only in the summer that there is a halfpipe, which hosts a number of European competitions. It's 300m long, with steep walls and excellent snow conditions due to its position at 3,300m. The Crêtes funpark, which is 500m long, is built on a medium gradient and has table tops plus a quarterpipe. There are plans to build a funpark and halfpipe at 2,600m, so check progress with the tourist office.

AT HIGH ALTITUDE, LES DEUX ALPES IS ONE OF THE ALPS' MOST SNOWSURE RESORTS

 Carvers

There are over 200kms of piste, of varying difficulties, to cruise.

 Lifts to avoid

The Diable gondola at rush hours. The lift giving the best access to the mountain is the Soleil D'or chairlift, just below the village.

 Mountain fare

La Pastorale at the top of the Diable gondola has great views of the area and good food at surprisingly reasonable prices.

Gumby - pic: Mark Junak

pic: J.M. Favre

Essential Contacts

Tourist office

Tel: 7679 2200   Fax: 7679 0138

Snowboard shops

- Milou Sports Tel/Fax: 7660 5042
- Yellow Cab Tel: 7679 0700

Board/boot hire: 180F/day

The independent, dedicated snowboard store.

Snowboard Schools

- Yellow Cab Surfing

Tel: 7679 0700 Fax: 7679 0143

6 days of tuition: 1,590F

A snowboard school teaching freeriding,
halfpipe, slalom and alpine.

- Luc Pelisson snowboard courses

Tel/Fax: 7679 0372

3 hours for 6 days: 1,290F

 ABOUT TOWN

**Les Deux Alpes is situated at the end of a large
plateau, at the top of a 900m precipice, from where
there are stunning views into the valley below. It has
everything based around a long high street that ends
at Place de Vénosc. A free shuttle bus tours the town
continually from 8.00am to 10.00pm.**

 Getting there

By air: The nearest airports, all a two to three hour
transfer away, are Chambery, Grenoble and, the most
popular, Lyon.

By train: The closest stop is Grenoble, from where
there are regular bus connections to Les Deux Alpes.
For more information, ring the station's information
line - Tel: 7647 7777.

By car: Follow the RN91 to the Lac du Chambon dam,
then turn right to the D213.

 Accommodation

Visitors are spoilt for choice. Hotels range from one
star to four star and there are numerous apartment
agencies organising self-catering and tailor-made
services. The centrally located Hotel Le Crêt is good
value, as is the Chalet, which has double rooms from
about 250F per night. The British-run tour operator,
Chalet Snowboard, comes highly recommended - their
all inclusive packages incorporate English-speaking
instruction - Tel: 01235-767 182 (in the UK). For more
accommodation information, contact the reservations
line - Tel: 7679 2438.

 Food

Supermarkets Le Sherpa and Casino are the best value
for self-caterers. There are many restaurants and
cuisines, such as Chinese, Moroccan, Italian and
traditional French, on offer. A handful of
recommended places are Charlie Burger for burgers,
Il Caminetto/L'Etable for pizzas, Smokey Joe's for
large portions of Tex-Mex hot salsa and big ribs, and
Chalet Mounier and the Bel Auberge for French food.
Prices range from 50F to 195F for a meal.

 Nightlife

The Boom Boom and Mike's bar have the liveliest
afternoon sessions. A beer at Boom Boom costs 20F a
pint and comes with a shot of tequila between the
hours of 4.00pm and 6.00pm. Either Smokey Joe's or
the Brazilian Club is the next port of call. Drinking-
dice, which feels like Russian roulette the following
day, is the favourite pastime at Smokey's, while the
Brazilian Club rocks with a large snowboard crowd.
Alternatively is to try riding the bucking bronco at the
Rodeo. For late night twisting and shouting, L'Opéra
is the most popular place with a 4.00am close and a
courtesy bus service. Also La Casa on the road out of
town is good for a late schmooze.

Other activities

A cinema, bowling centre, Turkish baths, paragliding,
Jacuzzi and a flotation tank at the Tanking Centre are
all up for grabs.

 Thanks

Adam Barnes (and his sponsors)

Serre Chevalier

Mountain Information

Mountain chain:

Haute Alpes

Vertical metre range:

1,630m - 2,830m

Length of season:

beginning of December -
end of April

Number of lifts:

9 gondolas, 16 chairlifts,
47 draglifts

Snow-making facilities:

There is a network of snow
cannons.

Safety:

There are avalanche indicator
boards at the base of the stations.

Guides:

Contact the Compagnie des Guides
de L'Oisans - Tel: 09224 7590

Lift pass prices:

1 day: 167F

6 days: 835F

Season: 3,255F

 ON THE MOUNTAIN

Thankfully, Serre Chevalier doesn't suffer the crowds that most of the big French resorts do. For some reason, it seems to have missed the hype and the whole area still maintains a rustic Provencal-type atmosphere. Serre Chevalier is best known as one of the finest resorts in France for freeriders. It has a mixture of terrain - wooded riding on the lower slopes and some open bowl riding above the tree-line.

❄ Snow conditions

The majority of the runs are north to north-west facing (with the exception of Briancon which faces south) and benefit from extensive snow cannon coverage. From Christmas onwards, Serre Chevalier has some of the best snow in the Alps.

Freeriders

The runs down to Briancon include the 'Grande Garguille', the piste du Luc Alphand, which lies above and below Jaques restaurant, and features fast natural rollers for catching air and speed. There are natural halfpipes below the Rocher Blanc chair, over Briancon way, and beneath the two higher Monetier chairs. For wide open cruising bowls, go above Chantemerle and Villeneuve. There is an abundance of tree areas - just make sure that you respect the fenced off areas. Enter the trees from the top of 'Predubois' drag and meander down by any route possible, but always in the direction of the road. There are steep ledges, board width tracks, rock-jumps, tree-slides, steeps and scary chutes. The trees here have everything and the snow keeps soft for weeks after a fall. Around the Aiguillete chia, there are prolific rock hits in the trees, and around Frejus, there are narrow steeps. There is endless off-piste by Cucumelle Peak (a 20 minute hike) around the back of the Yret chair (Monetier) and there is a massive route behind Pic de L'eyeret, but it is prone to big avalanches in the spring as is the back of La Balme leading to Cucumelle. Great couloirs for La Balme chair in both sides (go under the fence). If you are into serious cliff jumps, there is a 30 metre jump called Thierry's Leap between Echaillon and Grand Alpe. There are cornices to the left of the L'Echauda poma.

pic: Daniel Strasser rider: Jerome Catz

Freestylers

The funpark is high above Chantemerle in the Grand Serre bowl and below the top of Grand Serre chair.

Lifts to avoid

During the holiday season, try to avoid Fréjus gondola and the Chantemerle access lifts.

Mountain fare

There are quaint mountain restaurants dotted everywhere, but Jacques A. (above the Chantemerle chair) is the most popular, dishing up excellent eats such as main meals, pizzas, toasted sandwiches and snacks. An added bonus is the huge sun terrace, littered with deck chairs and playing live music at lunch-time.

pic: Ross Woodhall, Face Shots Photography

SERRE CHEVALIER IS BEST KNOWN AS ONE OF THE FINEST RESORTS IN FRANCE FOR FREERIDERS

 ABOUT TOWN

The resort is divided into four separate towns - Monetier, Villeneuve (La Salle), Chantemerle and Briancon. All are linked by a free shuttle bus.

Getting there

By air: Fly to Geneva, Lyon or Grenoble; all three to four hour transfer.

By car: Motorway to Grenoble, then RN91 in the direction of Briangon.

By train: Nearest station is Grenoble which has regular bus connections.

Accommodation

UCPA have three centres in this area and offer seven day packages from 2340F - Tel: 7650 3281. Apartments, chalets and even heated caravans are available through the Tourist office.

Food

All the facilities you'd expect from an international resort.

Nightlife

The resort is considered tranquil at night, although the Yeti bar kicks off with a happy hour from 4pm and regularly features live music. The Cav in Villeneuve sometimes has live bands and wild soirées.

Other activities

Loads! Toboggan slopes, natural ice skating rinks, heated swimming pool, sauna, turkish baths and sports centre.

Essential Contacts

Tourist office
Tel: 09224 7188

Snowboard shops
• Planet Surf Tel: 09224 4654

Snowboard schools
• ESF Tel: 09224 -1741

Les Pyrénées

France

Weather Information:

Eastern Pyrenees

Tel: 61 71 11 31/ 61 71 11 11

Central Pyrenees

Tel: 559 62 17 34/559 27 50 50

Western Pyrenees

Tel: 559 23 84 15/559 22 03 30

(for further information see page 126).

Les Angles	174
La Mongie	176
Piau Engaly	178
Luz Ardiden	180
Cauterets	182

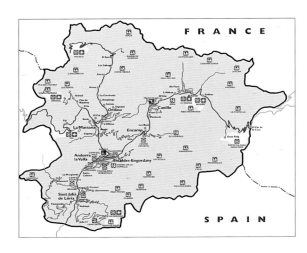

Andorra

Population: 64,311

Currency: Spanish peseta and French franc

Telephone information:

ISD code 376

Police: 110

Fire: 118

Ambulance: 118

Weather line: Tel: 86 43 89

Other resorts in Andorra:

Arinsal, Ordino-Arcalis, Pal,

Pas de la Casa-Grau and La Rabassa

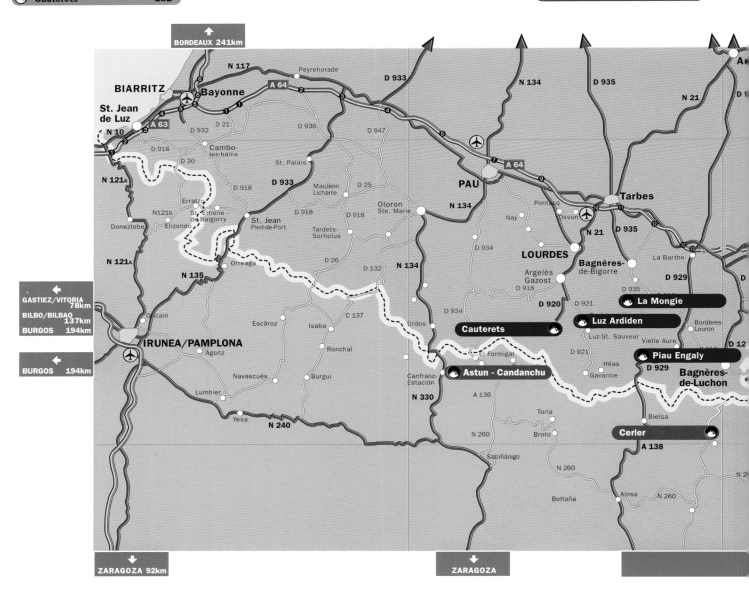

Spain

Capital: Madrid

Population: 38,542,000

Time: GMT + 1

Currency: Peseta

UK £1.00 = 200ptas

Telephone information:

ISD code: 34

International Operator: 099

National Operator: 118

Police: 091

Emergency: 088

National Snowboard/Surf Magazines:

Tres 60, Surfer Rule

Snowboard Association:

Tel: 34 01 43 59340

Mountain Weather:

Eastern Pyrenees

Tel: 34 93 21 25 666/21 25 816

Central Pyrenees

Tel: 34 976 23 43 36/23 09 01

Western Pyrenees

Tel:34 943 27 40 30

Main travel routes:

By Plane: Main airports for access to the Pyrenees

are: Bilbao, Zaragoza, Pamplona and Barcelona.

By Ferry: Portsmouth to Bilbao, P&O Tel: 01705 772244

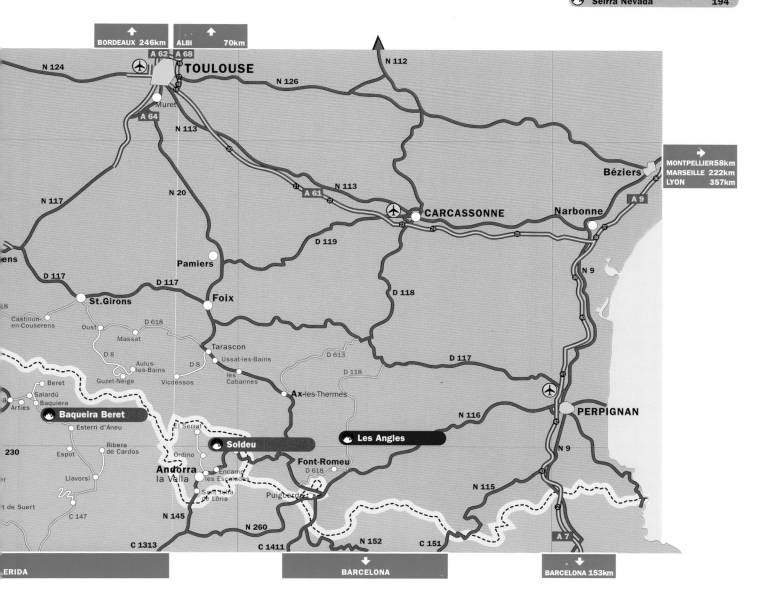

Les Angles

Mountain chain:

Capcir area

Vertical metre range:

1,600m - 2,400m

Length of season:

late November - late April

Number of lifts:

2 cable cars,

2 chairlifts, 19 draglifts

Snow-making facilities:

Massive amounts of artificial snow can be produced by 212 snow cannons.

Safety:

No real danger.

Guides:

The guide bureau is located next to the tourism office Tel: 6804 3922.

Lift pass prices:

1 day: 133F

6 days: 700F

Season: 1,870F

pic: Paul Palau

ON THE MOUNTAIN

Snowboarding was once banned in many resorts around the eastern Pyrenees, but not Les Angles. A traditional village, Les Angles is now a modern ski resort that welcomes riders, which is good news because it is by far the best suited to snowboarders in the area, and riders from Perpignan, Montpellier and Barcelona visit regularly. The beautiful views of Lake Matemale and heavily wooded forests are another plus point.

✱ Snow conditions

Located on the Mediterranean side of the Pyrenees, Les Angles receives less snowfall than the central Pyrenrees. This matters little as the slopes are either north-east facing or sheltered from the sun by a cover of fir trees, while underneath the snow lie meadows, with few rocks.

Freeriders

Most slopes are divided by forest which is too dense and hard to ride between, but there is some great freeriding in areas such as Balcere Lake and the Col Rouge. For a 3m-15m jump, try the cornice off the Roc d' Aude under the upper chairlift - ask the piste patrol about avalanche risks, as this is the only risky spot in the resort. Off the beaten track is the Versant pla del Mir, which has a good set of rocks and tree trunks close to an animal reserve; avoid the wolves!

Freestylers

Espace Surf, close to Lou Bac cable car exit, is a 450m 'snowboarders only' area, with all kinds of jumps and quarterpipes. It's well-maintained and often has music on the PA system. A halfpipe is built for the Pyrenees Snowboard Tour event, but it is not maintained for the rest of the season. Shame.

Carvers

Most runs are easy to carve as the declivity is not super steep. The trails, however, are often narrow and are to be avoided when crowded.

Mountain fare

Two snack places provide a quick bite; one at the Les Pélerins gondola exit, and the other at the Les Tassettes lift.

THE **SLOPES** ARE EITHER NORTH-EAST FACING OR **SHELTERED** FROM THE SUN **BY A** COVER OF **FIR TREES**

ABOUT TOWN

Les Angles is like the beauty and the beast; half of the architecture is that of a traditional old village while the rest are nightmarish, purpose-built constructions. Its setting, in the midst of a landscape of the lakes and forests, is magnificent. Out of peak season, it's very quiet, but in the weekends and in holidays, numbers can swell dramatically and the bars flow with people and beer.

pic: J.M. Favre

Getting there

By plane: The closest airport is Perpignan, (a 100km transfer by bus), or Toulouse (a 178 km transfer away).
By train: The closest station is Mont-Louis, a 12km transfer by bus.
By car: From Foix travel on the D117, and then the winding D118. From Perpignan, take the N116 and follow the D32 to Mont-Louis.

Accommodation

There are a handful of hotels offering double rooms at half board from 215F - 300F. Recommended are Le Coq D'or - Tel: 6804 4217, Le Bel Angle - Tel: 6804 4060 and Le Llaret - Tel: 6830 9090. There are apartments at Le Panoramic for up to four people priced from 1,900F - 3,500F - Tel: 6830 9020.

Food

There are two grocery stores, a heap of cheap fast-food places (Surf-Burger, Pizz n' Rock) and restaurants with varying menus: Ramballade, Arcades, Ty Yann, Casa de l'Ours, and Blue des Neiges, to name a few. Prices around 80F - 100F for a set menu.

Nightlife

Good vibes and beer flow both at La Troika and at L' Eden Rock. For late night dancing, try the nightclub La Tartane.

Other activities

There is a pool, an ice-rink with a disco, a sauna, bowling, a gym, and parapenting. More interesting pursuits are diving under the ice and ice-surfing, or windsurfing with ice skates.

Thanks to

Elizabeth.

Essential Contacts

Tourist office
Tel: 6804 3276   Fax: 6830 9309

Snowboard shops
• Carlit Sport   Tel: 6804 3899
• Freeride Shop   Tel: 6894 4314
• Mountain Surf   Tel: 6804 3777
Board/boot hire: 120F a day (average).

Snowboard schools
• ESF   Tel: 6804 4782
For youngsters, there's 'Le surf en 3D', a mix of pre-snowboard training (ie trampolining and skateboarding), freestyle training, and aprés-ride relaxing with videos and music at Capcir Room Surf Club - Tel: 6804 4551.

cabine Les Pèlerins
cabine Lou Bac
ski Pardal
ski Plateau
ski Cabanes
ski Fount
ski Rigals
siège Jassettes Express
siège Roc d'Aude
ski Llaret
Ski de fond
gement artificiel

11 Téléski Roc d'Aude
12 Téléski Bruyères
13 Téléski Bakère
14 Téléski Péborny
15 Téléski Col Rouge
16 Téléski San Père
17 Téléski Pla del Mir
18 Téléski du Cerf
19 Téléski du Faon
20 Téléski des Rhodas
Téléskis école
Parc Animalier

PIC CARLIT 2921
MONT LLARET 2377
PIC PERIC 2810
ROC D'AUDE 2375
ROC DE PEBORNY 2300
LAC DE BAL
PLA DEL MIR 1800
PISCINE PATINOIRE
LAC DE MATEMALE
Les Angles

La Mongie

pic: Claude Etchelecou

Mountain chain:

Vallée d'Aure

Vertical metre range:

1,800m - 2,400m

Length of season:

early December - late April.

Number of lifts:

1 cable car, 1 gondola,

6 chairlifts, 25 draglifts

Snow-making facilities:

Snow cannons link the valleys

when the real thing is thin on the

ground.

Safety:

Ask at the Service des Pistes,

located in the Centre Administratif,

before riding off-piste.

Guides:

Book through the tourist office -

the rate is 175F hour.

Lift passes:

1 day: 140F

6 days: 700F

NB: La Mongie passes give access

to Barèges (6kms away on the

other side of the Tourmalet pass)

However, most of the winter

Barèges is closed and there is no

linking bus.

 ON THE MOUNTAIN

Snowboarding in the Pyrenees began in La Mongie, when the Sarran brothers decided that surfing off the Côte Basque in winter was too much like cold work and turned instead to snow. Combined with Barèges, La Mongie offers the largest snowfield in the Pyrenees and boasts the biggest vertical drop. The icing on the cake is the view from the Pic du Midi - it's stunning.

 Snow conditions

Snow cover varies, but is assured on La Mongie Tourmalet, which is north-facing.

Freeriders

La Mongie tends to sprawl and so there's lots of freeriding terrain. For tree runs, ride below the Toulet cable car or frolic in the Coume Lounque area. Another renowned areas is the 'Brèche du Countadet' (so-called because it's where the shepherds used to count their flocks). Try also the long vertical drop from the Termes Four chairlift and the Pas de la Crabe, both of which head off towards Barèges, and you'll find a number of natural halfpipes en route. Another couple of good runs, especially for hits and windlips, are Violette from Taoulet and Combe de l'Espade.

Freestylers

There is no funpark as yet, but there are plenty of natural resources for freestylers, and jumps are built for the Snowboard Test Day* and the Quiksilver Cup in late March.

(* During the Snowboard Test Day, snowboard

manufacturers encourage riders to test the next season's range of goodies for free.)

 Carvers

Plenty of trails and lots of chairlifts.

 Lifts to avoid

The Les Petits Sapins draglift is too long and too steep.

 Mountain fare

There is a restaurant at Tourmalet, which (given that it's only at 2,115m) has a magnificent view, but the food is unexceptional. There is another café at L'Etape.

THE LARGEST SNOWFIELD IN THE PYRENEES AND WITH THE BIGGEST VERTICAL DROP

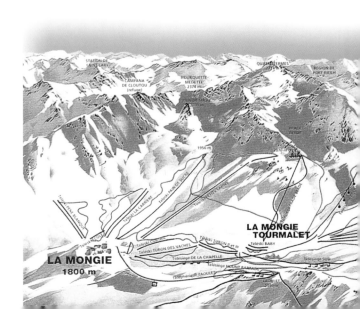

pic: Claude Etchelecou

ABOUT TOWN

The resort, which has all the essential amenities, stretches alongside the river between La Mongie and that of La Mongie Tourmalet. The best way to get around is on foot, although even short distances can seem extraordinarily long with burnt out legs.

Getting there

By plane: The closest airport is Ossun, between Tarbes and Lourdes, from where the resort is a 50km transfer.

By train: The closest SNCF station is Bagnères, from where there are connecting buses.

By car: If travelling on the main A64 motorway, take the Tournay exit and head to Bagnères on the D935.

Accommodation

There are 12,000 beds in town, providing a wide selection. There are half-board hotels from 230F, or rental apartments for rent; costing 2,000F to 4,000F per week. The Montana residential area is recommended for it's location. Contact the tourist office for more details - Tel: 6295 8181.

Food

The recommended restaurants are: the Brummel, Le Yeti, Pizzeria La Mama and Le Choucas. There are only two small, rather expensive food-stores/supermarkets in town.

Nightlife

The place to get drunk is the Mazot Bar. Once well-lubricated, head to La Tutte.

pic: Andy Jackson

Other activities

If you want spas, pools, jet-streams or saunas, go to Bagnères. For skidoos, parapenting or snow-biking, ask at Indiana Scoot or Ushualia.

Thanks to

Max Campays (tourist office) and Jean-François Arena (Snow Camp).

Essential Contacts

Tourist office
Tel: 6295 5071   Fax: 6295 3313
(Barèges - Tel: 6291 9415).

Snowboard shops
• L'Aventure (Rip Curl) Surf shop
Tel: 6291 9023
Board/boot hire: 150F/day
Contact: Laure or Olivier
• Ushualia (Quiksilver) Surf Shop
Tel: 6291 9419
Board/boot hire: 150F/day

Snowboard schools
• ESF   Tel: 6291 9244
Ski Ecole International   Tel: 6291 9430
• Snow Camp
Tel: 6291 9677 or 5943 7730
Contact: Jean-François Arena, director
The price for a weekend's tuition (including lift pass and video) is 630F. Other packages include accommodation.

Piau Engaly

Mountain chain:

Bigorre area

Vertical metre range:

1,850m - 2,500m

Length of season:

early December - early May

Number of lifts:

1 access gondola, 9 chairlifts,

11 draglifts

Snow-making facilities:

2.5 kms of tracks are covered by

snow cannons when necessary.

Guides:

Not needed.

Lift passes:

1 day: 122F

6 days: 610F

Season: 1780F

Nearby resort:

It is possible to get a pass which

includes Pia d'Adet/Esplaube,

but it's 20kms away.

pic: D. Julien

ON THE MOUNTAIN

Piau Engaly is the highest resort in the French Pyrenees and has one of the best snowfalls in the area. The slopes are steep and most of the off-piste titbits are easily accessible from the chairlifts.

Snow conditions

Due to its altitude, Piau Engaly is colder than most of the Pyrenean resorts and therefore retains quality snow throughout the season.

Freeriders

There are a number of off-piste rides. Here, we detail two of the best. To get to the awesome Badet valley, go to the highest point of the Piau chairlift, turn left, and there is a wild 900m descent with cliff jumps. The other option is to the left-hand side of the Gela chairlift - look out for the big jumps on the way to Pic de la Ludette and carry on down the black slope to Mephisto.

Freestylers

When contests are organised, jumps and a halfpipe are built, but generally there is nothing special set up for freestylers.

Carvers

There are a number of steep, well-kept pistes with banked walls on either side, making Piau Engaly possibly the best resort in the area for carvers.

Mountain fare

There are no restaurants on the slopes - everything is in the resort village.

THE HIGHEST RESORT IN THE FRENCH PYRENEES AND ONE OF THE BEST SNOWFALLS IN THE AREA

pic: Eric Chauché Hard to choose between a fresh dump and a spring swell

ABOUT TOWN

The village of Piau Engaly is the best place to stay because it is the closest settlement to the resort and access to the snow is easy. However, all other amentities are to be found in the closest main town of Aragnojet.

Getting there

By plane: Tarbes is about 80kms away, while Toulouse is 260kms distant. From Tarbes the bus and train to Piau Engaly both take 90 minutes.

By train: The nearest main station is Lannemezan, a 1 hour bus transfer away.

By car: Take the main A64 till Lannemezan and then the D929 to Saint-Lary. There is easy access from Spain through the Bielsa tunnel, which only closes in severe conditions.

Accommodation

There are 4,000 tourist beds in Piau. As an example; the Glavani charges 415F for one night with halfboard. The most common form of accommodation is a four person apartment, which costs 4,290F per week. Tel: 6239 6565 for more information. For budget travellers, there is a specially equipped area for camper vans where costs are minimal.

Food

There is only one small food store and a bakery in the town, so stock up on food before you arrive, otherwise you'll find supplies expensive and the choice limited. If you intend to eat out, try the Pizzeria Roma or Le Lys ou l'Engaly for provincial French food.

Nightlife

There are a couple of bars, such as Le Pub and La Bodega, on the main street. For some late night rare grooves, head for the Moonlight disco. As a mountain resort, Piau doesn't offer much other cultural action.

Other activities

There are not much aside from movies, night riding and skidoos.

Thanks to

Agnes (tourism office) and Jean-Luc Videau (president of the Pyrenees Snowboard Tour)

Essential Information

Tourist office

Tel: 6239 6169   Fax: 6239 6119

Snowboard shops

•Avalanche   Tel/Fax: 6239 6733

Board/boot hire: 130F - 150F/day

•Avaski   Tel: 6239 6733

Snowboard schools

•ESF   Tel: 6239 6283

Group 2 hour lesson: 100F

•Snow Fun   Tel: 6239 6899

Group 3 hour lesson: 140F

Luz Ardiden

Mountain Information

Mountain chain:

Bigorre

Vertical metre range:

1,700m - 2,450m

Length of season:

early December - late April

Number of lifts:

6 chairlifts, 13 draglifts

Snow-making facilities:

2 snow cannons cover

12 tracks of piste

when necessary.

Safety:

Check the daily report that is

posted at the tourist office or

Tel: 6292 8064 or 6292 8058

for up-to-date information.

Guides:

Maison de la Montagne - Tel: 6292

8728, Richard Dupont

(who charges 280F for a day) -

Tel: 6292 9610.

Henri Nogué - Tel: 6292 6973.

Lift passes:

1 day: 100F

6 days: 420F

Season: 1,600F

NB - A TOY ticket also allows you to

go either to Barèges

or Gavarnie.

 ON THE MOUNTAIN

Luz was the first resort in the Pyrenees to organise a snowboarding event and has a welcome attitude towards riders. The mountain itself has some great terrain which is split into two parts: the Bederet area, (best for beginners and intermediates), and the more interesting Aulian (suited to advanced and off-piste riders).

 Snow conditions

The resort has a northerly orientation, at a reasonably high altitude, so it is snowsure.

 Freeriders

The best off-piste options in Aulian are around the Caperete peak at 2,400m and Col de Cloze at 2,450m. Take the Cloze lift to ride off-piste around the Lagues Lake and arrive at Plateau de Bernazaou for wide, open bowls, with hits and gullies. The north-exposed couloirs preserve wonderful snow most of the time - look hard to find them.

 Freestylers

A 'snowboard space' with bumps and music, is serviced by the Pourtere draglift. It gets better every season, but is always at it's best during the Pyrenean Snowboard Tour contest.

 Carvers

The average gradient is good, and there is a lot of space to make wide turns.

 Lifts to avoid

Aulhères and Bergère in the Baderet area; both are long and tedious!

Mountain fare

There is nothing on the slopes, but there are two average restaurants close to the parking sites at Aulian and Baderet.

LUZ WAS THE **FIRST** RESORT IN THE PYRÉNÉES TO ORGANISE A **SNOWBOARDING EVENT**, AND HAS A **WELCOME** ATTITUDE TOWARDS RIDERS

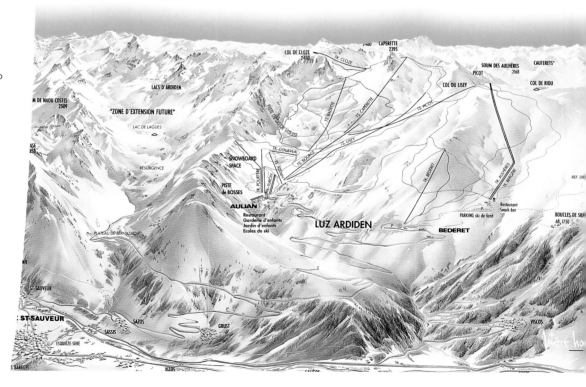

pic: FACE shots

ABOUT TOWN

The resort village of Luz Ardiden, is a 13km drive or bus ride along a road which may require chains if there has been a recent snowfall. An exemplary old mountain village, is steeped in history; there is a brook, castle, and a Templar church. The village exists without snow tourists, giving it some real atmosphere, in contrast to the other Pyrenean resorts. Costs in Luz Ardiden are low compared to most resorts, (including lift passes).

Getting there

By plane: Ossun airport is a 40km transfer away.
By train: The main station of Lourdes is a 30km transfer by bus.
By car: Take the main A64 till the Soumoulou exit, then travel to Lourdes by the D940. Take the N21 till Argeles Gazost and lastly the D921 till Luz Saint-Sauveur.

Accommodation

Luz Saint-Sauveur has 2,600 beds which gives scope for choice. There are 13 hotels which range in price from 110F to 350F per night. Les Templiers, a two star hotel is a good bet for ancient house and furniture lovers. For a four person apartment, expect to pay 1,900F - 2,300F per week. There are a lot of interesting package offers combining accommodation and pass. Contact the tourist office for more details.

Food

There are lots of cheap places serving traditional French cuisine costs from 65F to 120F for a meal; the restaurant at Hotel de Londres is great bargain. There is a Champion supermarket in town which can save big bucks also on food. In general the prices are comparable with rural France.

Nightlife

For an early evening drink, the Tasca, La Taverne and the Centrale Bar are all sound places for a pint or three. Later in the evening head for the Cocoloco or the Toy Club - both go off with crazy nights. Posters around town inform of one-off parties.

Other activities

Relax in a spa, jaccuzzi, gym, or at a movie.

Thanks to

Sophie Lebalch (tourist office), Loïc Cadiou (Mickey Snowboard).

More Essential Information

Tourist office
Tel: 6295 5071   Fax: 6295 3313

Snowboard shops
Mickey Snowboard   Tel: 6392 9640
Board/ boot hire: 100F/day

Snowboard schools
•Faz Surf Training
Tel: 6238 0916 Fax: 6238 0980
New courses start on Monday mornings.
Cocktail training for beginners, which includes three hours of tuition a day for five days, plus a video, and other material, costs 880F.
Spot surf training for medium to advanced riders, includes five to six hours a day, for five days, which costs 1,540F.

pic: Luz Ardidens Tourist Board

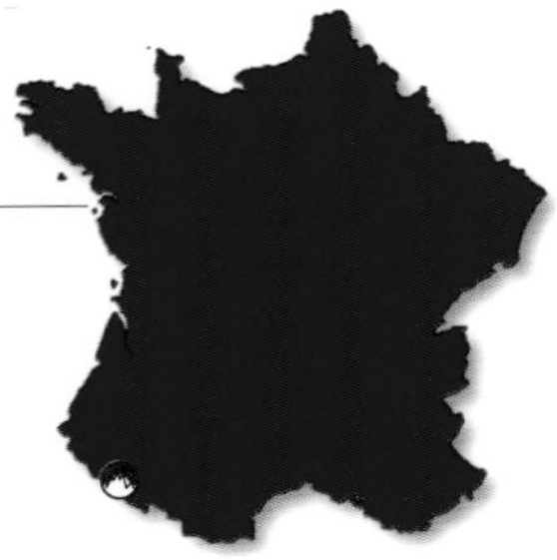

Cauterets

Mountain Information

Mountain chain:

Pyrénées, Bigorre

Vertical rmetre range:

1,400m - 2,400m

Length of season:

late November - early May

Number of lifts:

1 double cable-car, 1 gondola,

6 chairlifts, 12 draglifts.

Snow-making facilities:

There are five snow cannons

covering the lower runs.

Safety:

Most of the avalanche danger is on

the exposed south face, but for up-

to-date information ask at the

guide bureau.

Guides:

Contact the guide bureau

Tel: 6292 5983

Lift passes:

1 day: 115F - 105F

6 days: 690F - 652F

Season: 2,500F

Prices vary from high to

low season.

Nearby resorts:

Pont d'Espagne is a 7km drive from

Cauterets.

CONDITIONS ARE **EXCELLENT** FOR MOST OF THE SEASON, THANKS TO THE RESORT'S PREDOMINANTLY **NORTH-FACING SLOPES**

ON THE MOUNTAIN

Cauterets is one of the best resorts in the French Pyrenees, with the longest season, plus 40kms of piste linked by a fast and efficient lift system.

Snow conditions

Excellent for most of the season thanks to the resort's predominantly north-facing slopes.

Freeriders

There is one major off-piste run, which takes about two hours to complete. It's important to check with the guide bureau before setting off, as most of the faces are exposed to the south. Take the Brèche chairlift and ride down the other side - the first section is steep. Enter the national park (there's a refuge at Les Houlettes) and follow the river bed towards the Courbet car park. Another run is the ridge follows Les Crête, which has many long, wide snowfields waiting to be shredded.

Freestylers

The funpark for tricksters, located at Gentaines, was started two years ago. It has a number of jumps, including fun boxes and table tops located on a beginner's slope. A halfpipe is built during the Pyrenean Snowboard Tour and the Snowboard Test Day (late April).

Carvers

Looking up from the valley, all the chairlifts are on the right side and these are the best slopes for carving due to their steep gradient.

Lifts to avoid

None.

Mountain fare

There is a restaurant at the Lys cable car exit which has a large terrace and serves the usual fare. There is also a bar at the parking lot.

Tourist office

Tel: 6292 5027   Fax: 6292 5912

Snowboard shops

•Skilys Tel: 6292 5210

Board/boot hire: 120F - 150F/day

•Sport Evasion   Tel: 6292 0585

Laurent Descaves Shop Tel: 6292 6248

Board/boot hire: 120F/day

Snowboard schools

•ESF   Tel/Fax: 6292 5506

2 hour group lesson: 90F

•Snowfun

Tel/Fax: 6292 5983 or 6292 0305

2 hour group lesson: 90F

pic: Claude Etchelecou

ABOUT TOWN

Cauterets is the most developed mountain resort in the Pyrenees. Based around a natural spring, which after riding can assist in soothing away the day's aches and pains. It's a popular with the French and Spanish and so can get over-crowded in the holiday season.

Getting there

By plane: The closest international airport is Ossun, from where it is a 35km transfer by bus.

By train: The closest main station, Lourdes SNCF, is a 28km transfer by bus.

By car: Take the A64 and turn off onto the D940 to Lourdes at the Soumoulou exit. Then take the N21 till Argelès Gazost, the D921 to Pierrefitte and finally the D920 to Cauterets.

Accommodation

There are 20,000 tourist beds in Cauterets, so there is a wide variety of choice. Most are two star hotels offering halfboard and are priced from 210F (low season) to 240F (high season). However, there are one star and three star hotels where the prices vary accordingly. For four person apartments expect to pay 1,400F (low season), and 2,000F (high season) for a week. For more information, contact the tourist office.

Food

Cauterets has a number of restaurants (26 in fact!). The cheapest, and most quickly satisfying foods are fast foods, such as crepes, pizzas and burgers.

Nightlife

For a late afternoon drink, or two, the Saint Tropez and the New Pub both have relaxing bars. Dancing goes on at the 'stylish' Casino! Remember to bring your tie and paisley shirt.

Other activities

Pools, ice-rinks, gyms at the major hotels, spas, saunas, parapenting and tennis.

Thanks to

Jean-Pierre Florence (resort director) Christophe Fabre (local snow expert) and Catherine Toureille at the tourist office.

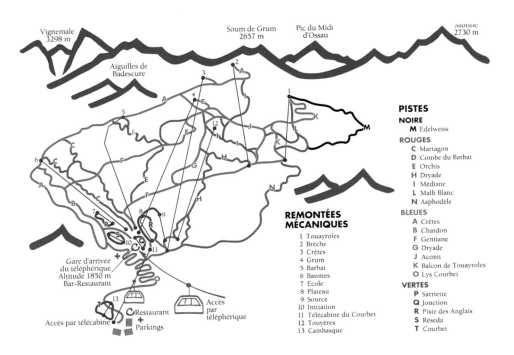

PISTES

NOIRE

   M Edelweiss

ROUGES

   C Martagon
   D Combe du Barbat
   E Orchis
   H Dryade
   I Médiane
   L Malh Blanc
   N Asphodèle

BLEUES

   A Crêtes
   B Chardon
   F Gentiane
   G Dryade
   J Aconit
   K Balcon de Touayroles
   O Lys Courbet

VERTES

   P Sarriette
   Q Jonction
   R Piste des Anglais
   S Réséda
   T Courbet

REMONTÉES MÉCANIQUES

   1 Touayroles
   2 Brèche
   3 Crêtes
   4 Grum
   5 Barbat
   6 Baumes
   7 Ecole
   8 Plateau
   9 Source
   10 Initiation
   11 Télécabine du Courbet
   12 Touyères
   13 Cambasque

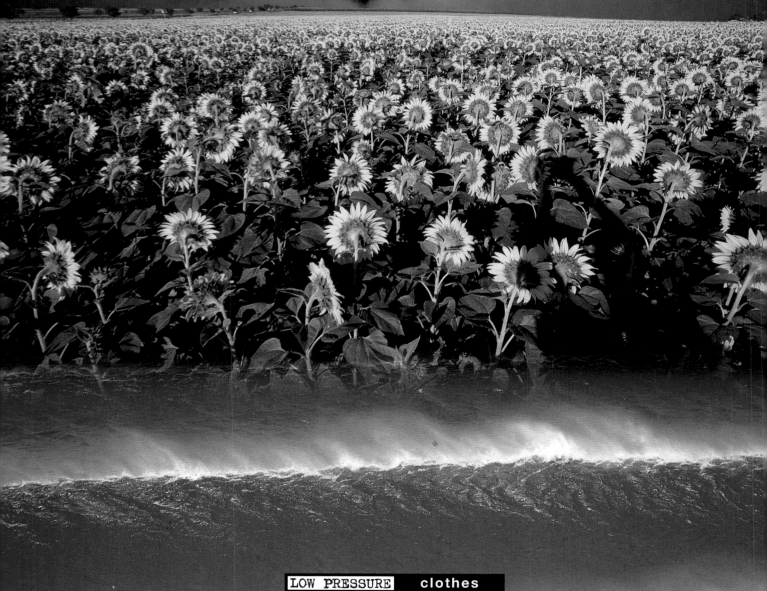

LOW PRESSURE

LOW PRESSURE clothes

Tactel®
Only by DuPont

POLARTEC
Climate Control Fabrics

LP

photos: DAN HAYLOCK
ALEX WILLIAMS

DEALER ENQUIRIES - tel or fax: 0181 960 1916

Spain and Andorra

Astun - Candanchu

Cerler

Baqueira Beret

Andorra - Soldeu

Sierra Nevada

Beret pic: Jakue Andikoetxea

pic: Jakue Andikoetxea

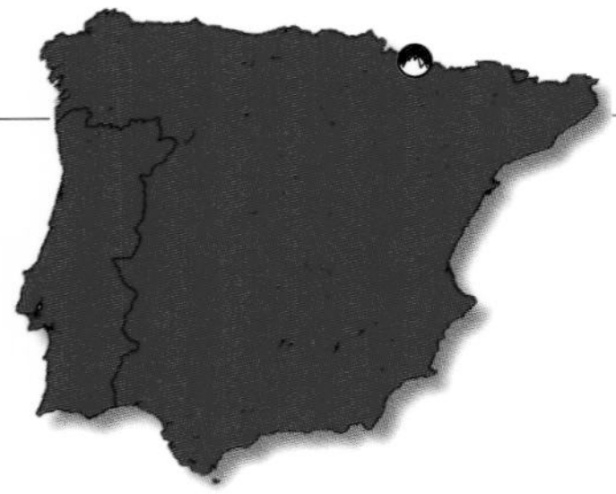

Astun-Candanchu

Mountain Information

Mountain chain:
The Pyrenées
Vertical metre range:
1,560m-2,400m
Length of season:
beginning of December - end of April
Number of lifts:
Astun: 3 chairlifts, 11 draglifts
Candanchu: 5 chairlifts, 19 draglifts
Snow-making facilities:
Astun has 100 cannons, when needed, and Candanchu has 109 cannons, when cover is scant.
Safety:
Check the avalanche indicator boards.
Guides:
Enquire at the ski school.
Lift pass prices:
1 day: 3,200ptas
6 days: 9,000ptas - 14,000ptas
Season: 57,000ptas

ON THE MOUNTAIN

These two resorts, which lie 4kms apart, are the best in the area. Both have extensive north-facing runs and pistes of varying grades. The off-piste possiblities are considerable, particularly after a snowfall - get a local to point out the best spots.

Snow conditions

As most of the main runs are north-facing and the resort is at high altitude, the snow conditions are generally good.

Freeriders

In Candanchu, black run 14 Pinos heads through some trees and is the steepest in the resort, lying just above the village. Runs 26, 27 and 28 in the centre of the ski area are steep - 50 degree slopes - with tight trees. In addition, run 28 has rock jumps. For a day trip, head towards the Cumbre del Aspe (2,500m) or visit the surrounding limestone cliffs.

Freestylers

There is a halfpipe at the bottom of the slalom course, to the east of Candanchu. Plans for a funpark are afoot and, with a little luck, it should be jumping by the '96/'97 season.

Carvers

At Candanchu, the popular snowboarding runs are the Tubo Del Tobazo and the Tubo de la Ollia. In Astun, the Arandaos is recommended for some smooth riding.

Lifts to avoid

There are lots of draglifts, so make sure you build up those thighs before you leave home.

ASTUN-CANDANCHU IS WHERE THE BASQUE SURFERS FIRST BEGAN TO RIDE THE SNOW

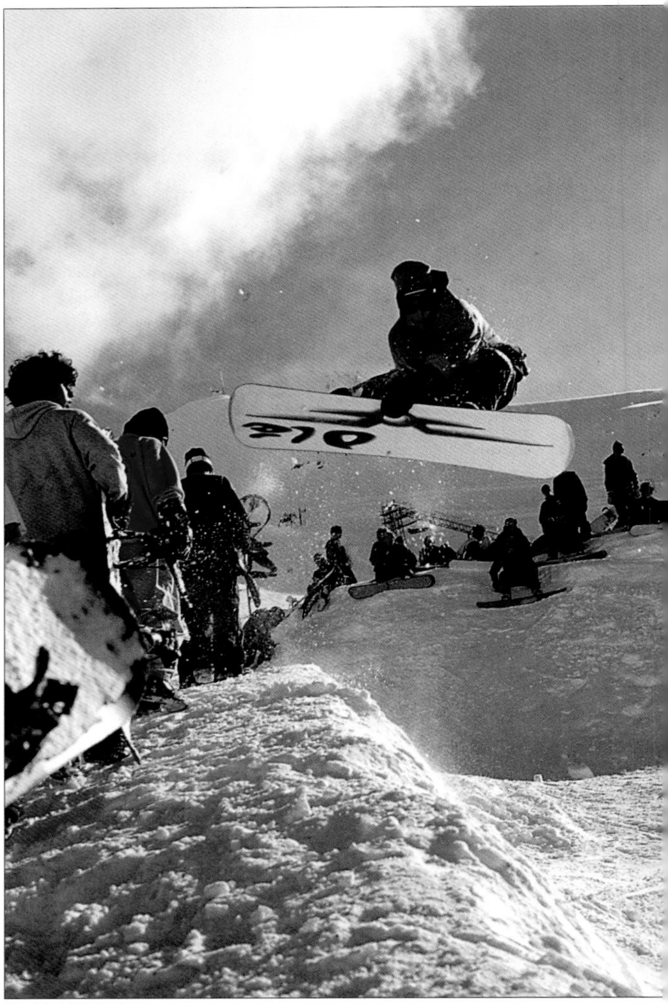

pic: Jakue Andikoetxea

Mountain fare

The mountain has many self-service restaurants.

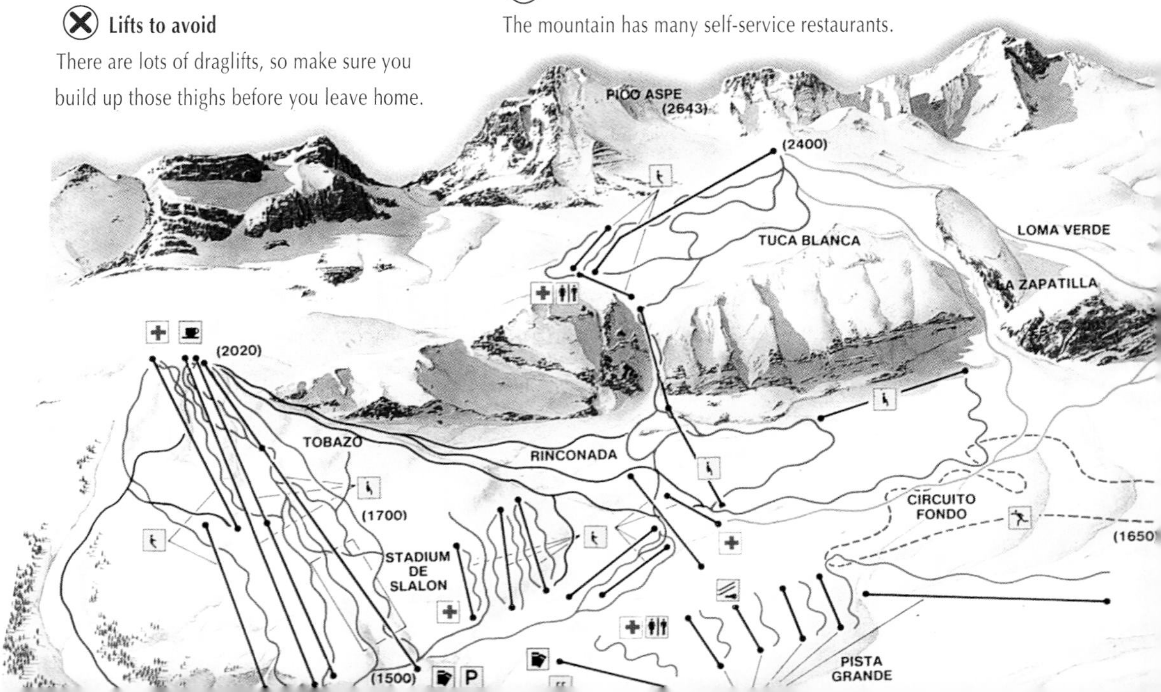

Mundaka - Basque training ground pic: Jakue Andikoetxea

pic: Jakue Andikoetxea

Essential Contacts

Tourist board

Valle de Astun

Tel: 974-373 088 or 974-373 034

Fax: 974-373 295

Local snowboard shops

There are many shops in Astun and Candanchu, many of which offer snowboard hire.

Board hire: 3,000pts/day

Boots hire: 1,000pts/day

Snowboard schools

The Spanish ski school have snowboard lessons on offer.

Price for 1-2 people per hour: 4,000pts

For 5 people: 6,000pts

ABOUT TOWN

Astun-Candanchu is where the Basque surfers first began to ride the snow. Unfortunately the resorts, while functional, are unaesthetic. Astun is the more recent of the two purpose-built resorts, but Candanchu has more facilities on offer.

Getting there

By air: The nearest international airports are in Pamplona and Zaragoza.

By train: From Zaragoza, take a train to Candanchu, from where there is a connecting bus service.

By car: Driving is easy and the roads are clear. It's a 138km drive from Pamplona and just 84kms from Pau in France.

Accommodation

The small resort of Astun offers little variation in accommodation and prices. The most expensive hostelry is the Hotel Europa, at 30,000ptas - 60,000ptas per room (depending on the season) - Tel: 0974-373 312. Cheaper options are apartments for 2 to 5 people: Hoserval has places for two starting

from 24,000ptas and for four from 16,200ptas - Tel: 0974-373 313, while the Atuva has apartments for two people from 25,000ptas and for four people from 15,500ptas - Tel: 0974-372 084.

Candanchu has more variety. We recommend the Hotel Edelweiss, where B&B starts from 14,600ptas and the Arusa - Tel: 0974-373 022.

Food

The eating options are pretty standard. Pizzerias, burger bars and cafés - Astun-Candanchu has them all, although the latter has a better selection. The prices are, in general, reasonable.

Nightlife

Nightlife is pretty much confined to a chin-wag, as the resorts are small, but the cheap Spanish-sized measures are bound to keep you happy and may even kick start you into creating your own party.

Other activities

In Candanchu, there's a sauna and massage. In Cantranc (6kms away), you'll find a sports centre and in Jaka (30kms away), there is another sports complex, with a covered swimming-pool and an ice rink.

Thanks to

Eduardo Boldán at the Candanchu tourist office.

Cerler

pic: Jakue Andikoetxea

 ON THE MOUNTAIN

Cerler, located in the valley of Benasque, a part of the Aragon Pyrenees, is the highest resort in the Pyrenees. Its position offers views of the peaks of Aneto, La Madaleta and El Posets, all of which rise above 3,000m. The area offers a multitude of possibilities. Experimental snowboarders will love the steep slopes and plenty of off-piste areas among pine trees, while beginners will enjoy the gentle slopes of the various pistes.

❄ Snow conditions

As Cerler is predominantly north to north-west facing and is on one of the Pyrenees' highest mountains, it is snow-sure.

 Freeriders

The brave-hearted seeking large surges of adrenaline should visit Gallinero's Canal Radical, an ungroomed piste with the unbeatable combination of steep slopes and smooth wide terrain. Access is via the chair Gallinero (up to 2,630m), from where you need to traverse 800 metres to the "wide canal", otherwise known as the Canal Amplia, and eventually you will reach the solitary Canal Radical, where silence, snow, wind and carving reign supreme. Take a local or a guide from Radical Snowboards, as this place, especially after a big dump, is avalanche prone and dangerous. Always allow the snow, which keeps for several days, settle. In the middle

section of the run, there are endless funnels and Passidizos, from which there are jumps. The last part of the run opens out, giving you time to pick up speed and take air from small rock hits.

 Freestylers

The only features to play on are 100 percent natural.

 Carvers

Plenty of good slopes, especially for beginners.

❌ Lifts to avoid

The draglift Faruserals is not open to snowboarders.

 Mountain fare

There are two reasonable restaurants: the Ampriu, where meals range from 1,000ptas to 1,500pts, and the Cota 2000, where meals cost from 1,500ptas.

Mountain Information

Mountain chain:

Upper Aragonese Pyrenees

Vertical metre range:

1,500m - 2,630m

Length of season:

beginning of December -
end of April

Number of lifts:

6 chairlifts, 7 draglifts

Snow-making facilities:

84 snow cannons service a wide area, when needed.

Safety:

There are avalanche indicator boards at all information and meeting points.

Snow report information:

Tel: 0974-551 111

Guides:

For more information, contact Casa de la Montana -
Tel: 0974- 552 094
or Compania de Guias de Benasque -
Tel: 974-551 351.

Lift pass prices

1 day: 2,300ptas - 2,800ptas
6 days: 13,500ptas - 15,000ptas
Season: 52,000ptas

Rider Robert Jofre pic: Jakue Andikoetxea

Essential Contacts

Tourist office

Benasque Tel: 0974-552 280/551 280

Cerler Tel: 0974-551 012

Snowboard shops

•Radical Snowboard   Tel: 0974-551 433

The staff know the resort like the back

of their hands.

Board hire: 2,300ptas/day

Boot hire: 800ptas/day

Snowboard schools

•Radical snowboard   Tel: 0974-551 433

1-2 persons: 3,500ptas/1 hour

1-2 persons: 5,500ptas/2 hours

Check out the special weekend deals,

including lift passes, half-board

accommodation and equipment hire,

from 19,000ptas.

 ABOUT TOWN

A short bus ride down the valley from Cerler is the old village of Benasque, which - with a population of only 1,000 inhabitants or so - has managed to maintain the original, quaint charm that is typical of the Spanish Pyrenees. Cerler is its rather unattractive, purpose-built sister, but it is closer to the mountain.

 Getting there

By air: The closest international airports are in Zaragoza and Barcelona.

By train: The closest station is Monzon, from where the resort is a 100km bus ride - Tel: 0973-5540 1244 for more information. Otherwise there are bus connections from all the main cities to Benasque - Tel: 0974-210 700 for details.

By car: From Barcelona, take the motorway to Lleide, then the N-240 to Huesia, the C-138 till Barbastro and the C-139 to Cerler.

Accommodation

There are a wide variety of options. The cheapest option is to hire a self-catering apartment; from 2,500ptas per person per day - Tel: 0974-551 124.

Alternatively, a room at the Casa Horgodo in Cerler costs 3,000ptas - Tel: 0974-551 067 and half-board at the Hotel Edelweiss (also in Cerler) starts at 4,000ptas per person, per day- Tel: 974-551 242.

Food

There is a wide range of supermarkets and restaurants, the most popular of which are La Borda del Martin and La Picada in Cerler.

Nightlife

In Cerler, in the afternoon, drink yourself silly on beer at La Cabana - half a litre only costs 200ptas, while a third of a litre sells for 165ptas. Later in the evening, go to Pub Paralelo, where beers will set you back 250-300ptas. In Benasque, La Nite has similar prices to Pub Paralelo, and both attract riders, who watch the snowboarding videos on show. For a change of scene, try Casa Porta and El Rincon.

Other activities

Parapenting, trekking, cycling and Nordic skiing.

Thanks to

Jordi Casas at Radical Snowboard and Ana Ventura at the tourist office.

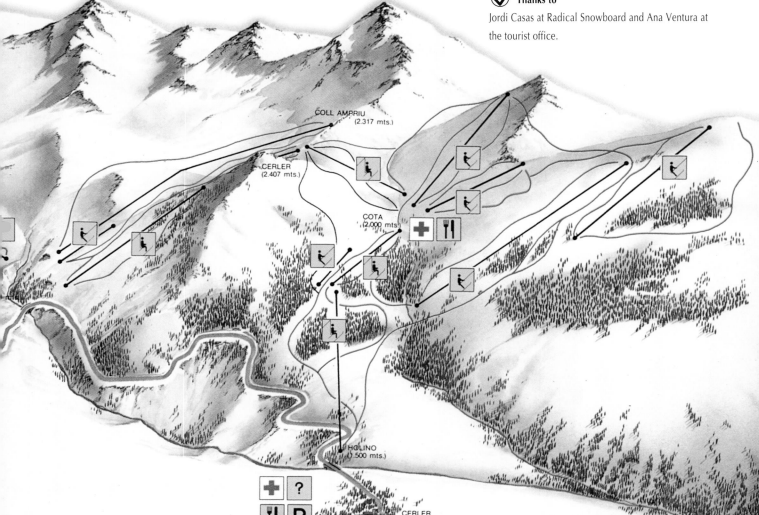

Baqueira Beret

Rider Luc Navarro pic: Jakue Andikoetxea

Mountain Information

Mountain chain:

The Pyrenees

Vertical metre range:

1,500m - 2,656m

Length of season:

beginning of December -
end of April

Number of lifts:

20 chairlifts, 8 draglifts

Snow-making facilities:

There are 244 snow cannons
covering an extensive area,
when needed.

Safety:

Check with the tourist office.

Snow information:

Tel: 0973-645 062/052.

Guides:

The Isuala Snowboard School and
Shop (see opposite page) can
provide mountain guides.
Otherwise, contact the tourist
office.
Isuala also organises freeriding
and heliboarding trips. Prices range
from 15,000ptas to 30,000ptas
per day.

Lift pass prices:

1 day: 3,900ptas
6 days: 20,100ptas
Season: 88,000ptas

ON THE MOUNTAIN

Baqueira Beret, developed by Luis Arias (who was Spanish national ski champion 24 times) is the biggest and best resort in the Spanish Pyrenees. A well-thought out area, which is large enough to get lost in, it has an efficient lift system and a snowboard friendly atmosphere. What's more, it offers conditions to suit all levels of snowboarders. There are three different sections: the main Baqueira area has beginner runs and north-facing slopes for experienced riders; Bonaigua-Argulls has substantial off-piste for intermediates and advanced riders; and the Beret area is where the halfpipe is located.

Snow conditions

The riding is mainly above 1,800m and the mountain's orientation is mostly north-facing, so snow cover is reliable.

Freeriders

La Bonaigua, where rivers have created great gullies, is the best freeriding area. For rock jumps and extreme riding, the left side of the Chozas lift is a great place to go, but watch out for the avalanche risk. Beret is the best area for beginners, because it tends to be less crowded and there are wide runs.

Freestylers

The halfpipe is located near the stadium in Beret, but is only maintained for competitions. However, the resort hopes it will be open throughout the season soon.

Carvers

Carvers can get their edges slicing a number of pistes.

Lifts to avoid

The Luis Arias drag is fast and difficult for boarders.

Mountain fare

There are a number of standard mountain cafés serving cheap Spanish fare.

La Bonaigua pic: Jakue Andikoetxea

Essential Contacts

Tourist office

Tel: 0973-644 455   Fax: 0973-644 488

Snowboard shops

• Mombi Surf   Tel: 0973-645 081

Board/boot hire: 2,900ptas/day

Board/boot hire: 12,000ptas/week

Snowboard schools

• Escuela de Snowboard Val D'Aran

Tel: 0973-645 126   Fax: 0973-644 154

• Isuala Snowboard School and Shop

Tel: 0973-644 022   Fax: 0973-644 039

Lessons: 4,300ptas/hour

ABOUT TOWN

Baqueira is a large, purpose-built resort, which is very popular with the French and the Spanish Royal family, who usually spend their winter holidays in the resort. The route to the resort winds through some stunning mountain scenery, with huge drops on either side of the road and sheer cliff faces up above.

Getting there

By air: The closest airport is Toulouse, 160kms away by bus or train transfer.

By train: From Toulouse, there is a train direct to Montrejeaur, from there a taxi is the best option.

By car: From Barcelona, it's a 330km hike through Lerida, up the scenic Valle de Aran to Baqueira Beret.

Accommodation

There are a number of options, many of which are part of a package deal. For example, the Hotel Montarto offers seven nights and a six day ski pass for 55,700ptas to 71,500pts (depending on the season) - Tel: 0973-644 444. The price of a self-catering apartment for six people for a week, including a lift pass, is 30,400ptas to 42,000 ptas - Tel: 973-644 353.

Food

More than 50 restaurants offer a huge variety of choices. The cheapest are the creperies and pizzerias, but there is local cuisine in abundance including Aranes, Catalan, Basque and French - prices per meal vary from 1,000ptas to 6,000ptas. For self-caterers, there is a supermarket.

Nightlife

There are various pubs and a couple of lively discos. Snowboarders tend to start at the Lobos Pub, which is open till 1.00am, and then move on to Tiffany's, which closes at 5.00am.

Other activities

Ask at the tourist office for information on the tennis courts, swimming-pools and horse-riding.

Thanks to

Roberto Buil, Mombi Surf and the tourist office.

DEVELOPED BY LUIS ARIAS, IT'S THE **BIGGEST** RESORT IN THE SPANISH PYRENEES

pic: Jakue Andikoetxea

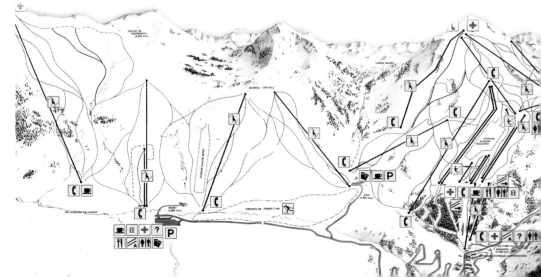

Andorra - Soldeu

Mountain Information

Mountain chain:

Pyrenees

Vertical metre range:

1,710 m - 2,650 m

Length of season:

December - April

Number of lifts:

1 telecabin, 10 chairlifts,

14 draglifts

Snow-making facilities:

There are 241 snow cannons

covering an extensive area.

Safety:

There are avalanche indicator

boards near the main station.

Guides:

Contact the ski school, where most

of the instructors double up as

guides - Tel: 851 269.

Lift pass prices

1 day: 3,000ptas -3,500ptas

6 days: 2,100ptas - 2,600ptas

Season: 57,000ptas

Lift pass alternatives:

There is a joint pass with Pas

available.

THE MOUNTAIN

Soldeu El Tarter, with its large, varied terrain, is well noted for its sunshine hours and snowfall. From the town of Soldeu, the resort is reached by crossing an Indiana Jones style foot bridge over a canyon, which leads to a double chair and draglift. It's worth noting that riders are not allowed to use the drag due to archaic rules still in force in Andorra. If there is a long queue for the chairlift (which there tends to be around midday), it's worth walking up the piste for 100m and taking the cat track down to El Tarter, from where there are two high speed chairlifts.

Snow conditions

Andorra had more snow than any other area in Europe in the '95/'96 season, which - along with the fact that most of the resort is north-facing - means that snow conditions tend to be reliable.

Freeriders

Take the quad chair from El Tarter, followed by the quad chair up to the top. Facing downhill, traverse left from the exit, continue past the piste boundaries and you'll one of the steepest areas in Soldeu, which is littered with cornices to drop and steep slopes to get your legs working - straight-line it right on to the piste. Once on the piste, take the entrance into the next gully and ride the banks all the way

back to the second chairlift.

Alternatively, from Soldeu's rickety chair, walk left and back on yourself, then pick a couloir and ride it! None of the couloirs ends in cliffs, so grab some friends and ride one each. At the end, keep on traversing right until you hit a piste. The pistes all converge into one large cat track that snakes back to the lift or go off-piste for some great untouched bits.

Freestylers

There is no official halfpipe, but the natural halfpipe under the Planell chairlift does the job just as well. In the El Tarter area, there is a funpark that is serviced by its own lift. A minipark sponsored by Red Bull should be up and running by February 1997, but if it's delayed, just jump the hundreds of cat tracks that traverse the mountain.

Carvers

Carve at full speed on the gentle slopes, which are perfect for beginners. All the pistes coming off the chairlift Planell-gran are recommended.

Lifts to avoid

None.

Mountain fare

There are two mountain restaurants serving cheap - a tenth of the price of Alpine resorts - international snacks and sandwiches. Try the restaurant at the top of Soldeu's two man chair as it serves the best hot chocolate (with whipped cream) in the world!

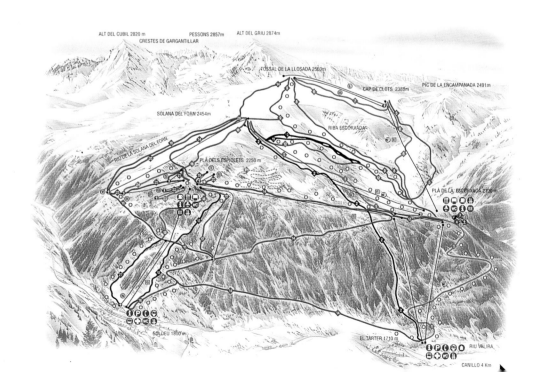

⌂ ABOUT TOWN

Soldeu is a small purpose-built resort that is better known for being functional, than aesthetically appealing. However, it's a great place to indulge in the Andorran habits of eating and drinking yourself stupid at night. Most of the bars are along the main high road, which runs parallel to the main street, and are ridiculously cheap as Andorra is a duty free zone - 'jus' like Blackpool but wi' snow 'n all.'

→ Getting there

By air: The nearest international airports are Barcelona, a 170km transfer away, and Toulouse, a 225km transfer away.
By train: Contact the tourist office for details.
By car: From Toulouse, take the N-20 to Ax - Les Thermes and keep on heading for Andorra, through Port d'Envalira. From Barcelona, take the A-18 to Manresa and then the B-1411 through the Tunel del Cadi.

⌂ Accommodation

Contact the tourist office for details or ask your local tour operator about cheap package deals.

🍴 Food

There are several restaurants and bars where you can eat from 2,000ptas to 6,000ptas. Our hot tip: the Underground where there are cheap pizzas, fat burgers, satellite TV stations, English waitresses and punk posters on the wall.

×× Nightlife

The drinking starts at happy hour in any one of the hotel bars, although the Aspen is the chosen hang-out for most riders and is a good place to meet local headcases. Also, go see Paul Coleman - a multilingual, seasoned veteran of the British Championships - who can be found in the Naudi bar every evening as he's the barman.
The one true nightclub in Soldeu has closed, but the Z-Bar and the Pussycat are both open till late. There are also weekly excursions to the Pas de la Casa Casion, a dodgy Spanish karaoke bar, and many organised Butlin style activities - be careful not to stumble in on a bingo night at one of the nightclubs!

Rider Ali Ashworth pic: Pete Webb

Other activities

At different times in the season, Soldeu has snow-biking events, carnivals and music concerts on its slopes. Both Hotel Lop Gris and Guilles have swimming-pools and gyms.

Thanks to

Marc Canavaopla, sales manager at Soldeu El Tarter, and Chris Moran.

Essential Contacts

Tourist office
Tel: 851 151 Fax: 881 337
Snowboard shops
• Pic Nagre Tel: 851 441
• Aspen Sport Tel: 851 580
• Calvo Tel: 851 251
Board/boot hire: 2,500ptas/day
Snowboard schools
• Soldeu El Tarter School
Tel: 851 269/852 752.
1 person: 3,600ptas/hour

Sierra Nevada

Mountain chain:

Sierra Nevada Penibetico

Vertical metre range:

2,100m - 3,300m

Length of season:

December - April

Number of lifts:

12 chairlifts, 5 draglifts,

2 telecabins

Snow-making facilities:

187 high pressure and 13 low

pressure cannons cover 20kms

of piste.

Safety:

Ask at the local tourist office.

Guides:

Ask at the local tourist office.

Lift pass prices:

1 day: 2,300ptas - 3,150ptas

6 days: 13,960ptas - 16,000ptas

Season: 57,000ptas

 ON THE MOUNTAIN

The mountain has pistes for all levels, but, in particular, has lots of high quality runs with good bowl sections. One of its main advantages is its open spaces - there's an infinite amount of off-piste riding with plenty of cliffs to suit all tastes. Another major plus is the Mediterranean climate, which means many days of T-shirt riding and clear panoramic views.

Snow conditions

Due to the winds, cold night temperatures and a lack of rain, the snow pack is often quite hard. As a result, lots of the locals tend to switch from soft to hard boot riding.

Freeriders

There are six off-piste runs, which are marked on the piste map. The best are the Barranco de San Juan, which is in the Valle de San Juan, and Tajos de la Virgen, located on the edges of Laguna de las Yeguas.

 Freestylers

There are only, for the moment, natural features - the resort has plans in the pipe-line!

 Carvers

All the black pistes have mad, fast runs.

 Lifts to avoid

None, although they are all cold on a windy day.

 Mountain fare

There are a number of cheap eats on the mountain - don't forget to try the local paella.

pic: Tim Rainger

THE MEDITERRANEAN CLIMATE MEANS MANY DAYS OF T-SHIRT RIDING AND CLEAR PANORAMIC VIEWS

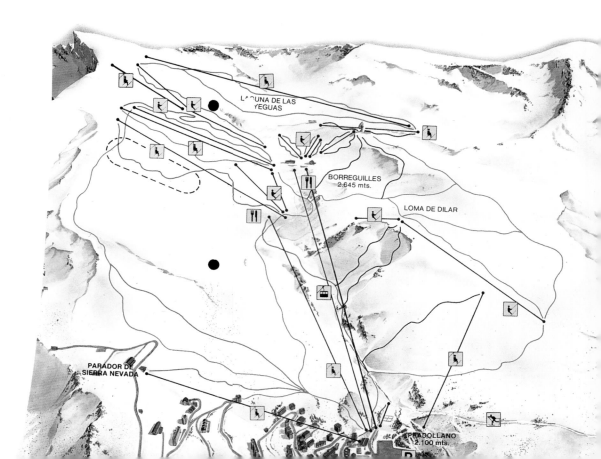

LAGUNA DE LAS YEGUAS

BORREGUILLES 2.645 mts.

LOMA DE DILAR

PARADOR DE SIERRA NEVADA

PRADOLLANO 2.100 mts.

ABOUT TOWN

Pradollano, the name of the resort town, is a fair size and is reasonably attractive. It has everything you need, and the general atmosphere is relaxed and friendly.

Getting there

By air: Granada a is the closest airport, 32kms away by bus or train. A taxi from the airport to the resort will cost you around 5,000ptas.

By train: For information on the trains - Tel: 0958-271 272.

By car: From Madrid, take the N-IV to Granada and then follow the local roads to Sierra Nevada. From Sevilla, take the A-92 motorway to Granada and then the N-346 to Malaga.

Accommodation

There are lots of options - contact the tourist office early and you may be able to make huge savings on week-long apartment stays.

 Eating

There are heaps of restaurants serving traditional Spanish and Andalucian cooking, as well as French, Swiss, Italian and Mexican dishes. Other options are the tea rooms, crêperies, croissant shops and supermarkets.

pic: Jakue Andikoetxea

Nightlife

There are a number of tapas bars serving cheap beer. But with some of the world's most sophisticated night-riding on offer, who needs to drink?

Other activities

The Trevenque Sport Club has a gym, indoor soccer, volley-ball, basketball, table tennis, massage rooms, saunas, Turkish baths, jacuzzi and an indoor swimming-pool.

Essential Contacts

Tourist office
Tel: 0958-249 100/111/119

Snowboard shops
Most of the ski shops hire out snowboarding equipment.

pic: J, Karm

Scottish Highlands

Glencoe 200
Nevis 202
Cairngorms 204
The Lecht 206
Glenshee 208

Country Information

Capital: Edinburgh

Population: 5,090,000

Time: GMT

Language: English, Gaelic

Currency: English, Scottish Pounds

Telephone Information:

ISD Code: 44

Operator: 100

International operator: 155

Directory Enquiries: 192

Int directory enquiries: 153

Emergancy Services: 999

Tourist Board Details:

Scottish Tourist Board:

23 Ravelston Terrace

Edinburgh. EH4 3EU

Tel: 0131-332 2433

Major airports:

Glasgow: 0141-887 1111

Aberdeen: 01224-722 331

Edinburgh: 0131-333 1000

Information: The cheapest way to get up to
Scotland from London is to catch an Easyjet
flight which goes from as little as £24.00
return. You can then catch a National Express
bus on to the resort of your choice.

Bus: National Express:

London: Tel: 0171-730 0202

Birmingham Tel: 0121-622 4373

Manchester Tel: 0161-228 3881

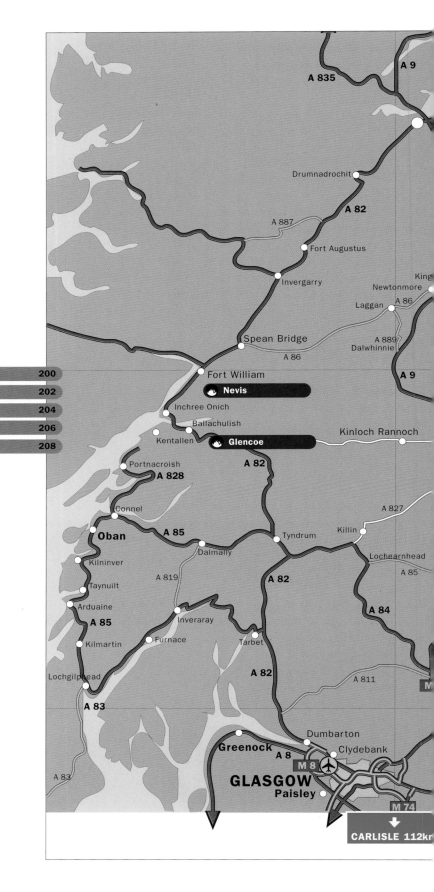

Further Information

Weather Reports
BBC1 Daily at 13.25, 18.25, 21.25
BBC1 Weekly forcast at Sunday
lunchtime
Newspapers: the Independent, the
Times & Sunday times have good
meterological maps.
The Met Office -
METFAX 0336-400 444
Met Office Helpline:
Tel: 01344-854 435
Calls are charged at 39p/min
cheaprate, 49p/min at all other
times.

What's On T.V.?
Sunday 1pm, Channel Four:
Board Stupid
National Snowboard Magazines
Snowboard UK. (SUK), White Lines,
Onboard, Fall Line
National Snowboard Associations:
British Snowboard Association:
Contact: Steve Davis
Tel: 01494-884 407
For up-to-date information about
what's going on in Britain.
**British Association of
Snowsports Instructors (B.A.S.I)**
Tel: 01479-810 407
For all information about teaching
and instruction.

kaipo jaquias

pic: Tim Rainger

Glencoe pic: Andy Shaw

Glencoe

Mountain Information

Mountain chain:

Meall A'Bhueridh

Vertical metre range:

310m - 1,110m

Length of season:

mid-December - early May

Number of lifts:

2 chairlifts, 4 draglifts,

1 trainer tow

Snow-making facilities:

None.

Safety:

Ask the piste patrol for daily

information on snow conditions.

Guides:

Not necessary.

Lift pass prices:

1 day: £9.00

6 days: £14.50

Season: £165.00

Lift pass alternatives:

Before November 1, a joint season

pass with Glenshee is available

(£225.00). Before December 31,

there is a special 'any 5 day' pass,

which gives you access to both

Glencoe and Glenshee (£60.00).

 ON THE MOUNTAIN

In terms of tows and facilities, Glencoe is tiny, so faces become familiar after only a day or two, leading to a congenial rapport among riders. That said, the mountain has some of the gnarliest terrain in Scotland and, on a clear day, the view from the top is stunning. However, mist can sometimes cause 'white-mares' - seek local advice in these conditions.

 Snow conditions

Due to its proximity to the west coast, the temperature and wind, and thus the conditions, can bounce up and down as fast as a yo-yo. Depending on the recent wind direction, a combination of ice and deep powder often prevails.

 Freeriders

Much of the terrain changes dramatically, even during the season, so although certain areas are recommended, general hits and rollers are better assessed first-hand. The Canyon has a natural pipe. The steep and exhilarating Fly Paper, with hits and gullies, has to be tried for its incredible off-piste. Off Thrombosis, there are windlips and another pipe. If it's a great gully jump you're after, try the Haggis Trap.

 Freestylers

Resort manager Peter Weir is a master-moulder, treating the piste like putty. If you want something, just ask for it!

 Carvers

For fast, pisted runs, carve the Main Basin, Happy Valley, Etive Glades, Mugs Alley and the Rannoch Glades.

(X) **Lifts to avoid**

Learners should avoid the top tows and the Wall T-bar.

Mountain fare

The Plateau Café is cheap and cheerful - we recommend their hearty, cockle-warming soups.

SOME OF THE GNARLIEST TERRAIN IN SCOTLAND AND, ON A CLEAR DAY, THE VIEW FROM THE TOP IS STUNNING

pic: Andy Shaw

Essential Contacts

Tourist office

Tel: 01397-703 781   Fax: 01397-705 184

Snowboard shops

•The Clan

Tel: 0141-339 6523

Board/boot hire: £15.00/day

A friendly specialist shop in Glasgow, which offers waxing advice and other services.

•Glencoe Ski Centre

Tel: 01855-851 226

Bard/boot hire: £17.00/day

•Mountain Madness

Tel: 01855-821 500

Snowboard schools

•Glencoe Snowboard Academy

Tel: 01855-851 226

Instruction at weekends: £10.00/day

pic: Tim Rainger

Gromms pic: Tim Rainger

🏠 ABOUT TOWN

Glencoe is in the heart of the Highlands and the scenery is spectacular. The villages of Glencoe, Ballachulish and Onich are closest to the resort, and offer an adequate array of facilities.

→ Getting there

By plane: Glasgow is the closest airport, a 200km train or bus transfer away.

By train: The nearest station is Fort William, from where there are bus connections.

By car: Take the A82 from Fort William to Glencoe.

🏠 Accommodation

The King's House Hotel has everything - a bar, food, beds and proximity (it's just a kilometre to Glencoe) - Tel: 01855-851 259. There is also a youth hostel, and a number of cheap B&Bs and hotels located in Glencoe village -Tel: 01855-811 303.

🍴 Food

All the hotels have restaurants with varied menus serving international and traditional Scottish food. The Clachaig Inn and Four Seasons (Inchree) serve cheap, solid pub food.

(x x) Nightlife

Sink a sumptuous pint at the Clachaig Inn. It's won an award for its real ales and has a roaring beer festival in March to celebrate the bevvy's virtues. The Four Seasons Pub is a relaxing place for a pint.

Other activities

Walking or whiskies - take your pick!

✓ Thanks to

Mark McLetchie, Gareth Lee and Jeff Fraser.

BE AWARE – SKI WITH CARE!

Welcome to our ski facilities. Help keep skiing fun for yourself and others, follow the FIS skier's code.

F.I.S. CODE OF CONDUCT

Respect for others - A skier must behave in such a way that he does not endanger or prejudice others.

Control of speed and skiing - A skier must be in control. He must adapt his speed and manner of skiing to his personal ability and to the prevailing conditions of terrain, snow and weather as well as to the density of traffic.

Choice of route - A skier coming from behind must choose his route in such a way that he does not endanger skiers ahead.

Overtaking - A skier may overtake another, above or below and to the right or to the left provided that he leaves enough space for the overtaken skier to make any voluntary or involuntary movement.

Entering and starting - A skier entering a marked run or starting again after stopping must look up and down the run to make sure that he can do so without endangering himself or others.

Stopping on the piste - Unless absolutely necessary, a skier must avoid stopping on the piste in narrow places or where visibility is restricted. After a fall in such a place, a skier must move clear of the piste as soon as possible.

Climbing and descending on foot - whether climbing or descending on foot a skier must keep to the side of the piste.

Respect for signs and markings - A skier must respect all signs and markings.

Assistance - At accidents, every skier is duty bound to assist.

Identification - Every skier and witness, whether a responsible party or not, must exchange names and addresses following an accident.

GLENCOE SKI CENTRE

MEALL A'BHÙIRIDH 3636 FT.

LIMIT OF SKI PATROLLED AREA

• Plateau Cafe

Licensed Log Cabin Restaurant

GLENCOE

The access lift takes you to the start of the plateau tow which offers access to the best nursery areas in Scotland. From here the real pleasures of Glencoe begin.

The Main Basin is the most popular run, and from the top, the entire mountain is at your feet.

Go left for challenging blue runs, right for stiffer red runs and the steep black Fly Paper. Cruise the Rannoch Glades, shoot the Spring Run, meander down Mugs Alley or take a tour of Etive Glades. There is something for every standard of skier.

LIFTS

A. Access Chair
B. Plateau Tow
C. Cliffhanger Chair
D. Lower T-Bar Tow
E. Top Button Tow
F. Top T-Bar Tow
G. Beginners Lift

SKI RUNS

1. Plateau
2. Mugs Alley
3. Thrombosis
4. Canyon
5. The Wall
6. Etive Glades
7. Happy Valley
8. Main Basin
9. Rannoch Glades
10. Spring Run

■ EXPERT
■ EXPERT - INTERMEDIATE
■ INTERMEDIATE

Nevis Range

Mountain chain:

Aonach Mor

Vertical metre range:

650m - 1,221m

Length of season:

end of December -

beginning of May

Number of lifts:

1 gondola, 3 chairlifts, 3 T-bars,

4 buttons, 1 trainer tow

Snow-making facilities:

None.

Safety:

Avalanche indicator boards at the

base station, the top gondola

station and at the summit of the

hill. Information and advice from

the ski patrol.

Guides:

Contact the tourist office.

Lift pass prices:

1 day: £17.00

6 days: £75.00

Season: £230.00,

(after November 1).

 ON THE MOUNTAIN

As Nevis Range includes Britain's eighth highest peak, Aonach Mor (4,006ft), the resort has the most reliable snow cover in Scotland, with frequent powder days. Beginners are well-catered for with several lifts and flat areas, while intermediate to advanced riders enjoy some excellent, and extreme, off-piste terrain.

 Snow conditions

Nevis Range is located in the Western Highlands. It therefore cops much of the wind and weather that lashes in from the North Atlantic. In spring, when the weather settles, the low pressure systems bring snow which can be as good as anywhere in the Alps.

Freeriders

Most freeriders at Nevis Range can be found 'off the back' in Coire Dubh, where extreme boarders will enjoy (the ironically named) Easy Gully and Summit Gully. For cornices and excellent drop-offs of up to 12 to 15 metres, head to Chancer, Easy Gully and Yellow Belly. The Nid Wall and the lower Nid area can provide some great steeps, with a natural halfpipe nicknamed the Gun Barrel. With good cover, the far west of the Goose Lift can provide eye-stinging powder runs with frequent outcrops for hits and ollies. Warren's Lift also has great freeriding.

Freestylers

A natural halfpipe forms seasonally in the Allt Sneachda run on the bottom half of the Goose Chair. Along with the Goose Gully, it is usually the longest lasting run and can be a good spring area right up till mid-May. To the right of the Goose T-bar, there's a funpark, which usually contains a gap jump, log and rail slides, table tops, quarterpipes and obstacles, such as barrels and picnic tables.

Carvers

The Goose Chair, the Goose T-bar and the Summit Run all provide scope for great carving. The Summit Run, the Sidewinder and the Fairway are a good combination, but it's a two kilometre long leg-burner.

Mountain Fare

The Snowgoose Restaurant & Bar is the main place for a sit-down-leg-rest. There are also two huts for refreshment stops at the Goose and Rob Roy T-bars.

Loch Lomand pic: Andy Shaw

Rider Frazer Duthie pic: ESP

ABOUT TOWN

Although there is accommodation closer to the mountain, Fort William (a 15 minute drive from the Nevis Range) is the best place to stay. The setting is fantastic, with the town located in the nook of the beautiful Loch Linnhe, while Britain's highest peak, Ben Nevis, towers in the distance. Visitors will not want for a thing, because the town has a full set of amenities and a lively nightlife - have a Highland fling in true tartan style!

Getting there

By plane: The nearest airports are Glasgow (a two hour transfer away) and Inverness (a 1.5 hour transfer away). There are bus and train links direct to Fort William from both.

By train: There is an overnight sleeper service from London to Fort William.

By car: From Glasgow, head straight along the A82.

Accommodation

Fort William offers a range of places to stay. Traditional B&Bs start from as low as £12.00 a night. Alternatively, hire a self-catering unit with beds for six people for £300.00 a week. For more information - Tel: 01397-703 781.

Food

There are a number of fast food outlets in Fort WIlliam serving fish and chips, pizzas and burgers, including the omnipresent MacDonalds. For a satisfying sit-down bar meal, the Nevisport Bar and the Grog & Gruel have reasonably priced fare. For delicious fresh, locally caught fish, try the Crannog by the pier.

Nightlife

The Nevisport Bar is a great place to unwind after a hard day's riding. Otherwise, try the whiskies at the Crofters and The Jack. For a late night jig, local discos such as the Waterfront, McTavish's and Malborough's have pumping, loud music.

Other activities

The Lochaber Leisure Centre in Fort William has a swimming-pool, a sauna, a gym, squash courts and a climbing wall. For tenpin bowling, snooker and five aside football, head for Marco's

at An Aird. In addition, there are the Ben Nevis Distillery Visitor Centre, a cinema and regular exhibitions. Mountain bikes can be hired all year round.

Thanks to

All the staff at Nevis Range.

'If ye cannay reed in Scotland, then ye cannay reed a' aa.'

THE SETTING IS FANTASTIC, WITH THE TOWN LOCATED IN THE NOOK OF THE BEAUTIFUL LOCH LINNHE, WHILE BRITAIN'S HIGHEST PEAK, BEN NEVIS, TOWERS IN THE DISTANCE

Essential Contacts

Tourist office

Tel: 01397-703 781   Fax: 01397-705 184

Snowboard shops

•Shred Shed (at the base station of Aonach Mor)

Tel: 01397-705 825

Board/boot hire: £15.50/day

•Boardwise   Tel: 01397-706 098

Board/boot hire: £15.00/day

•Mountain Madness (at Onich)

Tel/Fax: 01855-821 500

Board hire: £12.00/day

•Nevisport   Tel: 01397-704 921

Board hire: £12/day

•Ellis Brigham   Tel: 01397-706 220

Board hire: £12/day

Snowboard schools

•Nevis Range

Tel: 01397-703 781   Fax: 01397-705 184

2 hours of instruction: £9.00

4 hours of instruction: £14.00

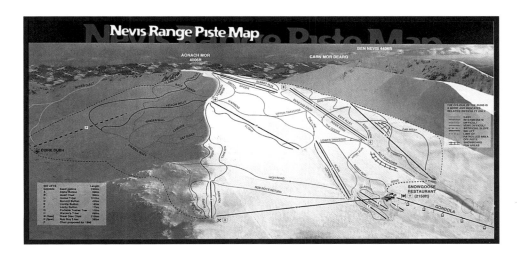

Nevis Range Piste Map

Cairngorms

Mountain Information

Mountain chain:

Cairngorms

Vertical metre range:

545m - 1,091m

Length of season:

December - early May

Number of lifts:

4 double chairs, 6 T-bars, 7 pomas

Snow-making facilities:

None.

Safety:

Information from the ticket office,
the ski patrol or daily reports on
Radio-ski 96.6FM.

Guides:

Boardwise prices range from
£15.00 to £30.00

Tel: 01479-810 336

Lift pass prices:

1 day: £17.00

6 days: £76.50

Season: £230.00

 ON THE MOUNTAIN

Cairngorm is a progressive snowboarding resort. The area piste map has a user-friendly Ride Guide, which details the location of everything from freestyle jumps to steeps and recommends freeride areas. From late February, when spring conditions soften the snow, the area, although small, is comparable to anything in the Alps. In the summer, Aviemore (the closest village) is also a dry slope Mecca for riders.

✳ Snow conditions

Conditions can be harsh in December and January, when it's often icy and the weather changeable. The best months are February, March and April extending, in a good season, into late May with the help of some spring snow showers. As in all the Scottish resorts, conditions can be changeable.

Freeriders

The Head Wall offers a large cornice drop, with a lovely bowl and run out back to the Coire Cas T-bar. The West and East Walls have steep runs leading back to the piste runs. Corrie Laogh Mor (the bowl behind Corrie Na Ciste) is accessible from the traverse that accesses the East Wall and will take you all the way back to the Ciste car park. For the more extreme, there is Corrie ant Sneachda, which has serious cornices and chutes. One in particular, Aladdins Couloir, is for experts only - guides and avalanches are prescribed. Lurcher's is the next gully along and is a nice long powder run. Both runs end at Sludge Gully, where cornices and a quarterpipes can be found by those who don't mind the hike out. The traverse from the M1 to the Cas offers great drop-offs right along its length, leading to the excellent 105 run. This also has good drop-offs along its length, but you'll have to ollie the fences. A large quarterpipe also forms at the top of 105, but usually only at the beginning of the season. There are no tree runs and cliff drops are very rare, but can form on the east-facing slopes, next to the White Lady or the Corrie na Ciste. None of the features mentioned above is permanent - they form according to wind direction and snow.

Middle station at Cairngorms pic: Andy Shaw

Freestylers

There is a funpark that is maintained all season, snow conditions permitting. Two boardercross courses are built, and maintained throughout March and April.

Carvers

The best places to carve are the Coire Cas, the Ptarmigan Bowl, the Ciste run and the Ciste No.1 Gully.

✗ Lifts to avoid

Later in the season, watch the west wall lifts and the Aonach Poma. When these lifts close and the snow has gone in the Lower Ciste, it's a long walk back to the car parks.

Mountain fare

In the main car park, the Day Lodge has a restaurant, café and bar selling snacks. The Ptarmigan restaurant near the summit and the Sliding Snack Bar at the mid station offer simple snacks. Both are reasonably priced.

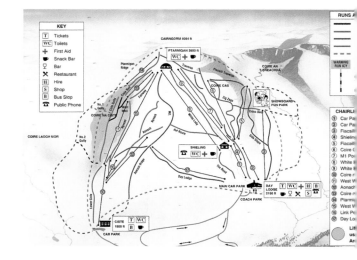

pic: Tim Rainger

ABOUT TOWN

The village of Aviemore boomed with the ski industry in the late '60s. The result? An odd mixture of - then stunning - new, but now unsightly, high-rise hotels and traditional, more austere buildings, such as the Cairngorm Hotel. The village is currently undergoing more development in an attempt to increase its appeal. A massive sports complex and cinema are being built, which should be completed by the late '90s. It's a 12km, or 20 minute, drive from the village to the resort. Buses travel regularly between the railway station and the resort in the season.

Getting there

By plane: The closest international airport is Glasgow and the nearest domestic airport is Inverness.

By train: There are daily British Rail train services from Glasgow and Inverness to Aviemore -Tel: 01479-810 229.

By bus: City Link, which is cheaper than British Rail, runs buses from both airports to Aviemore - Tel: 0990-5050 5050.

By car: The A9, off which there is a turning to Aviemore, is the main road from Perth to Inverness. If there are heavy snows, the road may be closed at Drumochtor Pass, from where diversions will lead to Fort William and then north again, along Loch Laggen, to the A9. If the road is clear, it is only a 2 hour drive from both Glasgow and Edinburgh.

Accommodation

Aviemore has something to suit all pockets, from top hotels to good B & Bs. B & B prices start at £13.00 (i.e. Kinapol Guest House - Tel: 01479-810 513) and rise to around £24.00 (i.e. the Lynwig House - Tel: 01479-811 685). There are also camping and self-catering facilities, both in the village and on the road to the ski area. Prices at the High Range start at £120.00 per week - Tel: 01479-810 636. There is a Youth Hostel located at Loch Morlich; prices from £7.00 (packages with equipment rental and lift passes are also available) - Tel: 0131-229 8660.

Food

Most of the bars and hotels offer a wide selection of cheap meals and snacks. For a fair sized meal and a friendly atmosphere, the Ski-ing Doo and Little John's are both recommended. There are a number of take-aways, including a delicious (but expensive) Indian and a very tasty (and reasonably priced) Chinese. For self-caterers, there is a large supermarket, a late night Spar shop and a 24-hour garage offering an array of foods for late night munch-outs.

Nightlife

There are over 20 bars and clubs to suit all tastes, from families to single boarders and winter climbers (who tend to congregate at the Old Bridge Inn). The liveliest bar in the village, and the main snowboarder hangout, is Chevvy's, which has good music, videos and a wide selection of beers. For pool tables, head to the Illicit Still. Later in the evening, the Crofters Show Bar is the local nightclub, with DJs playing dance music till late. The Summit Bar also does the occasional party night, with house music and pumping dance tunes.

pic: Tim Rainger

Other activities

There is a skateboard halfpipe outside the Boardwise Snowboard Shop, plus two gyms, a swimming-pool with a sauna, steam room and Jacuzzi. Chevvy's Bar organises beach volley-ball! Ask at the tourist office for details about squash, ice-skating, ice go-carting, fishing and mountain biking.

Thanks to

Ross Dempster from Boardwise Snowboarding and Tania Adams from the Cairngorm Chairlift Company.

Essential Contacts

Tourist office
Tel: 01479-810 363   Fax: 01479-811 063

Snowboard shops
•Boardwise Snowboarding
Tel: 01479-810 336   Fax: 01479-811 046
Board/boot hire: £15.00/day
Boardwise is the main snowboard shop, where you'll find local contacts and guides, a full board repair service, plus sales and rentals. From February to May, demo boards for the following season are available for hire.

Snowboard schools
•The Cairngorm Snowboard Bothy
Tel: 01479-861 261   Fax: 01479-861 207
2 hours of instruction: £15.00
This is the only recognised snowboard school operating in the Cairngorms. It offers professional i.e. qualified instruction, equipment hire and technical support.

FROM LATE FEBRUARY, THE AREA IS
COMPARABLE TO THE ALPS

The Lecht

Mountain Information

Mountain chain:

East Cairngorms

Vertical metre range:

610m - 823m

Length of season:

December - end of April

Number of lifts:

7 pomas, 5 trainer tows

Snow-making facilities:

None, but proposed for '96/'97 season.

Safety:

Not high enough for serious avalanche danger.

Guides:

Not necessary!

Lift pass prices:

1 day: £11.00

6 days: £66.00

Season: £155.00

ON THE MOUNTAIN

The Lecht is a good place to head when the weather - which tends to change every day, if not three times a day - or queues are dire elsewhere in the Scottish highlands. Great for both learning and improving, there is limited scope for experts, although there are a few bowls, cliffs and some steep sections. In short, the Lecht is a very small, friendly resort with a built-in dry slope for year-round riding.

Snow conditions

Due to its low altitude, snow reliability can be a problem at the Lecht, although the proposed snow-making will assist levels. However, due to its inland location, the Lecht doesn't suffer from the coastal winds that lash Glencoe and the Nevis Range.

Freeriders

Due to the constantly changing terrain, it's hard to recommend a particular place, because it's unlikely to be there next season! For some steep and fast riding, with good hits, seek out the Harrier and the Buzzard.

Freestylers

There is no halfpipe or formally organised funpark, but the friendly piste-bashers will help build jumps if you ask nicely.

Carvers

Carvers will have most fun on the Buzzard and the Harrier.

Lifts to avoid

None, but a general word of warning: watch out for fast take-offs!

Mountain fare

The café at the base area has a bar and reasonable food at 'normal' prices.

THE LECHT IS A VERY SMALL, FRIENDLY RESORT WITH A BUILT-IN DRY SLOPE FOR YEAR-ROUND RIDING

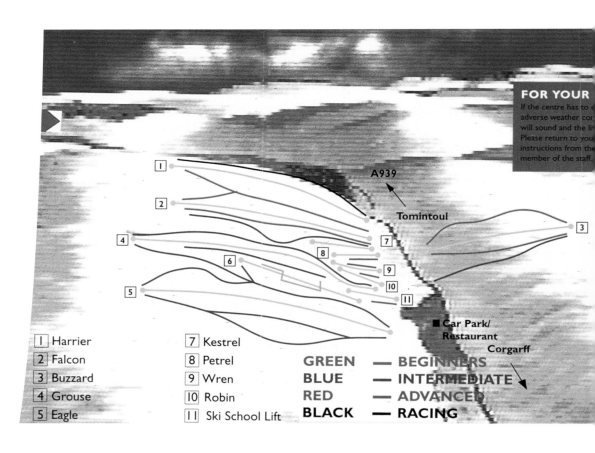

		GREEN	—	BEGINNERS
1	Harrier	7	Kestrel	BLUE	—	INTERMEDIATE
2	Falcon	8	Petrel	RED	—	ADVANCED
3	Buzzard	9	Wren	BLACK	—	RACING
4	Grouse	10	Robin			
5	Eagle	11	Ski School Lift			

FOR YOUR

If the centre has to c adverse weather cor will sound and the l Please return to you instructions from the member of the staff

A939

Tomintoul

Car Park/ Restaurant

Corgarff

🏠 ABOUT TOWN

Tomintoul, the nearest settlement, is roughly a 10 minute drive from the resort, and is a typical highland town with a handful of pubs and hotels. If you don't want to be restricted by the riding offered by the Lecht, stay in the Speyside villages which are also well placed for the Cairngorms.

➔ Getting there

By plane: The closest airport is Aberdeen, from where it's a 120km drive.

By train: Travel to Aviemore, Aberdeen or Inverness and then hitch on local transport to Tomintoul.

By car: Head towards Cairngorm, take the A93 through Glenshee and drive on to the Lecht.

🏠 Accommodation

A couple of bunkhouses have beds from £7.00 - Tomintoul - Tel: 01807-580 450 and Carrbridge in Invernesshire - Tel: 01479-841 250. B&Bs, from £13.50, include the Carn Daimh - Tel: 01807-580 439. Contact the tourist office for more details.

🍴 Food

There are a number of local bars serving meals. For a slap-up meal, Scottish style, try the Gordon.

Nightlife

Sample every one of the plethora of whiskies at the Gordon... in a single night, fall down, crawl to bed.

Other activities

Curling, ice-skating, a cinema and... more whisky!

✓ Thanks to

Jeff Fraser.

Rider Paul Jeremiah pic: ESP

It can be done on the cheap pic: Tim Rainger

Essential Contacts

Tourist office
Tel: 01975-651 440   Fax: 01975-651 426
Snowboard shops
The Lecht Ski Centre   Tel: 01975-651 440
Board/boot hire: £17.00/day
Snowboard schools
Part of ski school   Tel: 01975-651 440
2 hours of instruction: £12.00

pic: Tim Rainger

Glenshee

Mountain Information

Mountain chain:

Cairngorms

Vertical metre range:

604m - 1,068m

Length of season:

December - April

Number of lifts:

2 chairs, 24 draglifts

Snow-making facilities:

6 snow guns service the

Claybokie run

Safety:

If there has been a heavy snowfall,

seek the advice of the piste patrol.

Guides:

Contact the ski school.

Lift pass prices:

1 day: £16.00

5 days: £64.00

7 days: £86.00

Season:

£190.00 (before November 1)

£235.00 (after November 1)

Lift pass alternatives:

Before November 1, a joint season

pass with Glencoe is available for

£225.00. Before December 31,

there is a special 'any five day'

pass, which gives you access to

both Glenshee or Glencoe

(£60.00).

ON THE MOUNTAIN

Glenshee, spread over three valleys and with 26 lifts, is the largest of Scotland's resorts. Given the right snow conditions and weather, the wide variety of terrain can offer good snowboarding. All the beginners' areas are well situated on flats near central facilities, intermediates have a large choice of terrain, and experts can look forward to interesting and challenging riding.

Snow conditions

The snowfall is often erratic, but when the weather settles later in the season the conditions can be superb.

Freeriders

The best runs for boarders are the Butcharts Coire, which normally has a huge natural quarterpipe, table tops and a gigantic roll-over jump near the bottom. All the runs on Meall Odhar can be amazing, with cornices, drop-offs, hits and powder pockets. Coire Fionn, on the other side of the mountain, has an intense banked gully run, which was the site of the '95/'96 British boardercross. Adrenaline junkies will enjoy the cornices, which - as ever - are seasonal. One cornice is on the right-hand side of the Tiger, cutting off the Bunny Run down to Claybokie. Another cornice, normally larger, is a 10 minute hike along the Meall Odhar ridge. Ask someone with local knowledge before you leap, as the area can be avalanche prone.

Freestylers

The chairlift company tried to build a halfpipe in the '95/'96 season, but an early thaw thwarted their construction plans. Another is planned for the '96/'97 season. On the left-hand run at Meall Odhar, there is a small funpark,

with a table-top, a quarterpipe, a banked snake run and a handrail. However, it had a short lifespan last season, due to the early thaw.

Carvers

The right side of Cairn Aosda and Glas Moal are the best places for carving, as they are wide open fields harbouring deep powder.

Lifts to avoid

Snowboarders, for their own safety, were once banned from the infamous Tiger T-bar, which has now been replaced by an easy-to-ride poma. The access lift queue can be plain ugly.

Mountain fare

There are three restaurants, all fully licensed, which serve standard hot and cold food at slightly expensive prices. A cheap alternative is a packed lunch.

The origonal mad cow pic: Chris Power

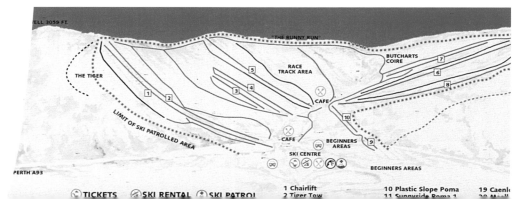

SPREAD OVER THREE VALLEYS AND WITH 26 LIFTS, GLENSHEE IS **THE LARGEST** OF SCOTLAND'S RESORT

ABOUT TOWN

As with the other Scottish resorts, there are no towns near the resort - just a couple of hotels. Braemar and Blairgowrie, a 21km and a 60km drive away respectively, are the nearest two settlements of any size. Braemar is a beautiful highland village, but besides hotels it lacks facilities. Blairgowrie has all the amenities of a town, including a recreation centre with a swimming-pool and games hall.

Getting there

By plane: The closest airports are Aberdeen and Edinburgh, which are both a 2 hour drive away.
By train: The nearest train stations are in Dundee (72kms away) and Perth (57kms away), from where bus transfers are available.
By car: The only road to Glenshee is the main Aberdeen to Perth road (A93), which passes right through the ski centre. It may close in severe weather.

Accommodation

The closest lodging is near the spittle of Glenshee, where the Glenshee Hotel has rooms from £18.00 to £25.00 - Tel: 01250-885 215. The cheapest options for budget travellers are the youth hostel and the caravan park (located at the Bridge of Cally), which charge from £6.00. Other alternatives are the Braemar Bunk House - Tel: 01339-741 242 and the Braemar Youth Hostel - Tel: 01339-741 659 with beds from £7.00. In Braemar, more up-market accommodation can be found at the Fife Arms and the Invercauld Hotels. The Glenshee Tourist Association has more details - Tel: 01250-875 509.

Food

Braemar and Blairgowrie are the only places with a choice of places to eat. The food at both the Bridge of Cally Hotel and the Moorfield House Hotel in Blairgowrie is excellent. Both villages have supermarkets and take-aways, of the Chinese and fish and chips variety.

Nightlife

There is not much in the way of nightlife in this area, but the local pubs are a great place to enjoy a dram or ten. There's always a good cross-section of people at the bar and the atmosphere is friendly, becoming ever more friendly as the whisky works its magic. There are occasional discos at the Invercauld in Braemar and tawdry karaoke or disco nights at the Spittal Hotel.

Other activities

There's lots of other sports in this area, such as curling at Pitlochry and Perth, golf on Britain's highest course at Braemar, walking, climbing, mountain biking, bird-watching, shooting and stalking. Sport of another kind comes in the shape of a whisky trail.

Thanks to

Alex Craig, Andy Gooday and Jeff from the Clan.

Essential Contacts

Tourist office
Tel: 01339-741 600 or 01250-872 960
Snowboard shops
•Cairdsport   Tel: 01250-885 216
Board/boot hire: £17.00/day
•Glenshee Chairlift Co   Tel: 01339-741 320
Board/boot hire: £17.00/day
Board/boot hire: £65.00/5 days
Board/boot hire: £84.00/7 days
Snowboard schools
•Glenshee Snowboard Academy
Tel: 01339-741 320
1 day of instruction: £12.00.

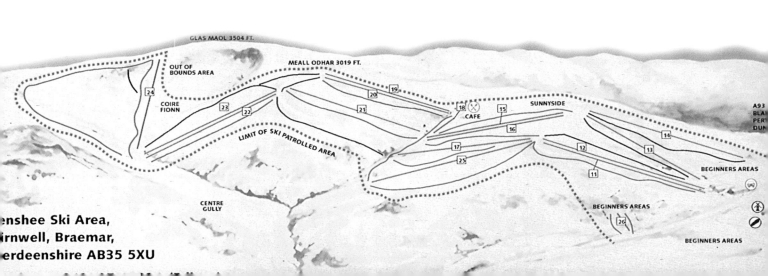

GLAS MAOL 3504 FT.
MEALL ODHAR 3019 FT.
OUT OF BOUNDS AREA
COIRE FIONN
LIMIT OF SKI PATROLLED AREA
SUNNYSIDE
CAFE
A93 BLA PER DUN
BEGINNERS AREAS
CENTRE GULLY
BEGINNERS AREAS
BEGINNERS AREAS

enshee Ski Area,
irnwell, Braemar,
erdeenshire AB35 5XU

GLOBAL EYEWARE

England

compiled with the assistance of the B.S.A.

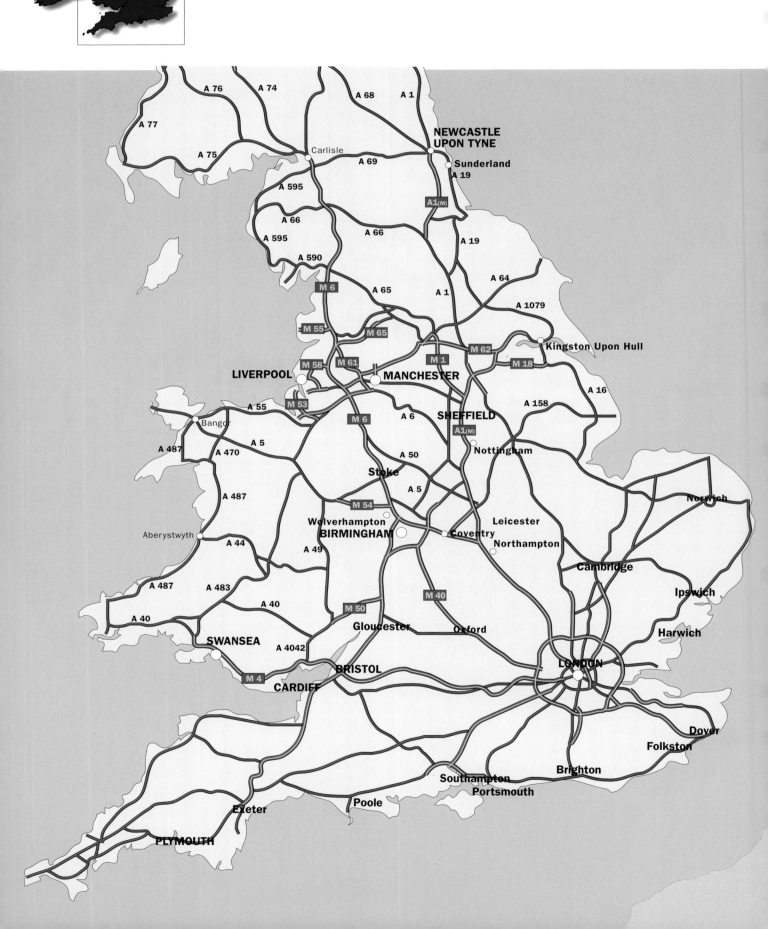

Greater London/South East

Location	Details	Surface/Slopes	Season	Facilities
Chatham:	Alpine Ski Centre, Capstone Farm Country Park, Capstone Rd, Kent - Tel: 01634- 827 979	dendix, skitech, 200 X 40m, nursery 40 X 30m	all year	2F, R, O
Guildford:	Bishop Reindorp School, Larch Avenue, Surrey, GUI IJY - Tel: 01843-37373	dendix, 33 X8m, nursery 20 X 12m	all year	T, F
Newhaven:	Borowski Ski Centre, New Road East Sussex - Tel: 01273-515402	dendix, 33 X 8m, 30 X 12m, nursery 10 X 8m	all year	T, F, R, O
Tunbridge Wells:	Bowles Outdoor Pursuits Centre, New Road, East Sussex - Tel: 01892-665 665	dendix, 76 X 50m	Call for times	T, F, R, O
Folkestone:	Folkestone Sports Ski Centre, Radnor Park Ave, Kent - Tel: 01303-850 333	dendix, skitech, bowmat 56 X 12m, nursery 20 X 8m, 40m	all year	3T, F, R
Uxbridge:	Hillingdon Ski Centre, Park Road - Tel: 01895 5183	dendix, skitech, 135m, 80m, 30m, 25m	all year	3T, F, R
Alpine Way:	Beckton Ski Centre, Beckton Alps Lane, E6 4LA	dendix, skitech, 200 X 40m	all year	3T, R, F, O
St Paul's Cray:	Profiles Ski Centre, Sandy Lane, Orpington, Kent, BR5 3HY - Tel: 01689-878 239	dendix, 120 X 30m nursery 40 X 45m	all year	2T, F, R, O
Esher:	Sandown Ski School, More Lane, Surrey, KT10 8AN - Tel: 01372-465 588/467 132	dendix, skitech, and powder pack, 100 X 30m	all year	2T, F, R, O

Southern England

Location	Details	Surface/Slopes	Season	Facilities
Bracknell:	Bracknell Ski Centre, John Nike Way, Binfield - Tel: 01344-860 033	dendix, skitech, mogul run and toboggan run	all year	3T, F, R, O
Southampton:	Southampton Ski Centre, Sports Centre, Basset - Tel: 01703 768 732	dendix, 110m, 100m and 20m	Clsd August	2T, F, R
Calshot:	Calshot Activities Centre, Calshot Road, Southampton, SO4 1BR - Tel: 01703-892 077	dendix, 30m X 22m nursery 12 X 10m	all year	T, F, R, O
Norwich:	Norfolk Ski Club, Whitlingham Lane, Trowse - Tel: 01603-662 781	dendix, 170m and 40m	all year	T, R, F, O
Ipswich:	Suffolk Ski Centre, Bourne Terrace, Wherstead, Suffolk, IP2 8NG - Tel: 01473-602 347	dendix, skitech, 110m X 30m, 70 X 30m, 100m mogul run	all year	T, F
Welwyn Gdn	Ski Centre, Stanborough Road, Herts - Tel: 011707-331056/330780	skitech, 160m wave slope, 160 X 40m, 2 x nursery	all year	2T,F,R,O

East Midlands

Location	Details	Surface/Slopes	Season	Facilities
Nottingham:	Carlton Forum Ski Slope, Foxhill Road - Tel: 01159-8723 333	dendix, skitech 6 X 30m	all year	T, F, R
Leicester:	Leicster outdoor pursuites Centre, Loughborough Road - Tel: 01533-681 426	dendix, 34m	all year	R, O
Rushde:	Skiew Bridge, Ski School, Northampton Raod, Northants, NN10 9AP - Tel: 01933-59 939	skitech, curver, 95 X 11m, 75 X 11m, nursery 10X 7m	all year	2T, F, R, O
Stamford:	Tallington Ski & Snowboard Centre, Tallington Lakes, Lincs, PE9 4RJ - Tel: 01778-344 99	80m		T, F, R

West Midlands

Location	Details	Surface/Slopes	Season	Facilities
Birmingham:	Ackers Trust Ski Centre, Golden Hillock Road, Smallheath - Tel: 021-771 448	dendix, 100m X 10m, nursery 30 X 18m	all year	2T, F, O
Stoke	Stoke Ski Centre, Festival Park, Staffs, ST1 5SN - Tel: 01782-294 159	dendix, skitech,130m nursery, 75m	Call for times	2T, F, R, O
Swadlincote:	Swadlincote Ski Centre, Hill Street, Burton-on-Trent, Staffs - Tel: 01283-217 200	dendix, 140 X 21m, nursery 46m X 36m	Call for times	4T, F, R, O
Telford:	Telford Ski Slope, Court Centre, Madeley, Telford - Tel: 01952-586 862	dendix, skitech, low friction, 85 X 21m, nursery 30 X 21m	all year	F, R, O
Tamworth:	Tamworth Snowdome, Castle Ground River Drive, Tamworth, B79 7ND - Tel: 01827-67 905	real snow - indoor		

North West

Location	Details	Surface/Slopes	Season	Facilities
Lancaster:	Lancaster and Morecambe Col FE, Ski Slope, Morecambe Road -Tel: 01534-662 15	dendix, 50m	Sept-April	
Reading:	Ski Carter, 99 Caversham Road, Berks - Tel: 01734-55 589	dendix, 20 X 6m	Call for times	
Aldershot:	Stainforth Ski Centre, Hurwst Road, Hants, GU11 2DJ - Tel: 01252-258 89	dendix, 95 X 11m, nursery, 70 X 11m	Oct-April	2T, F, R, O

South West

Location	Details	Surface/Slopes	Season	Facilities
Gloucester:	Gloucester Ski Centre, Robinswood Hill, GL4 9EA - Tel: 01452-114 300	dendix, 240m, 200m and 40m	all year	3T, F, R, O
Churchill:	Avon Ski Centre Lycombe Lodge, Nr Bristol, BS19 5PG - Tel: 01934-852 335	dendix, 180m X 8m, 3 nursery slopes	all year	2T, F, R, O
Christchurch:	Christchurch Ski Centre, Matchams Lane, Hurn - Tel: 01202-199 155	120m X 34m	Call for times	T, F, R, O
Dorchester:	Warmwell Ski Centre, Warmwell, Dorset, DT2 8JE - Tel: 01305-853 245	dendix, 110 X 22m (max), nursery incorporated in main slope	all year	T, F, R, O
Wellington:	Wellington Sports Centre, Corams Lane, Somerset, TA21 OLL - Tel: 01823 473 010	dendix, 50 X 10m (max), nursery incorporated in main slope	all year	T, F, R, O
Yeovil:	Yeovil Ski Centre, Addlewell Lane, Nine Springs, Somerset - Tel: 01935-21 702			
Exeter:	Exeter & District Ski Club, Clifton Hill Athletic Center, Belmont Rd - Tel: 01392-211 422	dendix, 70 X 20m, nursery, 120 X 8m	Call for times	T, F
Torquay:	Wessex Ski Club, Barton Hall, Kingskerwell Road, Devon - Tel: 01803-313 350	dendix, 112 X 12m, nursery 50 X 30m	all year	T, F, O
Plymouth:	John Nike, Leisure Sport Complex, Marsh Mills, Devon PL6 PLQ - Tel: 01752 600 220	skitech, 150m, 60m, nursery	Call for times	T, F, R, O

Eastern

Location	Details	Surface/Slopes	Season	Facilities
Royston:	Bassingbourn Ski Centre, Rose Villas, Jacksons Lane, Herts, SG8 8AB - Tel: 01763-848 114	dendix, 90 X 30m,	Call for times	T, F
Brentwood:	Brentwood Park Ski Centre, Warley Gap, Essex, CM20, 2JF - Tel: 01277-211 994	dendix, skitech, 180m X 10m, 1900m X 10m, 60m X 10m	Sept-April	3T, F, R, O
Harlow	Harlow Ski Centre, Hammarskjold road, Essex CM20 2JF - Tel: 01279-422 265	dendix, 170 X 20m, nursery 80 X 20m	all year	3T, F, R, O
Herts:	Tel: 01442-241 321	dendix, 180m, 30m and 65m	all year	2T, F, R
Oldham:	Oldham Ski Centre, Counthill road, Moorside, Lancs - Tel: 0161-678 4054	dendix, 75m	Call for times	T, F
Bebington:	Oval Sports Centre, Old Chester Road, the Wirral, L63 7LF - Tel: 051-645 0551	dendix, 50m	all year	R,O
Blackburn:	Pendle Ski Club, 13 Whitham Cres, Whalley, Clitheroe - Tel: 01253-822 347	dendix, skitech, 100 X 10m, nursery 20 X 10m	all year	2T,F, R, O
Runcorn:	Ski Runcorn, town park, Palacefields, Cheshire - Tel: 01928-701 965	dendix, 60m	all year	T, R

North East

Location	Details	Surface/Slopes	Season	Facilities
Catterick:	Catterick Indoor Ski Centr, Loos Road, DL9 4LE - Tel: 01748-833 788	Curver 50 and 15m	all year	2T, F, R, O
Sheffield:	Sheffield Ski Village, Vale road, Parkwood Springs, Sheffield, S3 9SJ - Tel: 01742 -769 459	dendix and Norski, powder pack, various slopes from 35m nursery areas (6) to blue red and black runs up to 330m	all year	2T, F, C

Northern

Location	Details	Surface/Slopes	Season	Facilities
Carlislie:	Carisle Sk Slope, Edenside, Carlisle, Cumbria - Tel: 01228-561 634	dendix, 50m	Sept-April	T, F, R
Alston:	High Plains Lodge Ski Slope, High Plains Lodge - Tel: 01434-818 86	dendix, skitech, 75m	Sept-April	T, F, R
Kendal:	Kendal Ski Club, Thronyhills, Kendal, Cumbria - Tel: 01539-235 51	dendix, skitech 75m	Sept-April	T, F, R
Keswick:	Keswick Ski Slope, Vicarage hill, Keswick, Cumbria - Tel: 01768-772 605		Call for times	
Morpeth:	Morpeth Ski Slope, Cuttingwood Lane, Northumberland - Tel: 01670 841200 ext: 333	skitech, 60m	Call for times	
Willington:	Spectrum Ski Slope, Hunwick Lane, Co Durham, DL15 OJA - Tel: 01388-747 000	dendix, 70 X 15m	all year	T, F, R, O
Sunderland:	Silksworth Ski Centre, Silksworth Lane, Tyne and Wear, SR3 3AW - Tel: 091-522 9119	dendix, skitech, 160 X 30m, nursery 50 X 20m	all year	3T, F, R, O

T = tow
F = floodlighting
R = refreshments
O = other facilities

Rider: Steve Bailey, Rossendale. pic: Stig

Newcastle pic: Stig

Gloucester pic: Stig

Sheffield pic: Sang Tan

Brentwood pic: Stig

Lowlands

As the best part of the Dutch and Belgian surface area is below sea level, the only option for snowboarders in these nations is a wide range of artificial slopes. Hills, and even small mountains, have been built from domestic waste and construction debris. Although these artificial slopes are usually short and lacking in steepnesss, jumps and hits, their numbers are growing fast. In addition, to provide riders with something closer to the genuine white powder, more and more 'real' snow slopes, with small funparks and special runs and lifts for snowboarders, have opened in recent years. While these simulated slopes are never going to reach the dizzy heights of true snow, they are great places for ride freaks to practise their rad tricks. They're also good for testing the latest equipment before you hit the real slopes. The Lowlands even have a small competition scene, with contests being held on the manufactured slopes in the disciplines of alpine and freestyle riding. Still, nothing beats the real thing and before long, you find most of the Lowland riders heading for the hills of central Europe.

✓ Thanks to:
Information: Gijs Vroom,
Air 22 Snowboarding Magazine
Photos: Arjan Kruik, Funsports
Magazine

General Information

Nederlandse Ski Vereniging and
Snowboard Holland:
P.O. Box 82100, 2508 EC
The Hague
Johan van Oldenbarneveldlaan 9,
2582 NE The Hague
Tel: (+31) 070 - 352 58 00
Snowboard Club Holland
Tel: (+31) 070 - 352 58 25
Travel information
Tel: (+31) 070 - 352 58 05
Fédération Belgique de Ski:
Avenue Reine Astrid 26,
B-1410 Waterloo.
Tel: (+32) 023 - 54 88 94

General Prices

free boarding:	approximately 20 NLG (400 BFR) per hour and with gear approximately 25 NLG (500 BFR)
day pass:	between 40 NLG (800 BFR) and 70 NLG (1400 BFR)
10 hour tickets:	approximately 150 NLG (3000 BFR) and, with gear, approximately 250 NLG (5000 BFR)
season tickets:	between 300 NLG (6000 BFR) and 700 NLG (14000 BFR)
board rental:	approximately 15 NLG (300 BFR) per hour and 125 NLG (2500 BFR) for 10 hours
bindings rental:	approximately 1 NLG (20 BFR) per hour and 8 NLG (160 BFR) for 10 hours
boot rental:	approximately 3 NLG (60 BFR) per hour and 25 NLG (500 BFR) for 10 hours
snowboard course:	between 200 NLG (4000 BFR) and 350 NLG (7000 BFR)
average season:	most artificial slopes open in September and close in April (some stay open year round)

Rider Denis Muldle - Nieuwegein pic: Funsport Snowboard mag - Kruik

MAIN OUTDOOR AND COVERED ARTIFICIAL SLOPES

Name	Address	Tel	Type	Opening times
Skibaan Drenthe	Oranjekanaal NZ 10, 7853 TA Wezuperbrug	tel: 059 - 138 20 82		
Indoorski De Vlinder	Sportcentrum de Kloek, Insulindeweg 11, 1462 MJ Middenbeemster	tel: 029 - 968 38 65	indoor slope	Saturday: 09.30 - 12.30
Skigebied Ennerveld	Molenweg1, 8191 KA Wapenveld	tel: 038 - 447 85 52/444 27 06		always
Sigi Moser Ski & Fun School	Heuvelweg 6-8, Velsen Zuid (Recreatiegebied Spaarnewoude)	tel: 025 - 553 58 90	outdoor slopíe (ski tiles)	Monday - Friday: 17.00 - 19.00 Thursday: 17.00 - 22.30 Saturday - Sunday: 16.00 - 17.00
Skiclub de Wolfskamer	P.O. Box 389, 1271 AA Huizen	tel: 035 - 526 17 09	outdoor slope (bristles)	call for opening times
Skipiste Hoofddorp	Arnolduspark 10, 2132 CR Hoofddorp	tel: 023 - 563 47 46	outdoor slope (bristles)	Monday - Friday: 17.00 - 18.00 Wednesday: closed Saturday - Sunday: 16.40 - 18.00
Skicentrum Sousterberg	Sportpark Kerklaan, Soest	tel: 034 - 635 26 74		Monday: 12.00 -17.00/19.00 -22.00 Saturday - Sunday: 10.00 - 17.00
Skicentrum Bergzicht	Doornseweg 23, 3931 MH Woudenberg	tel: 034 - 344 26 92	outdoor slope	Wednesday: 16.30 - 21.30 Saturday: 17.00 - 18.00 Sunday: 17.45 - 19.00
Skischool Duinrell	Duinrell 1, 2242 JP Wassenaar	tel: 070 - 511 76 27		
Ski sportief	Groeneweg 52, 3521 VG Utrecht	tel: 030 - 294 01 44/251 77 89		on request only
Skipiste Nieuwegein	Recreatiegebied N†edereindseplas, Nedereindseweg, 501 a, Nieuwegein	tel: 030 - 687 31 39	outdoor slope	Monday - Friday: 14.30 - 23.00 Saturday: 10.00 - 20.00 Sunday: 10.00 - 18.00
Duijvestein Snow World	Buytenpark, Zoutermeer	tel: 079 - 320 22 02	covered slope (real snow)	all year from 9.00 - 24.00
Skicenter Bergschenhoek	Rottebandreef 10-12, 2661 JK Bergschenhoek PO Box 30, 2665 ZG Bleiswijktel:	tel 010 - 522 07 55 (fax: 010 - 522 11 39)	outdoor slope, pins	Monday - Friday: 14.00 - 22.00 Saturday - Sunday: 10.00 - 17.00
Skicentrum Wijchense Berg	Heumenseweg 180, 6603 KT Alverna	tel: 024 - 641 13 41 (fax: 024 - 641 97 81)	outdoor slope	Monday -Thursday: 18.00 - 21.00 Friday: 18.00 - 19.30 Saturday: 17.00 - 18.00 Sundays: 16.00 -18.00
Skibaan Molenhoek	Lierweg 4, 6584 DC Molenhoek	tel: 024 - 358 40 16	outdoor slope	Monday - Friday: 13.00 - 23.00 Saturday - Sunday: 10.00 - 18.00
Portres Du Ski Ridderkerk	Kerkweg 219, 2985 AS Ridderkerk	tel: 018 - 042 65 65	covered slope & escalating ski-slope	Monday - Friday: 14.00 - 23.00 Saturday - Sunday: 10.00 - 17.00
Holland Indoor Ski	De Ritte 3, 3201 LE Spijkenisse	tel: 018 - 161 32 51	indoor slope	Monday: 16.30 - 21.30 Tuesday: 12.30 - 22.30 Wednesday: 16.00 - 22.30 Thursday: 15.00 - 22.30 Friday: 13.00 - 22.30
Skicentrum Dordrecht	Vogelaarsweg 1, Dordrecht	078 - 621 03 55	outdoor slope (bristles)	Monday - Friday: 13.30 - 23.00 Sunday: 9.30 - 18.00
Skischool Oss	Aengelbertlaan 50, 5342 LA Oss	tel: 041 - 262 35 86	outdoor slope, (bristles - alpine)	Monday - Friday: 14.00 - 23.00 Saturday - Sunday: 10.00 - 17.00
De Schans	Vluchtoordweg 5, 5406 XX Uden	tel: 041 - 326 71 66		Monday - Friday: 18.30 - 22.30 Saturday - Sunday: 09.00 - 17.00
Skiberg Beekse Bergen	Beekse Bergen 1, 5081 NJ Hilvarenbeek	tel: 013 - 536 00 32	outdoor slope (bristles)	Monday - Friday: 18.00 - 19.00 Saturday - Sunday: 14.00 - 18.00
Skibaan de Kempervennen	Kempervennendreef 8, 5563 VB Westerhoven	tel: 040 - 208 32 47		Monday - Friday: 18.00 - 23.00 Saturday - Sunday: 09.00 - 20.00
*De Nederlandse Skischool,Sigi Moser	Parallelstraat 21, 6372 XD Landgraaf	tel: 045 - 542 06 68	outdoor slope, ski tiles (with chairlift)	Monday - Friday: 17.00 - 19.00 Thursday: 17.00 - 22.30 Saturday - Sunday: 16.00 - 17.00
Skibaan de Dousberg	Dousbergweg 90, 6216 GC Maastricht	tel: 043 - 347 03 56	outdoor slope	Monday - Friday: 20.30 - 22.00 Sunday: 14.00 - 18.00
Skibaan Casablanca	Wouwerstraat 15, B-2970 's Gravenwezel, Belgium	tel: 036 - 58 52 06	indoorslope, real snow	Monday - Sunday:09.00 - 21.00 (summer) Monday - Thursday:22.00 - 23.00 (winter)

*(longest in Europe, 530 meters)

TIM VLANDIS

Rider Danny Hiebert Nieuwegein pic: Funsport Snowboard mag - Kruik

Indoor escalators in the Netherlands

Indoor Ski Hemrik	Jupiterweg 6, 8938 AE Leeuwarden	tel: 058 - 280 05 34	
Indoor Skischool	Holenweg 14 a, 1624 PB Hoorn	tel: 022 - 923 44 64	Monday - Friday: 12.00 - 24.00
De Binding			Saturday - Sunday: 09.00 - 24.00
Ski-inn	Eeducalaan 25, 8251 GC Dronten	tel: 032 - 131 46 07	Monday: 18.00 - 23.00
			Tuesday - Thursday: 10.00 - 16.00
			Friday: 18.00 - 23.00
			Sunday: 10.00 - 18.00
Ski Inn	WG Plein 281, 1051 SE Amsterdam	tel: 020 - 618 49 46	Monday - Sunday: 10.00 -23.00
Ski-promotion	Emdenstraat 18 a, 7418 BR Deventer	tel: 057 - 063 63 54	Monday: 10.00 - 23.00
			Tuesday - Friday: 14.00 - 23.00
			Saturday: 10.00 - 23.00
			Sunday: 10.00 - 18.00
Indoorski Gooi	Industrieweg 10 (Panda-Hallen), 1231 KH Nieuw-Loosdrecht	tel: 035 - 582 44 04	Monday - Friday: 10.00 - 12.00 and 14.00 - 17.00
Indoorski Discovery	Waterpas 99, 2267 AS Leidschendam	tel: 070 - 399 10 14	Monday: 18.00 - 23.00
			Thursday: 18.00 - 23.00
			Saturday - Sunday: 10.00 - 13.00
Indoor Ski Rotterdam	Folkert Elsinggasltraat 11, 3067 NW Rotterdam	tel: 010 - 456 61 60	Monday - Sunday: 08.30 - 23.30
Ski-fit	Groenstraat 3a, 4845 AE Teteringen	tel: 076 - 581 08 31	Monday - Friday: 19.00 - 23.00
			Saturday - Sunday: 10.00 - 20.00
Skischool Nicky Broos	Baanvelden 13, 4715 RH Rucphen	tel: 016 - 534 31 34	Everyday - 09.00 - 23.00
Sport-Inn Maerlant	St. Josephstraat 75 a, 6245 LL Oost-Maarland Eijsden	tel: 043 - 409 49 49	Monday - Sunday:10.00 - 24.00

Scandinavia

Norway

Capital: Oslo

Population: 4,000,000

Time: GMT + 1 hour

Currency: Krone (Kr)

UK = 9.7Kr

Telephone information

ISD Code: 47

International directory: 181

Local directory enquiries: 180

National airline: Braathens

Tel: 0191-214 0991

Snowline information

0171-321 0666

Snowboard Associations:

Tel: 47 67 154825

Fax: 47 67 132989

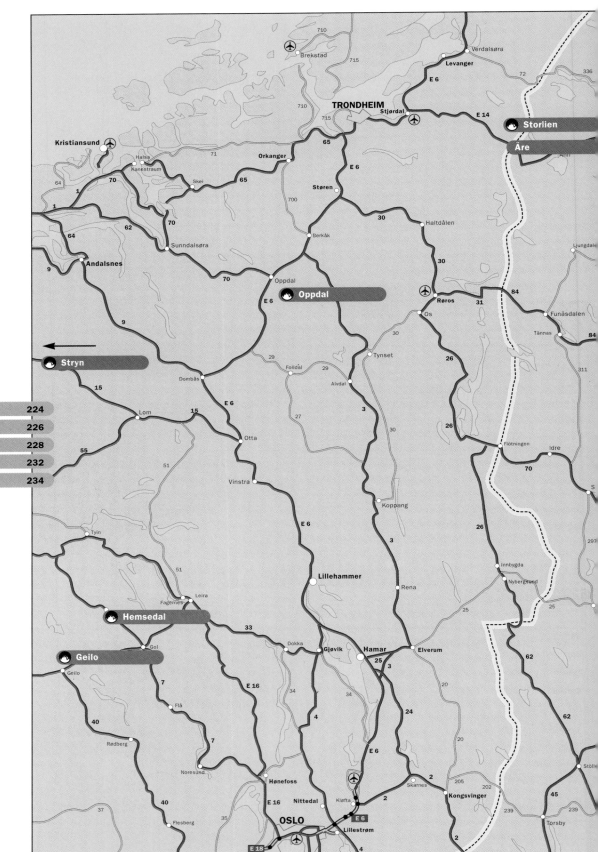

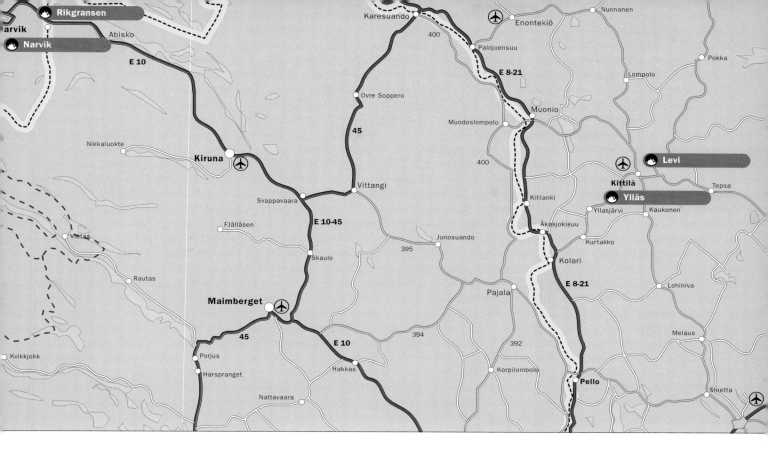

Geilo
Hemsedal
Stryn
Oppdal
Narvik

Rider Steve Bailey

Geilo

Mountain Information

Mountain chain:

Hallingskarvet

Vertical metre range:

800m - 1,175m

Length of season:

mid-November - first week of May

Number of lifts:

4 chairlifts,

14 draglifts

Snow-making facilities:

50 percent of the runs are covered by snow cannons.

Safety:

There is hardly any avalanche activity.

Guides:

Contact the ski school for local guiding services - Tel: 3209 0650.

Lift pass prices:

swatch access

1 day: 195kr

6 days: 765kr

Lift pass alternatives:

If you purchase a 6 day ticket, an extra 20kr buys a Winterland Pass, giving you access to the five resorts of Gol, Hallingskarvat, Uvdal, Hemsedal and Al.

pic: Peter Grant

 ON THE MOUNTAIN

Geilo is one of the oldest resorts in Sweden, having been created when it was still considered extreme to slide down the slopes strapped to a wooden board. The resort is split between the two sides of a valley, both with intermediate rolling hills that flatten out towards the lower slopes providing easy gradients for learners. Most of the runs are well-groomed pistes, with some steeps. The resort has limited scope for advanced riders, although there are some off-piste titbits. The lift system is incredibly efficient and a cheap taxi service links the two sides of the resort. The mountain can get quite crowded at weekends with holidaymakers heading north from Oslo.

 Snow conditions

By January and February, which are the best powder months, Geilo normally has a 1.5m snow base. For snow conditions - Tel: 3209 1809.

 Freeriders

The most accessible forested areas are between runs 21 and 23, which are reached via the Geilo Heissen Lift. Black runs 58 and 23 on the Vestilla side are split-groomed, creating great bump runs. Beneath the Geilo Heiser chair line, in between the trees and pop-off rocks, are short and steep chutes.

The biggest hits (up to four metres) are located on the lower part of run 14. On a powder day, the back side above the tree-line on run 47 is the most exhilarating place to frolic in deep, dreamtime snow.

 Freestylers

When not on the jibber's tracks, runs 13 and 14, freestylers can hit the two halfpipes on either side of the resort. Run 44 has the best pipe, which has been made on top of a natural halfpipe. It has snow-sculptured three metre walls and a smooth transition. The halfpipe and funpark are next to each other on the Vestlia side, at the bottom of runs 58 and 59, but the pipe was too low so another is being built for the '96/'97 season. The funpark has limited space, but two table tops, one fun box, two gap jumps, one rail slide and a rubber tyre hit have been squeezed in.

 Carvers

The pistes are well maintained, packed, firm and excellent for carving. Runs 23 and 14 are the best for wide, low turns.

 Lifts to avoid

Don't go to Slatte Jordet lift as run 35 is too flat.

 Mountain fare

There are six cafés on the mountain, all with indoor and outdoor areas, similar food and prices (starting at 50kr for lunch). None serves alcohol.

pic: Peter Grant

Essential Contacts

Tourist office

Tel: 3209 9130   Fax: 3209 1850

Snowboard shops

There are two sports shops, but neither of them specialises in snowboarding. If you want to hire equipment, go to the ski school.

Snowboard schools

•Geilo Ski School

Tel: 3209 0650

Lessons: 150kr/day

Board/boot hire: 250kr/day

 ## ABOUT TOWN

The village is small, friendly and relaxed. Visitors are well catered for and all the facilities are easily accessible. Traditionally, Geilo is a family resort and, at first, 20-something visitors may think there is little action, but look beyond the veneer and there is an oozing underground party scene.

 ### Getting there

By air: Dagali airport is a 20km bus or train transfer from Geilo.

By train: Three or four trains operate daily between Oslo and Geilo.

By car: It is only a four hour drive from Oslo and the road is always kept clear.

Accommodation

The cheap, snowboard friendly option is the campsite, which has self-catering cabins for one person ranging in price from 60kr to 100kr (depending on the season). The Youth Hostel, located in the town centre, is good and clean - it provides self-catering facilities at a cost of 130kr (including breakfast). For other options, contact central reservations on
- Tel: 3208 8400.

 ### Food

There are two supermarkets, which are both open late but close on Sunday. Just below the main station is a pizzeria, where pizzas cost around 60kr. The Beeferia Restaurant has a large, varied menu, with prices at around 100kr. The up-market Vestlia Hotel's restaurant serves traditional Norwegian dishes, such as grilled mountain trout, which will set you back, on average, 180kr.

 ### Nightlife

The most popular place for late afternoon sessions is Doctor Holm's Prescription Bar - so-called because doctors ensure that you take your medicine. There is often live music and the place has undoubtedly seen many great nights. Nightclub Bardola, with a 50kr entry fee, is the red mouth of Geilo's dance scene.

Other activities

All the hotels have saunas, pools and gyms - the entry fee for non-residents is 20kr. Geilo is also a popular destination for ice fishing - learn the traditional method of survival for 100kr.

WELL-GROOMED PISTES, WITH SOME STEEPS. THE RESORT HAS LIMITED SCOPE FOR ADVANCED RIDERS, ALTHOUGH THERE ARE SOME OFF-PISTE

Hemsedal

 ON THE MOUNTAIN

Hemsedal has been dubbed the 'little Matterhorn of the north' on account of its craggy peaks, which are unusual for Norway. You can find every type of terrain imaginable and the best nuggets are easy to pick out at a glance. As Hemsedal is within striking distance of Oslo, the weekends and holidays can be crowded, so time your visit accordingly.

 Snow conditions

Variable, particularly in the early season, so Hemsedal often relies on man-made snow. However, plenty of powder days arrive in February and March. Most of the slopes are north-facing and hold good snow, which is even better preserved in the wooded areas.

 Freeriders

From the Hamaren summit, you'll find some great bowls and open faces. Look out for good lines and cliff jumps above runs 23 and 24. The tree riding is excellent all over the mountain, but the west side is tighter and steeper with rock hits in-between, and, if you can find them, great little gullies. Extreme terrain, cliffs and couloirs are found off the back side of the Totten Summit. The most noted chute is the Annus Couloir, a 200 metre vertical drop that twists and turns through rock walls.

Below the ride out is a beautiful avalanche-controlled descent to the road, from where a bus returns to the resort. Off the front side of Totten is the undulating run 1 - try the path going right into Devil's Valley, which leads to a great tree run with a natural halfpipe, leaving you 500m short of the Hemsedal Café.

 Freestylers

The jibber's track is located off Lift E, from where runs 24 and 10 have plentiful hits on either side of the groomed piste all the way down to the funpark. In the '95/'96 season, the park included a couple of ramp jumps, a big table top and a log slide, but there are plans to make it bigger and better for the '96/'97 season, with floodlights, quarterpipes and fun boxes. A decent halfpipe is also in the planning as, due to poor snow conditions in the '95/'96 season, the halfpipe did not function.

 Carvers

For pure carving, runs 8, 9, 22 and 10 offer a good choice of well-groomed, fast steep slopes, which are at their best when freshly mowed in the early morning, before the crowds arrive.

Lifts to avoid

The K lift is known as the 'party lift', as it's extremely slow, and the only way to bide your time is to party.

Mountain fare

There are three cafés, two at the base and one on top. They all serve the usual fast food, priced from 45kr.

Tommen Bjerknaes pic: Peter Grant

DUBBED THE 'LITTLE MATTERHORN OF THE NORTH' ON ACCOUNT OF ITS **CRAGGY PEAKS**, WHICH ARE UNUSUAL FOR NORWAY

Essential Contacts

Tourist office

Hemsedal Tourist Information

Tel: 3206 0156/3560 Fax: 3206 0537

Snowboard shops

•TottenSport Skiutleie

Tel: 3206 2390

Board/boot hire: 250kr/day

•Hemsedal Sport Skiutleie

Tel: 3206 2110

Board/boot hire: 250kr/day

Snowboard schools

•Hemsedal Ski School   Tel: 3206 2330

1 hour lesson (minimum): 190kr

Hemsedal locals pic: Peter Grant

 ABOUT TOWN

Hemsedal is divided between a clump of hotels and bars at the base of the resort, and a one street town, 2kms away. At one time, its sole source of income was farming, hence the large barns dotted across the landscape. How times change... Hemsedal now has the highest concentration of millionaires in Norway and, as a result, it's pretty expensive. Still, it manages to retain a rural atmosphere and, simultaneously, knows how to throw a great party.

 Getting There

By plane: There are flights to Dagali (70kms away) and Oslo (220kms away) - buses are then available from both.

By train: The nearest station is Gol, from where there are regular bus transfers (price 35kr) taking 30 minutes.

By car: Hemsedal is a three hour drive from Oslo, along roads which are always open.

 Accommodation

The cheapest option is to hire a self-catering caravan or cabin (price 2,000kr per week) for four to five people at Orjukandefoss, 4kms from the resort. For hostel-type self-catering accommodation, Club Hemsedal has rooms for up to six people, starting at 4,000kr per week (prices reach 7,000kr in the peak season). Apartments, with saunas, suitable for groups of ten range from 7,500kr to 12,500kr per week (depending on the time of year). There are only three hotels. The best is Harahorn (on the mountain) where prices range from 1,300kr to 1,500kr for a weekend - Tel: 3206 2380. For more information, contact central reservations - Tel: 3206 0700.

 Food

There are four grocery stores-cum-supermarkets. The Hortun Pub & Grill and the Hemsedal Café are good, basic places to drink and eat - a hamburger will cost around 70kr. The Stallen restaurant does Mexican meals priced between 60kr and 150kr. The Skogstad Hotel's restaurant does traditional Norwegian food for around 190kr.

Nightlife

A good place for a relaxing drink after riding is the A-Frame Bar. The snowboarders' fave hang-out for happy hour and pre-disco drinks is the Hemsedal Café, which plays good sounds and serves up lethal 20kr shots of Carollan's coffee liquor. The Garasjen Pub, where the tables have been reinforced for dancing, is another action-packed place for slightly older, trendy types. For late night moves and grooves, all the hotels have clubs, the most popular of which is in the Hemsedal Hotel.

Other activities

'Up-skiing' (going up hill behind a parachute) is popular, as is paragliding, which costs 400kr for a tandem ride. There is a free skateboard ramp at the base of the resort (near the Skogstad Hotel), and all the hotels have saunas and swimming-pools.

 Thanks

Tom Bjerknaes, Lars Eriksen, Andreas Haugen, Morten Berg and Tommas Nilsen.

Building a hit pic: Peter Grant

Stryn

Mountain Information

Mountain range:

Strynefjellet

Vertical metre range:

830m - 1,350m

Length of season:

middle of May -

beginning of October

Number of lifts:

1 chairlift, 1 T-bar

Snow-making facilities:

Not needed - the average snowfall in Stryn is over five metres, so it never closes due to lack of snow, only too much snow!

Guides:

Contact Stryn Fjell or Breførarlag -

Tel: 057-871 200

Fax: 057-872 222

Lift pass prices:

1 day: 190kr

1 week 860kr

Season: 2,500kr

 ON THE MOUNTAIN

Stryn is not your average summer glacier. While most glaciers are flat and have unrideable slushy snow after midday, Stryn is fairly steep (so it's not the best for beginners) and has cold snow year-round. The bottom area is serviced by a double chairlift, the queues for which can be long, and the upper part is serviced by a T-bar lift. Much of the glacier is packed with various national ski teams training through the summer. Just in case you feel the urge, here's a warning: don't eat the snow in the ski area as there's so much salting during the year it's like a frozen Dead Sea.

 Freeriding

As Stryn is a glacier, freeriding off-piste can be deadly. The best freeriding season is mid-May - mid-June, when there is fresh cold snow in inconceivable amounts. You can see more or less all the rideable terrain from the lifts and, if it has snowed recently, it's good, although there is a lack of drops and cliffs. However, the best freeriding is not visible from the lift as it's on the other side of the mountain. In the early season, you can ride nearly 1,000m in fresh snow with a local guide. There are giant crevasses all over and every year some snowboarders get stuck. Stryn will never be famous for its terrain, for although it's steep, there are too few drops, windlips or cliffs. Go to Stryn for the freestyle scene, the forested area and the little anti-clinal valley. There are two or three hairy off-piste descents from the Scex-Rouge, but these should not be attempted without a guide. A young rider died the day we rode there, attempting to find a line down an unrideable face. No guide, no life.

Freestyle

The halfpipes are built in the upper part of the mountain and are mostly used by the camps, but there is a public pipe. The pipes are dug down into the glacier and hold up well due to the rock-hard snow. The camp pipes are maintained every day and offer superb training. The public one is OK and you can borrow a shovel from the lift station if you want to shape it yourself. There are several fun boxes and other obstacles - of all shapes and sizes - in a long run on the bottom part of the

Rider. Jaha Tenkku pic: Richard Walch

mountain, which are maintained daily. From the top of the chairlift, a wide cat track - full of natural hit and jumps - winds down the mountain. However, beware of descending cross-country skiers - their tiny skis feel like spears if you crash into them. The pipes and the lower part of the mountain are open in June and July. After that, only the upper part is open for riding - call to see which pipes are rideable. The road jumps in Stryn are legendary and separate the boys from the men, and the girls from the Amazons.

 Carving

The pistes are too narrow to be good for carving, but if you are into bashing gates it's one of the best places in the world as it's steep and the snow is rock hard. If you want to put up gates, ask at the information centre and you will get a numbered run where you can race, but bring your own gates and timing equipment.

 Lifts to avoid

There are only two, so they're unavoidable. The queues are at their worst an hour after opening and just after lunch. Be there at the crack of dawn and take an early lunch.

ABOUT TOWN

Stryn's summer ski centre is a boring concrete structure that you will want to leave as soon as your bindings are unstrapped. The closest village is Hjelle (15kms away), which consists of farmers, a gas station, a pub and a few camping grounds. It's not worth staying in for its scenery, but if you travel a further 30kms along the fjord, you'll find some of the most beautiful views in the world.

Accommodation

There are many camping grounds along the road from the ski centre down to Stryn. The farther from the glacier, the cheaper the rates. Strynefjell Tourist Centre in Hjelle is the most popular spot for snowboarders - it has a mini ramp and pub; prices from 400kr/day for a four bed cabin. Camping prices start from 15kr. Beware of thieves - leaving your wet gloves to dry outside your cabin is not a good idea. For more information - Tel: 057-871 946, Fax: 057-875 300. A more salubrious option is the Hotel Alexandra in Loen - it's a pleasant place with a restaurant, bar, disco, sauna and swimming-pool; a double room with breakfast costs 460kr per person. It's a long way from the glacier, but it's close to all the amenities in town - Tel: 057-877 660, Fax: 057-877 770.

Food

There is a gas station in Hjelle that sells all the pasta, bread and cheese you can eat. In Stryn and Loen, there are all types of restaurants serving food from hamburgers to delicious fish freshly caught from the fjord. The Skicentre offers the usual fare: hamburgers, pizza slices, sandwiches, chocolate bars and ice-cream. Generally food prices in Norway are high - a pizza costs around 100kr.

Nightlife

If you want to party when you are in Stryn, there are really only two alternatives: either go to one of the two beer outlets in Stryn or head back to your camping ground to make your own party and BBQ. If you are into dancing, the place to go in Stryn is Båhn Ski, which is open from Wednesday till Sunday, between 10.00pm and 3.00am.

Other activities

At the Skicentre, you can try telemarking, alpine or cross-country skiing. If you are a hard-core boarder, you will love the new mini-ramp at the camping ground in Hjelle. When it's raining, the indoor swimming-pool in Stryn is a popular hang-out. Watch out for Ingemar Backman and Daniel Franck, who try double back flips on the trampolines... and miss!

Thanks to

Martin Wilners.

pics: Richard Walch

Stryn is the perfect place for training. In summer you'll have a chance to test next year's equipment on snow before it gets to your local store. When it's sunny, it's a paradise; but when it's raining, it's hell. And it rains a lot... Bring stuff to do when it's raining or you will die of boredom. A car is good to have but not necessary. The best place to get information about riding is at the camping ground in Hjelle. There are always snowboarders there.

pic: STIG

Essential Contacts

Tourist board

Tel: 057-87 5340   Fax: 057-87 5300

Snowboard shops

• Skicentre Rentals

Tel: 057-87 1062

Board/boot rental: 190kr/day

Board/boot rental: 700kr/week

A number of snowboard companies have test stations with the next season's models at Stryn in the summer. The pro riders also sell their stuff before leaving, so there are some bargains to be struck, but be wary as there is a bit of stealing and dealing at the camping ground and at the Skicentre.

REEF BRAZIL

6'3'

Sheila – Relaxing

Blinder

The Tool
Quad Stitching

Oppdal

Mountain Information

Mountain chain:

Oppdal

Vertical metre range:

680m - 1,280m

Length of season:

first week of December
- end of May

Number of lifts:

14 draglifts, 2 chairlifts

Snow-making facilities:

Snow cannons cover six groomed
runs.

Safety:

Back-country equipment can be
hired at the base of the mountain.

Guides:

Contact the ski schools for back-
country tours or the ski patrol for
free group orientation tours.

Lift pass prices:

1 day: 185kr

6 days: 745kr

Season: 2,000kr

 ON THE MOUNTAIN

Oppdal is a big resort covering four mountains, so it offers a wide range of terrain. Beginners will enjoy the Vangslia's G lift, intermediates will have plenty of choice on the groomed slopes and advanced riders will find the off-piste good fun - there are rolling hills with steep sides, cliffs, rocks, huge windlips and gullies. Much of it is left untouched, as crowds are never a problem. In fact, the resort is often deserted.

 Snow conditions

The snow base, which averages two metres, is at its best around February and March.

 Freeriders

Vangslia is the mountain most popular with Norwegian snowboarders. Some of its most notable features are a great natural halfpipe on run 5 and the Beckkdalen ('valley of the stream'), which is deep and steep with windlips, and leads onto the funpark and a couple of quarterpipes. Approaching Beckkdalen from H lift on the Adalen side, a five minute hike takes you to extreme cliff lines. A good place for trees, rock and air is to the right of run 21, on Hovden. On the other side of Hovden, beyond run 24, is the Paradise Zone, a steep powder face. Below, among the

cliffs, is the 'Hammer Hul' (Hammer Cave), a huge hit. On Stølen mountain, run 37, there is a great, wind blown quarterpipe - not too steep and perfect for intermediates.

 Freestylers

Jibbers are spoiled in Oppdal, for loads of reasons. The main one is that it has a 600m vertical track on Vangslia with tons of hits. Start at the Beckkdalen valley and ride to the funpark, located where run 5 meets run 6. It has a great gap jump, six fun boxes, a log slide and a funky, twisty quarterpipe in the middle. In the '95/'96 season, the halfpipe was a joke, but the resort is planning something that will kick for '96/'97.

 Carvers

Hovden is the place for laying low on steep, wide groomed pistes.

Lifts to avoid

Vangslia D is a 1.6km T-bar, which, although unavoidable, becomes painful after a few runs.

Mountain fare

There are six cafés in the resort, all doing the usual burgers, fries and pizzas. None is cheap, with prices rising from 80kr. The café at the top of Hovden has outdoor facilities with a beautiful view.

pic: Peter Grant

ABOUT TOWN

Despite its claim to be Norway's largest resort, Oppdal retains a rural charm and welcomes all visitors, snowboarders in particular. Like the resort, the town tends to sprawl and, unless your hotel is close to the town centre, you will need a vehicle. There are some interesting old museums and buildings, which are almost as fascinating as the live culture - watch out for old ladies riding Zimmer-frame sleds!

Getting there

By plane: The nearest airport is Trondheim, which is a 150km bus or train transfer away.
By train: There are overnight trains from Oslo and connections from Stockholm.
By car: From Oslo, it's a 6 hour drive. The roads are good, but requirements for driving on ice, such as special tyres, apply. The drive from Trondheim takes 90 minutes.

Accommodation

Hellaugstøl Hytter is a collection of family run cabins (for up to four people), which are self-contained and in a convenient board-to-door location. The price per night, per cabin is 450kr - Tel: 724-214 19. Lainsbytorget has five person apartments for self-catering, board-to-door convenience; prices start at 64kr - Tel: 724-222 11. Oppdal Stunet is a youth hostel, with TV, shower and kitchen facilities, that has four person rooms; prices are from 110kr - Tel: 724-223 11, Fax: 724-223 13.

Essential Contacts

Tourist office

Tel: 724-21 760   Fax: 724-20 888

Snowboard shops

• Intersport   Tel: 724-21 637

Board/boot hire: 220kr/day

• Auna Sport   Tel: 724-20 810

Board/boot hire: 220kr/day

• Grøsdh   Tel: 724-21 690

Board/boot hire: 220kr/day

Snowboard schools

• Hovden   Tel: 724-222 0660

• Stølen   Tel: 724-20 630

• Sletvold   Tel: 724-22 311

*All these ski schools have boarding as part of their curriculum. 3 days of group lessons: 260kr.

pic: Peter Grant

Food

There are a several supermarkets in Oppdal's town centre. For fast food, try the Grillkroa, which delivers for free; prices range from 50kr to 90kr per meal -Tel: 724-224 95. Café Ludvik, located in the centre of town, is a great place to eat, with classy meals for around 100kr. The Perrongen Restaurant in the Oppdal Hotel is an exclusive place to savour traditional Norwegian food; prices start from 160kr.

Nightlife

After a hard day's boarding, the Jager'n Pub does happy hour beer specials for 25kr a glass. The George Pub is an Irish bar, where it's good to get legless with the local farmers. The nightlife is pretty grim during the week. The Hovden nightclub, underneath the Hovden lift, is the happening place at the weekend. There is an entry charge of between 50kr and 100kr. N.B. You can't buy alcohol around the resort before 3.00pm, and then it costs 38kr for 0.4 litres of beer, 36kr for a shot and 45kr for a glass of wine.

Other activities

Opplev Oppdal is an outdoor adventure group organising back-country extreme tours, ice climbing and overnight stays in snow caves, among other things - Tel: 724-222 42, Fax: 724-225 05. Alternatively, try paragliding, which costs 500kr for a tandem flight. If you're looking for a gym or pool, there is a training centre near the Hovden base - Tel: 724-213 30.

Thanks to

Snorre Renander and Ole Morten Hordel.

THERE ARE ROLLING HILLS WITH **STEEP** SIDES, **CLIFFS, ROCKS, HUGE WINDLIPS AND GULLIES.** MUCH OF IT IS LEFT UNTOUCHED AS THE RESORT IS OFTEN **DESERTED**

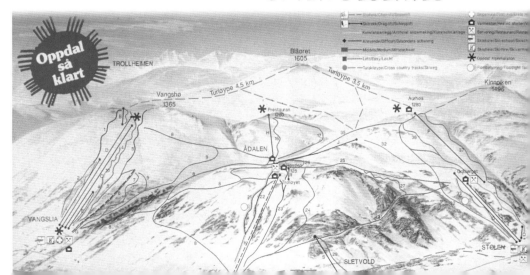

Narvik

Mountain chain:

Fagernesfjellet

Vertical metre range:

125m - 1,002m

Length of season:

December - June

Number of lifts:

1 gondola, 1 chairlift,

3 draglifts

Snow-making facilities:

Snow guns cover 50 percent of the

pistes when needed.

Safety:

An avalanche indicator board is

located at the top of the main

gondola.

Guides:

Contact the Narvik Ski Centre for

rates and details.

Lift pass prices:

1 day: 150kr

6 days: 900kr

Season: 2,200kr

pic: Peter Grant

 ON THE MOUNTAIN

Narvik is unique. It is one of the few places, if not the only place, in the world where boarders can ride to the ocean's edge. And beyond the resort lies a breathtaking panorama of some of Norway's most beautiful fjords. The mountain is best for intermediate and advanced riders. The top half of the mountain is all off-piste and the terrain is wild, with many open bowls, windlips and wooded runs. Lower down, there are some short, easy groomed slopes. A separate field called Amkenes, located on the adjacent side of the fjord, caters for learners.

 Snow conditions

When Narvik has fresh snow, its riding is world class, but due to its closeness to the sea, the snowfall is inconsistent and the powder often gets heavy in the damp climate. Due to the warming air from the Gulf Stream, the temperature rarely falls below -5°C.

 Freeriders

A 15 minute hike towards the summit will take you to the east face of Mørkholla, which has a long varied off-piste run, finishing by the sea. Ride over a massive windlip, drop into an open bowl, which is steep in places, and eventually funnel into a natural halfpipe, 'the river run' with many hits and banks. It's a five minute walk back to the lifts by

road. Otherwise, cross the road and railway line, ride through the forest and, eventually, you'll end up at the shore. Another run to the beach is on the adjacent side of the mountain. At the top, there's a natural halfpipe, which leads into a tight tree area leading down to the sea. On both routes, it's a bus ride back to the resort from the coast. For another open tree run, which often preserves soft snow, go to the right of Lift Two.

 Freestylers

A funpark and halfpipe are planned for the '96/'97 season. There are a couple of small, fun, natural halfpipes to the right of Lift Two. For great cliff and rock jumps, turn right off Lift Four.

 Carvers

Off the top lift is Fjellheimløypa, a downhill race track which is long and undulating, fast and wide.

 Mountain fare

Fjellheis Reståvranten, located at the top gondola station, must have the most awe-inspiring panorama in the whole of Norway. It sells snacks and meals for around 80kr, plus alcohol - a rare and expensive treat. At the bottom of Lift One is Asbjørnstua, a café offering a selection of fast foods including hot dogs (15kr), waffles (a must!) and coffee.

IT IS ONE OF THE FEW PLACES IN THE WORLD WHERE BOARDERS CAN RIDE TO THE OCEAN'S EDGE

ABOUT TOWN

The town of Narvik, at the base of the slopes, has little in common with the mountain, as it's a burly, working-class industrial town with a lively university scene. However, it's a wonderful place to observe Norwegian coastal life and, after a day's riding, it's easy to get swept along with the local ways. Pick the time of your visit carefully, as there are only a few hours of daylight in December, but by May there's 24 hours of sunshine.

Getting there

By plane: Harstad airport is a 70km bus transfer away.

By train: From Oslo or Stockholm, it's a 20 hour direct connection to Narvik station.

By car: The journey is a marathon 1,400kms from Oslo and the appropriate road knowledge is required for driving in extreme, icy conditions.

Accommodation

The Nordkalotten hostel provides self-catering services and a good café; price 110kr a night - Tel: 769-425 98. Another cheap alternative is the camping ground which has cabins and caravans; price 355kr a weekend for one person, including the price of a three day lift pass - Tel: 769-458 10. There are two big hotels: the Grand Royal - Tel: 769-415 00 and Norrlandia Narvik Hotel - Tel: 769-457 00; prices from 750kr/night. For more details, contact the tourist office.

Food

There are ten supermarkets and grocery stalls in Narvik. On the fast food front, there is Arild's and Burger, where meals range from 60kr to 80kr. The Rallarn Pub beside the Grand Hotel is a cosy bar/restaurant serving beef dishes and pizza; the price of an average meal is 100kr. The best place to take a date is the Astrupkjelleren

Rider Sergio Burtina pic: Jeff Webb

restaurant (beside the library) which has an ambient, candlelit basement and good quality food for an average of 100kr.

Nightlife

On the east side of the resort, the Fossen bar has great music and is perfect for after riding relaxation. The town disco, Malmen's, is popular with youngsters; entry fee 50kr. Peco is the town's 'cool' bar, which has alternative music and no cover charge, but drinks are expensive - 43kr for 0.4 litres of beer, 38kr for a glass of wine and 42kr for a shot.

Other activities

Next to the swimming-pool, a ten minute walk on the opposite side of the river, is the skateboard park, which has a mini ramp and boxes. Paragliding is also popular - ask the tourist office for details.

Thanks to

Fredrik Lindgren, Rikard Edman, Ronny Dahl and Ketil Singstad.

Essential Contacts

Tourist office

Narvik Ski Centre

Tel: 769-485 69   Fax: 769-458 18

Snowboard shops

•Bike and Surf   Tel: 769-436 31

The place to buy snowboard equipment. In the '95/'96 season, no shop hired out boards.

Snowboard schools

•Narvik Ski Centre

Tel: 769-485 69   Fax: 769-458 18

10 hours of lessons: 600kr

This small independent ski school offers snowboard lessons.

SWATCH/ISF WORLD BOARDERCROSS® TOUR

presented by

swatch® ✚   O'NEILL®

Riksgränsen pic: Jeff Webb

Swedish Lapland pic: Peter Grant

Storlien

ON THE MOUNTAIN

Storlien is good for learners and non-aggressive intermediates. There are a few nice off-piste rides through trees and gullies, but nothing for experts. It's a laid-back family-oriented place, often frequented by the Swedish royals.

Snow conditions

As one of the highest resorts in Sweden, Storlien receives a great cover of powder, often left untouched by skiers.

Freeriders

The only black run in the resort is a natural halfpipe called 'the Ravine', which twists and rolls down to Vargklyftanf (Woolf Creek). If you traverse for five minutes west off the Slalomliftarna, you'll find some forested areas where the trees are tight at the top and there are little gullies lower down. Traverse further out west from the top for more cliffs and windlips, plus a forest through which the Swedish-Norwegian border cuts.

Freestylers

The resort has plans for a proper funpark and halfpipe. In the '95/'96 season, there was only one fun box and two small ramps.

Carvers

Off the Slalomliftarna, the pistes are straight and steepish in spots - perfect for learning to carve fast.

Lifts to avoid

The Banggardsliften is a dodgy long, flat draglift.

Mountain fare

The Roedluvan restaurant at the bottom of the Slalomliftarna does fast food, such as burgers and pizzas which average out at about 60kr for a meal. At the bottom of the Banggardsliften, there is an open hot dog stand that also sells soft drinks.

pic: Peter Grant

Mountain Information

Mountain chain:
Åre

Vertical metre range:
up to 658m

Length of season:
end of November -
first week in May

Number of lifts:
7 T-bars

Snow-making facilities:
95 percent of the pistes are
covered by snow cannons.

Safety:
Hardly any avalanche activity.

Guides:
Contact the Sports Centre -
Tel: 647-70 444.

Lift pass prices:
1 day: 150kr
6 days: 600kr

Lift pass alternatives:
Potentially, as there plans
to link the resort with Åre.

We get the low down on all the good parties, No? pic: Peter Grant

 ABOUT TOWN

Built in 1887, Storlien was one of the first ski resorts in the country. Generations of Swedish royalty have patronised Storlien and they have two humble cottages on the slopes - one for the Royal Family, the other for their bodyguards. The resort has a warm, cozy atmosphere and an air of great history, which make up for the lack of bars and restaurants.

 Getting there

By plane: The closest airport (75kms away) is Trondheim, from where there are frequent bus and train transfers.

By train: There are overnight services from Stockholm straight to the resort.

By car: It takes 8 to 9 hours to drive from Stockholm, routing through Oestersund.

Accommodation

The Storlien Hotel has a wide range of rooms: the budget ones cost 195kr per person (including breakfast), while the top of the range deluxe suites (with butler service) are priced at 2,190kr - Tel: 647- 701 70. The Lyor Hostel has self-catering apartments for three people costing 350kr - Tel: 647-70 170. For more details, contact the tourist board.

 Food

The supermarket in the village is open throughout the weekend. Le Ski - don't be put off by the name - is an easy-going, inexpensive restaurant where prices for meals start at 50kr. The Storlien Hotel has the most wonderful restaurant if you want to splash out - try the reindeer dishes.

 Nightlife

The nightlife is limited. The Old Skier's Pub, in the basement of the Storlien Hotel, is a good place to start and/or finish. Le Ski, in the village, is a popular drinking hole and late night disco.

Other activities

There are snowmobile safaris, a swimming-pool, saunas and a fitness centre.

 Thanks to

Jonas Eriksson and Morton Olsson.

ONE OF THE **HIGHEST** RESORTS, STORLIEN RECEIVES A GREAT COVER OF **POWDER**, OFTEN LEFT **UNTOUCHED**

Essential Contacts

Tourist office

Tel: 647-70 170   Fax: 647-60 446

Local snowboard shops

•The Sports Centre (in the Storlien Hotel)

Tel: 647-70 444

Boot/board hire: 135kr/half day, 250kr/day

Snowboard schools

•The Sports Centre   Tel: 647-70 444

1.5 hour group lesson: 225kr

Äre

Mountain Information

Mountain chain:

Jäintlandsjällem

Vertical metre range:

376m - 1,274m

Length of season:

first week of December
- first week of May

Number of lifts:

1 mountain railway, 1 cable car,
1 gondola, 5 chairlifts, 36 draglifts

Snow-making facilities:

Most of the groomed slopes are
covered by snow cannons.

Safety:

Flashing lights on the lifts warn of
an impending avalanche risk. Off-
piste equipment, such as Ortovox
Systems, and snowshoes can be
hired from The Garage.

Ortovox hire:

100kr/day

300kr/week

Tel: 647-521 00.

Guides:

Contact the ski school; prices from
2,270kr/day.

Lift pass prices:

swatch access

1 day: 230kr/200kr

6 days: 1,060kr/930kr

Season: 2,400kr

(* Prices for high season/mid
season respectively.)

Linked resorts:

Riders can either board, or take a
free bus, to Duved, a family resort
that is good for learners. An hour's
drive from Åre is Edsåsdalen, a
small, old-fashioned resort with a
halfpipe. There are also plans to
link Åre with nearby Storlien.

ON THE MOUNTAIN

Äre is a huge resort with 64 groomed runs and
extensive off-piste terrain spread over three
mountains. The resort has an extensive maze of
lifts, runs and slopes going in all directions,
which makes it difficult to find the best areas
without local guidance. Every type of terrain is
available for all riders - there are five learner
areas, easy intermediate slopes and much to
choose from for the advanced rider. As one of
Sweden's most popular resorts, it can be
crowded over weekends and holiday periods.

Snow conditions

Pre-Christmas, the snow is unreliable. January
is the best month for powder with average
temperatures around -8°C, so the snow almost
never hardens, but the days are short (only five
hours long!). For snow information -
Tel: 647-130 30.

Freeriders

To access magnificent terrain, 30kr extra pays
for a snow-cat tow from the top station to the
Åreskutan summit. From there, head east over
the 50° steeps and carry on to Björnänge; a
long beautiful back-country run. Extreme
riders should try the wild east and west
ravines, which have steep walls and big
windlips. The west ravine can be reached by
traverse from the lifts. Lower down, the run out
becomes tight with more hits.
There is an open bowl with steep faces below
Lifts 18 and 27. On either side of Lift 25 are
superb tree runs, which have natural halfpipes
running through them. The Duved side is
mainly an intermediate zone, except for the
great forest runs between Lifts 38 and 41. If you
are prepared to hike from the top of Lift 38 for a
couple of hours, you'll find some great steeps
and cliffs.

Freestylers

The funpark cost 500,000kr to build and was
designed by Dennis Lenberg, the resort's chief
snowboard instructor - it's outstanding as it's been
well-executed and is maintained in top-notch
condition. It has two fun boxes, two massive
jumps, four big quarterpipes creating a
hippodrome, one wooden table jump, one wrinkle
jump, one goofy and one regular spine jump. The

park is located on Åreskutan mountain off S Lift, run
13. Äre's halfpipe - a 100m vertical pipe with 4m
walls and a great transition - is said to be the best in
Sweden. A short walk up from the village, underneath
Lift 10, it is floodlit until 11.00pm.

Carvers

Run 17 is a wide and consistent blue run. Runs 27
and 11 are steeper, groomed pistes on Åreskutan. Run
22 on Björnänge has no crowds and a good gradient,
while run 35 on Duved is sublime and people free.

Lifts to avoid

The traverse from run 22 to 29 is an uphill walk.

Mountain fare

There are nineteen places to devour everything from
coffee and cake to full meals, but none of them is
cheap (50kr for an average meal). Buustamon, west of
the funpark, is a cosy old-fashioned timber house that
is reputed to serve the best goulash around.
Hummelstugam, at the top of Lift 5, has a great view
and sun-deck.

Rider. Mårtin Axelsson pic: Martin Willners

pic: Martin Willners

EXTENSIVE MAZE OF LIFTS, RUNS AND SLOPES GOING IN ALL DIRECTIONS

🏠 ABOUT TOWN

Åre is primarily a winter holiday resort and 15 percent of its visitors are currently snowboarders. That figure looks set to rise as the resort management has invested heavily in snowboarding and has an open-armed attitude to riders, which makes a visit to the resort a real pleasure. The town itself is an ugly mix of boxy hotels built in the '70s and '80s, but there are stunning views over a frozen river of ice and thirty restaurants, fifteen bars and half-a-dozen nightclubs to ensure that the entertainment carries on well beyond the slopes.

➡️ Getting there

By plane: The nearest airport is Östersund (domestic flights only), from where Åre is an 85km bus or taxi ride.

By train: There is a railway station in the village, where overnight trains arrive from Stockholm and Oslo.

By car: From Stockholm, it's 620kms (roughly 8hrs) and from Oslo, it's 720kms (about 12hrs).

🏠 Accommodation

For budget accommodation, there is a Youth Hostel providing self-catering facilities and a dormitory bed for 150kr. Another option is the Åre camping ground, which has caravans available for 180kr. For B&B, the Diplomat Ski

Lodge starts at 295kr for a double room. Café Villan is a popular snowboarder respite at 400kr a night (including breakfast, and use of the gym and sauna). Engmam's Apartments, in the centre of the village, start at 2,200kr per week (seasonal rates apply) for up to four people. To ensure a cheap deal, it's advisable to book in advance, as the resort is particularly popular among the Swedes. For more information. contact central reservations - Tel: 647-52 100.

🍴 Food

There are two supermarkets open every day of the week. On the north side of the square there is a satisfying hamburger bar where a burger, fries and a drink cost around 48kr. Paminoteca, located in the square, is a reasonably priced Italian sandwich and pancake shop. The Broken Dreams, above the square is a lovely, inexpensive restaurant serving generous portions of food. Bykrogen's, a pizzeria under the cable car station, does delicious pizzas for 50kr. For traditional Swedish fare such as grouse, Villa Tottebø is highly recommended; main meals cost from 100kr.

✖️✖️ Nightlife

One of the best places for happy hour is the Sundial Hotel, which often has live music. The most popular nightclubs with local riders are the Diplomat (Tuesday and Sunday nights) and the Country Club (where there's an entry fee of 50kr).

Other activities

There is a skateboard ramp (open: 4.00pm-10.00pm) next to the internet cafe. There is also a climbing wall (20kr entry fee) and two schools for paragliding, which is extremely popular.

✅ Thanks to

Ullä Wiklund, Dennis Lenberg and Martin Willners.

pic: Peter Grant

pic: Courtessey of Åre Tourist Board

Riksgränsen

Mountain Information

Mountain chain:

Riksgränfjället

Vertical metre range:

530m - 950m

Length of season:

mid-February - end of June

Number of lifts:

2 chairlifts, 4 draglifts

Snow-making facilities:

None - Riksgränsen is one of
the most snow reliable resorts
in the world!

Safety:

The avalanche indicator board is in
the lobby of the Riksgränsen Hotel.
Flashing lights at the top station
warn of danger. Back-country
equipment can be hired from
Riksgränsen Hotel Sports Shop.

Guides:

The ski school organises
orientation and back-country tours;
prices start at 1,300kr/day.

Lift pass prices:

1 day: 190kr

6 days: 950kr

Season: 1,950kr

ON THE MOUNTAIN

The resort is on the north and south-facing sides of a butte. Most of the lift accessible terrain is intermediate with some steep tricky sections, plenty of off-piste areas and great powder hideouts. It's not a good place for beginners, unless they snowmobile (it's a free service!) to the learner zone. From May onwards, the resort opens its lifts on Wednesday and Saturday nights from 10.00pm to 1.00am - you can ride all night and never loose sight of the sun.

Snow conditions

Riksgränsen is located at 68 degrees latitude north, placing it 250kms inside the Artic Circle and guaranteeing late season snow till June and July. The best powder months are February and March, but the weather is often windy and foggy with flat light. For a couple of weeks in April, the snow turns hard as the temperatures rise and then the jib season starts in perfect sunny, spring conditions.

Freeriders

If you head west over the Norwegian boarder from the top of the Ovre Lift, you'll find great natural terrain: halfpipes with windlips, small cliffs to drop-off and a large quarterpipe. Further out, the best powder areas are found by walking to the top cabin and riding straight down. At the bottom, it's a 1km walk along the railway line back to the resort.

For a steep run, follow the fall-line off the Nedre Lift; the area has some funky gap jumps, including one over an old copper mine shaft. A thirty minute hike from the back side to Nordalsfjäll brings you to an extreme zone. Pick a line through the cliffs or go right for the safer, rock-free 50°-55° pitch and enjoy the huge hit at the bottom. Further round from the top of Nordalsfjäll is a safe, easy area that always has great snow. Recco tracking, the system of electronic avalanche detection was developed here... not without reason.

Freestylers

Any freestyler will be happy among the natural terrain built up by the weather conditions. The strong, prevailing westerly winds make great windlips and quarterpipes, the best of which are found west of runs 1, 5 and 6. Work starts on the funpark in the second week of May. A 100m vertical pipe is crafted and maintained daily by professional riders in preparation for the summer snowboard camps and competitions. A big jump and a couple of fun boxes are made at the same time just above the halfpipe, west of run 5.

The Swedish Snowboard Camp

Held around the last week of May, hundreds of snowboarders from round the world, including many of the elite, gather in Riksgränsen for this camp and associated competitions. The event is always accompanied by much media hype, but it's still a relaxed affair for the competing pros and 200-plus campers. The party atmosphere is due to the fact that the event falls outside the world cup circuit, so there are no career affecting falls and the pros can go all out to pull new tricks. A package deal, including a pipe pass and hotel accommodation for a week, costs 1,890kr. An extra 1,000kr buys a return train ticket from Stockholm.

Carvers

Runs 5 and 6 are well-groomed, long and end with a steep gradient.

pic: Andy Jackson

Mountain fare

Apart from a restaurant at the base of the lifts, which opens infrequently, there is a café called Nordalskiosken located at the bottom of the back side lifts. It serves the usual burgers, hot dogs and BBQ items for about 40kr.

 Thanks to

The staff at Riksgränsen and Jacko.

The bottom line
The night riding is unique - "spring is the best" says a local, Jacko, "as it's hot, wet and fun."

 ABOUT TOWN

Riksgränsen is a small, cosy place with a tiny local population. All the action is centred around the Riksgränsen Hotel, which is a hive of activity, particularly in June when the pro riders and other dedicated thrill seekers come to brain-storm and party.

 Getting there

By plane: There is a local airport, from where a train transfer is essential.
By train: It's a 20 hour train ride from Oslo or Stockholm to the station, which is a snowball's throw from the hotel.
By car: It's a long way from everywhere!

Riksgränsen pic: Jeff Webb

 Accommodation

In the spring, it is possible to bring your own tent and stay at the campsite, which has a kitchen, showers, bathroom and sauna, for 40kr/day. The Riksgränsen Hotel deal includes apartments for 1,000kr, per person, per week. Luxury three bedroom apartments are available for 9,000kr.

 Food

There is a small, predictably expensive, grocery shop in the hotel. The Rikgränsen Hotel has two menus, the eat-as-much-as-you-like buffet for 195kr or the up-market à la carte menu featuring Lapp and international cuisines. In the high season and at weekends, Café Lappis, where a big buffet costs 125kr, is open at the base of the slopes.

 Nightlife

The Riksgränsen Hotel bar swings most weekends with live music and old fashioned dancing. For a good time, bring your disco outfit and the locals will accept you like an old friend. Alcohol is expensive - 0.4 litres of beer costs 49kr (39kr at happy hour). A glass of wine or a shot goes for about 40kr.

Other activities

In the spring, there is a mini ramp for skateboarding at the hotel, which also has a gym, pool and sauna, plus a rock-climbing wall in its lobby. Ice climbing is available on some incredible waterfalls.

The best quarter pipe in the world pic: Martin Willners

THE HOTEL BAR SWINGS MOST WEEKENDS WITH LIVE MUSIC AND OLD FASHIONED DANCING. FOR A GOOD TIME BRING YOUR DISCO OUTFIT AND THE LOCALS WILL ACCEPT YOU LIKE AN OLD FRIEND

Essential Contacts

Tourist office, Snowboard shop and Snowboard school
• Riksgränsen Hotel
Tel: 0980-400 80   Fax: 0980-431 25
3 days of lessons: 260kr

Other alternatives

Heliboarding is available. It costs 700kr for one ride, 900kr for two rides, including a guide and off-piste equipment. So too is island riding - take a boat through the fjords where you'll be dropped off to ride mountain islands. For both activities, ask at the Riksgränsen Hotel for details.

ISS WZP 299   Number

SAUL D. GLUCKSMAN
PH.D., A.T.R., NCC

MOUNT SINAI MEDICAL CENTRE,
2301 PARK AVENUE, NEW YORK 10014, NEW YORK.

COPY FOR YOUR
INFORMATION

PATIENT'S SURNAME Poulton   OTHER NAMES Bradley, Thomas

D.O.B. 06.26.65   SEX Male   OCCUPATION   Accountant

ADDRESS Apt. 6b, 1054 E. 72nd Street, NY 10058, New York.

AIM
Brad - uncommunicative in repeated sessions with psychiatrist.
Referred for art therapy to aid diagnosis.

OUTCOME
Brad needed little prompting to draw - spent whole session scribbling
frenetically. When offered, preferred ball point to coloured pencils.

Sketches depict demons. When asked why the demons were
beheaded, Brad said "they had to die" or else they would kill him
and the "game" would be "over".

FINAL DIAGNOSIS
The use of black suggests Brad is suffering from depression.
The demons come from his PlayStation games. Brad feels worthless
and depressed because he has lost every game he has ever played.
(Apparently there are over 150 of them).

SIGNED
[signature]   DATE   06.24.96

Poulton B
6/24/96

GAME OVER

SONY
PlayStation

DO NOT
UNDERESTIMATE
THE POWER

Finland

Ylläs
Levi

Rider. Tero Ainonen pic: Jeff Webb

Ylläs pic: Peter Grant

Ylläs

Mountain Information

Mountain chain:

Ylläs

Vertical metre range:

255m - 718m

Length of season:

beginning of November
- end of May

Number of lifts:

15 draglifts

Snow-making facilities:

Only on the Äkäslompolo side,
where seven slopes are covered.

Safety:

No serious avalanche risk.

Guides:

The ski school and Ylläs Holiday
Service both organise tours.

Lift pass prices:

1 day: 120M

6 days: 500M

Season: 4,500M

Lift pass alternatives:

A lift pass for three days or more
includes Levi (see review) and
Olos, a small family field.

Snowboard schools

•Akas

Tel: 569 171

2 hour group lesson: 100M (price
of lesson includes lift pass)

ON THE MOUNTAIN

Ylläs is a 'tunturi', a Lappish hill with a flat plateau. Groomed intermediate slopes run down its sides ending in long, flat run outs, which are typical of Finnish resorts. While the terrain is not very challenging, Ylläs's main attraction is the powder, which stays light due to cool winter temperatures (averaging between -5°C and -15°C). Also, most skiers stay on the piste leaving plenty of untouched off-piste morsels for riders. However, most of the resort is above the tree line, so it can be exposed to foggy conditions and bitter winds.

✳ Snow conditions

Ylläs usually has ample snow cover by Christmas, but the best powder month is February. Low temperatures keep it fluffy.

Freeriders

For a great powder face, turn right at the top of the Kuruhissit lift and hit run 14, a natural halfpipe with high walls. Out beyond the Cänsiraja lift, run 15 is the most interesting off-piste region with bowls, jumps and bumps - keep your speed up for the flat run out. For guaranteed fresh tracks, head over the back side from the top, but be prepared for an arduous traverse and walk

back. A 30 minute hike from below Jokeri Hissit to the adjacent mountain, Kellostapuli, will lead you to short, steep descents of advanced terrain, with windlips and many other choice features. Again, it's quite a trek back.

Freestylers

On the Ylläsjärvi side, there is 'Lumilauta Street', the funpark. Made from artificial snow, it features two gap jumps and a couple of small ramps. For the '96/'97 season, the resort is planning a halfpipe.

Carvers

All the runs are cool for carving, but the longest and widest is the Jättipitka, run 15.

✖ Lifts to avoid

The whole mountain can be very exposed to high winds, so take some good gear for the chilly lift rides.

Mountain fare

On the Ylläsjärvi side, there is a Lapp tent 'Kata', which serves traditional food and steaming hot coffee. There are three 'regular' cafés, with expensive international foods - the pick of the three is the Sun Place, located on the Sun Lift.

ABOUT TOWN

Ylläs is a large hill in the middle of a flat plain, with two villages - Äkäslompolo and Ylläsjärvi - (25kms apart) on either side. Both villages are spread out and require a vehicle to go from hotel to restaurant to watering hole, which means most car-less visitors stay in their hotels or go out only on organised events. There is no real town centre or square, it's all in the woods!

Getting there

By plane: Kittilä is the nearest domestic airport, from where it's a 60km transfer by frequent bus connection.

By train: During the week, there are two or three trains to the main station of Kolari. At the weekends, there are only buses.

By car: It's a long way from anywhere and drivers must know to how drive in extreme, icy conditions, as well as have specially adapted tyres. It is possible to put a car on the train from Helsinki to Kolari for 1,300M, which also covers the cost of three people sleeping in a carriage.

Accommodation

For an interesting cultural experience, stay in a local home, B&B style; prices from 80M - Tel: 569 158 or call the tourist office for details. Cottages for up to six people are available for 1,200M - 4200M, depending on the season. There is a caravan camp next to Äkäshotelli, charging from 100M - 200M per caravan. Hotelli Ylläskaltio has good low season deals, charging around 360M for a room, plus free sauna and breakfast - Tel: 569 401, Fax: 569 251.

Food

There are expensive grocery stores in the middle of both villages. On the Äkäs side, Evåskori is the place to hang-out, drink beer and eat pizzas for 55M. Ylläksen Kaivohuone is a bar/café with cheap, hearty food; prices from 20M for a burger. Ylläs Humma Pub serves traditional Lapp food costing from 60M.

Nightlife

Peräkamary at the Äkäslompolo Hotel is the only place to attempt après drinking, even though there is no happy hour - most Finns go to the sauna at this time of day! Get naked with the locals. Ylläs Humina Pub in the main road of the village is the place to sing and drink, but remember: karaoke rules! The Ylläskaltio Hotel has a disco like all discos, with racy music and expensive drinks.

Other activities

At the base of the Ylläsjärvi side, there's a skateboard ramp. All the hotels have pools and saunas. Try the popular 'Skimbat', which entails skiing or riding uphill tied to a sail or parachute. Contact the Ylläs Holiday Service for more information.

Thanks to

Heidi Gardin and Hannu Väärälä.

Essential Contacts

Tourist office
Tel: 561 721   Fax: 561 337
Local snowboard shops
•City Sport Shop
Tel: 569 666   Fax: 569 777
Board servicing facilities.
Board/boot hire: 110M/day

pic: Peter Grant

Levi

Rider. Janne Kaitala pic: Peter Grant

Mountain Information

Mountain range:

Western Lapland

Vertical metre range:

200m - 531m

Length of season:

October - May

Number of lifts:

16 draglifts

Snow-making facilities:

Snow cannons cover four runs
and two halfpipes, when needed.

Safety:

No significant avalanche risk.

Guides:

Contact the ski school for services;
prices from 190M/hour.

Lift pass prices:

1 day: 120m

6 days: 520m

Season: 1,450m

Lift pass alternatives:

A 3 day (or longer) lift pass gives
you access to the nearby resorts of
Ylläs (see review), Olos and Pelles.

pic: Peter Grant

LEVI'S DRAW CARD IS THE PRIME POWDER BETWEEN FEBRUARY AND MARCH

ON THE MOUNTAIN

Like Ylläs, Levi is a 'tunturi', a typically
Finnish 'mountain' that is better described as
a hill in the middle of a great plateau. There is
limited terrain for beginners and experts, but
intermediates (and carvers) will enjoy the
well-groomed pistes. Off-piste riders will find
small tree runs and fun, undulating natural
terrain.

Snow conditions

Good snow cover usually graces Levi by
Christmas. Levi's draw card is the prime powder
in February and March, when the snow stays
light thanks to cool temperatures.

Freeriders

A natural halfpipe, with steep walls and good
drops, is located below run 12. Head below Lift
11 and ride towards Lift 10 for fun in the trees.
The best powder faces are off Lifts 5 and 7. The
resort's steepest slopes are the north-facing ones
between Lifts 5 and 6, from where there are fast
groomed runs and interesting off-piste areas.

Freestylers

When not looking for a new line on the north faces,
the jibbers can be found in the halfpipe below the
mid-station of Lift 3. At the time of our visit, the
halfpipe was 90 metres long, with both high walls and
good transition. There is no funpark, although there
are a couple of fun boxes located near Lift 1.

Carvers

The well-groomed runs off Lifts 5 and 6 are tops for
fast riding.

Lifts to avoid

None.

Mountain fare

There are four cafés serving the usual fast food and
costing from 20M to 50M. The best food is at
Åurinkøpaikka Tuikken Restaurant, which has a
stunning view and is a great place to relax after
a hard day's riding.

ABOUT TOWN

The resort town, at the base of the mountain, is centred around three big hotels, which contain nearly all the bars, restaurants and nightclubs. As Levi is Finland's biggest resort, the nightlife is lively, particularly during weekends and holidays, when there are things for every age group to do.

Essential Contacts

Tourist office

Tel: 643 466   Fax: 643 469

Local snowboard shops

•Levi Ski Shop

Tel: 641 246

Board/boot hire: 100M/day

Snowboard schools

•Lappish Ski School Levi

Tel: 641 246   Fax: 641 247

2 hour group lesson: 120M

Contact Janne Kaitala, halfpipe ruler, through the ski school.

Getting there

By plane: There are domestic flights to Kittilä, from where there are regular bus connections.

By train: The nearest main station is Kolari, which is an 80km bus transfer away.

By car: It's a long way from anywhere and all the roads in are gnarly. It's possible to put your car on the train from Helsinki to Kolari at a cost of 1,300M, which includes the cost of three people sleeping in a carriage.

Accommodation

There are three hotels and 350 cottages, with prices varying from 100M to 500M. For more details - Tel: 643 466, Fax: 643 469

Food

There are two supermarkets and ten restaurants. The Myllyn Aija (aka the 'Wild Indian') is casual and inexpensive - you can either sit down and eat or take food away. Most of the restaurants are in the hotels, where - after eating - Finnish folk furiously dance the 'hoppa-hoppa', a fast native waltz that has been known to cause indigestion! Don't forget your rhinestone studded boots.

Nightlife

Other than a drink at the Åurinkøpaikka Tuikken on the mountain, immediate après-ride activities are limited. Later in the evening, however, try Finland's most famous resort bar, the 'Crazy Raindeer' (aka 'Hulluporo'), where the price of entry varies between 20M and 40M. It rocks every night of the week and there is no option but to lubricate yourself on hot galliano shots at 10M apiece. If you're looking for alternative music, head for the Sirkantabiri Hotel. The Levitunturi Hotel is the place where over 40s do the hoppa-hoppa - try it, it's surprisingly fun.

The bottom line

A very compact resort with a truckload of slopes, which are probably the cleanest in Europe.

Other activities

The Levi Hotel has a big sports centre with a gym, sauna and pools.

Thanks to

Janne Kaitala.

Notes

Index

RIDER: SEBASTIAN PHOTO: JEFF WEBB LOCATION: CERVINIA

EUROPE SUCKS

ONBOARD
european snowboarding magazine

if you don't go...
you don't know

 # LOW PRESSURE  MAIL ORDER
the world's first portable web site

t-shirts

LONG PLAYER

GUT LOGO

Buddah Sticks
BUDDAH STICKS

I wanna get high
I WANNA GET HIGH

the snowboard guide europe
SNOWBOARD GUIDE

PANORAMIC

SPUN OUT

INFINITY SPINITY

colours Black, White, Green, Navy, Brown, Red, Grey Marl (subject to availability)   **sizes** Small or Big

publications

All the Breaks

europe
STORMRIDER GUIDE   £19⁹⁵

All the Spots

the snowboard GUIDE
europe
SNOWBOARD GUIDE   £19⁸⁵

other clothing

LONG ANTIFREEZE   £45

BOARDING SHORTS   £35

Polartec 100 Chassis
Flatlock Construction
Thermo-active
Stylish
Anti-fungicidal capabilities
Prophylactic storage facility

RASH V   £29

Short sleeved
High Necked
UV Protective
Anti Carcinagenic
Long Player logo

board bags

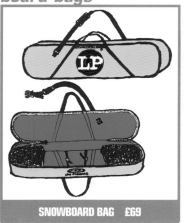
SNOWBOARD BAG   £69

10mm Padding
Oxford Nylon Shell
Plasweave Straps & Bumpers
100% Top Access
Rip-Stop water repellent-
boot & kit compartments
Board Straps
Flat front pocket for flat-stuff
Rubber shoulder-thing

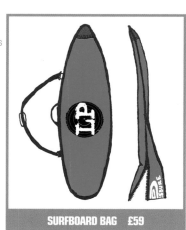
SURFBOARD BAG   £59

6 mm or 10mm Padding
Oxford Nylon Shell
Plasweave Straps & Bumpers
100% Tail Access
Fin Conservatory
6' to 9'6"
Removable Strap
Rubber shoulder-thing
Long Player logo

hats

CAP   £20

Winterweight or
Summerweight
Very Excellent

BEANIE   £19

Classic Beanie
Different Colours
What more can we say

**you need to have
some LP stuff call or
write to us and we'll
send it to you free**

GOTTA HAVE IT HOTLINE - 44 (0) 1896 01916

**Mail Order Dept
Unit 33 Pall Mall Deposit
124-128 Barlby Road
London England W10 6BL
Tel/Fax: +44(0)181 960 1916**

MARCO LUTZ, NARVIC, NORWAY PHOTO: JEFF WEBB